D1146235

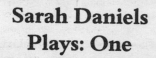

Sarah Daniels
Plays: One

Ripen Our Darkness, The Devil's Gateway, Masterpieces, Neaptide, Byrthrite

Ripen Our Darkness: 'This rough-cut scenario of role-playing musical chairs and outlandish social comment marks a most promising debut and gives off the unmistakable aroma of new talent.'

Michael Coveney, *Financial Times*

The Devil's Gateway: 'Ms Daniels' strength lies in her ability to write comically but incisively about the lives of women and to prove that the personal is political . . . gloriously funny.'

Lyn Gardner, *City Limits*

Masterpieces: 'The play has bite, anger and tenacity and many of its arguments are true . . . the supreme merit of Ms Daniels' combative work is that it makes me want to argue back.'

Michael Billington, *Guardian*

Neaptide: 'A lacerating wit subversively exposing how, under patriarchy, women are pushed to the very edge of lunatic behaviour.'
Carole Woodis, *City Limits*

Byrthrite: 'Daniels puts her case with vigour and wit.'
Claire Armistead, *Financial Times*

Sarah Daniels' plays include *Ripen Our Darkness* (Royal Court Theatre Upstairs, London, 1981); *Ma's Flesh is Grass* (Crucible Studio Theatre, Sheffield, 1981); *The Devil's Gateway* (Royal Court Theatre Upstairs, London, 1983); *Masterpieces* (Manchester Royal Exchange, 1983; Royal Court Theatre, London, 1983/4); *Neaptide*, winner of the 1982 George Devine Award (Cottesloe, National Theatre, London, 1986); *Byrthrite* Royal Court Theatre, London, 1986); *The Gut Girls* (Albany Empire, Deptford 1988); *Beside Herself* (Royal Court, London, 1990); *Head-Rot Holiday* (Clean Break Theatre Company, 1992) and *The Madness of Esme and Shaz* (Royal Court, London 1994).

SARAH DANIELS

PLAYS: ONE

Ripen Our Darkness
The Devil's Gateway
Masterpieces
Neaptide
Byrthrite

Methuen Drama

METHUEN WORLD CLASSICS

This collection first published in Great Britain in 1991
by Methuen Drama
an imprint of Reed Consumer Books Ltd
Michelin House, 81 Fulham Road, London SW3 6RB
and Auckland, Melbourne, Singapore and Toronto
and distributed in the United States of America by Heinemann,
a division of Reed Publishing (USA) Inc.,
361 Hanover Street, Portsmouth, New Hampshire NH 03801 3959
Reissued with a new cover design 1994.

1000 675472 T ISBN 0-413-67990-X

A CIP catalogue record for this book is available from the British Library.

Printed and bound in Great Britain
by Cox & Wyman Ltd, Cardiff Road, Reading

Contents

	page
Sarah Daniels: A Chronology	vii
Introduction	ix
RIPEN OUR DARKNESS	1
THE DEVIL'S GATEWAY	73
MASTERPIECES	159
NEAPTIDE	231
BYRTHRITE	329

A Chronology

Ripen Our Darkness, Royal Court Theatre Upstairs, London   1981

Ma's Flesh is Grass, Crucible Studio Theatre, Sheffield   1981

Masterpieces, Manchester Royal Exchange   1983

The Devil's Gateway, Royal Court Theatre Upstairs, London   1983

Neaptide, Royal National Theatre, London   1986

Byrthrite, Royal Court Theatre, London   1986

The Gut Girls, Albany Empire, London   1988

Beside Herself, Royal Court Theatre, London   1990

Head-Rot Holiday, Clean Break Theatre Company, touring   1992

The Madness of Esme and Shaz, Royal Court Theatre, London   1994

A Chronology

Ripen Our Darkness, Royal Court Theatre Upstairs, London   1981

Ma's Flesh is Grass, Crucible Studio Theatre, Sheffield   1981

Masterpieces, Manchester Royal Exchange   1983

The Devil's Gateway, Royal Court Theatre Upstairs, London   1983

Neaptide, Cottesloe, Royal National Theatre, London   1986

Byrthrite, Royal Court Theatre, London   1986

The Gut Girls, Albany Empire, London   1988

Beside Herself, Royal Court, Theatre, London   1990

Head-Rot Holiday, Clean Break Theatre Company, touring   1992

The Madness of Esme and Shaz, Royal Court Theatre, London   1994

Introduction

I didn't set out to be a 'feminist playwright'. I didn't set out to be a playwright at all. I can't remember wanting to be a writer when I was at school. I didn't even like drama, not the 'taught' sort anyway. My introduction to Shakespeare was Henry V for 'O' level, which was 'learnt' by having to read it out loud, around the class, in turn. Most of the lesson was spent trying to ensure that you would be able to pronounce the words without making a fool of yourself when the time came. To my amazement, I found that the first time I went to the theatre I enjoyed it. The two experiences were just incomparable.

When I started work, I went to the theatre once a week, and gradually became more discerning, seeing fewer and fewer West End shows and more and more plays. Convinced that my life needed 'putting in order' (an idea I got from Doris Lessing, or more accurately, one of her books) I started to write a play. I'd read an article in the London weekly listings magazine Time Out, which said that the Royal Court Theatre replied to anyone who sent in a play. So in October 1978 I did just that and received this response from the reader. (I discovered several years later that John Burgess who directed Neaptide, had written it.)

The problem with the play, like all works dealing with exposed personal emotion, is that it hovers on the edge of melodrama. It is probably too packed to be quite workable. The tone blurs into the sensational. What I enjoyed about it was the vigour of the dialogue. Not many people are writing like this for women— casual, angry talk, shrewd, bitter, violent, witty, etc. Ruth's breakdown rang absolutely true and the various appalling men are drawn with an accuracy that makes you wince.

Not only did the report encourage me to write another play, I now

Introduction

I didn't set out to be a 'Feminist Playwright'. I didn't set out to be a playwright at all. I can't remember wanting to be a writer when I was at school. I didn't even like drama, not the 'taught' sort anyway. My introduction to Shakespeare was *Henry V* for 'O' level, which was 'learnt' by having to read it out loud, around the class, in turn. Most of the lesson was spent trying to ensure that you would be able to pronounce the words without making a fool of yourself when the time came. To my amazement, I found that the first time I went to the theatre I enjoyed it. The two experiences were just incomparable.

When I started work, I went to the theatre once a week, and gradually became more discerning: seeing fewer and fewer West End shows and more and more plays. Convinced that my life needed 'putting in order' (an idea I got from Doris Lessing, or more accurately, one of her books) I started to write a play. I'd read an article in the London weekly listings magazine *Time Out*, which said that the Royal Court Theatre replied to anyone who sent in a play. So in October 1978 I did just that and received this response from the reader. (I discovered several years later that John Burgess, who directed *Neaptide*, had written it.)

The problem with the play, like all works dealing with exposed personal emotion, is that it hovers on the edge of melodrama. It is probably too packed to be quite workable. The tone blurs into the sensational. What I enjoyed about it was the vigour of the dialogue. Not many people are writing like this for women – casual, angry talk, shrewd, bitter, violent, witty, etc. Kath's breakdown rang absolutely true and the various appalling men are drawn with an accuracy that makes you wince.

Not only did the report encourage me to write another play, I now realise it was an astute piece of criticism relevant to the other plays in this volume. The bit about melodrama was absolutely true, but then to think that writing a play will put your life in order is rather a melodramatic notion. The worst thing a play can be is embarrassing. Being unintentionally melodramatic is equally high in the 'cringe' awards. The second worst thing a play can be is boring. I think I still write first drafts which are too packed. I have to keep reminding myself that putting more in does not necessarily make a more interesting play.

Ripen our Darkness was deliberately written in a sort of semi-detached style so that it couldn't be accused of the dreaded 'M' word. I also tried to keep it from being boring. Re-reading it now I am struck by the energy of the piece, the underlying unselfconscious anger. I don't think it is too packed, but nobody, except women, thought the men were drawn with any accuracy.

In the introduction to her book *Letters from a War Zone* Andrea Dworkin described her feelings after the publication of her first book: 'I thought that was it – I was a writer. (Sort of like being an archangel.) Forever.' When *Ripen our Darkness* was produced, so did I.

Still in my archangel state, I attended a workshop as part of 'Women Live' in 1982, led by Caryl Churchill and Annie Castledine. Annie suggested I write a play about Greenham Common, which I started to do, but became very stuck and decided to write about a woman living in Bethnal Green instead. I have never written to become immortal but I do wish now I hadn't put in quite so many references to television programmes. *The Devil's Gateway*, incorporating a flavour of the *Radio* and *T.V. Times* of the period, now, like a lot of contemporary plays, looks dated.

I have since discovered that writing gets harder not easier. I have also learnt about the collective nature of theatre. Bryony Lavery has described it as 'a big nutty fruit cake made up of the script, the director, the designer, actors, technicians and audience'. When it works, it does so because everyone has invested their own talent and passion in it. A brilliant script does not necessarily make a brilliant play. Similarly, a dull script can glow with brilliant direction, design and acting. The playwright has to learn to 'let go' to enable the process to happen. There will always be things in a production which were not how I saw them in my head. The skills and imagination which directors and actors bring can enhance a play greatly. (Although, I am sometimes left feeling like a big nutty fruit cake all on my own and, at the risk of sounding sensational, hover dangerously on the edge of wanting to shout 'No, I didn't mean it like that at all'.)

I tried to ensure that nobody could misinterpret *Masterpieces*. Unashamedly an issue-based play, I started writing it after talking to a friend of mine who was doing a dissertation on women and male violence. I'd also read Andrea Dworkin's book *Pornography – Men Possessing Women*, and attended a meeting at the University of London where members of 'Women Against Violence Against Women' were speaking. I was recently introduced to someone who took it upon himself to inform me that I'd done the Women's Movement a disservice by 'making Rowena behave in such an irrational manner'. (He was referring to Scene fourteen.) Somehow harassing women is seen as rational behaviour. Being angry, or worse, fighting back, is seen as irrational behaviour. I felt so strongly about the ideas in the play that, in an attempt to guard against being misunderstood, I censored myself from writing the detail and contradictions which give a character depth.

Claire in *Neaptide* suffers slightly from this authorial self-censorship. For, like Radclyffe Hall, *vis à vis* her heroine in the *Well of Loneliness*, I was so aware of the prejudice which exists against lesbians that I made Claire a bit too good and/or 'right on' to be true. I was determined not to provide anyone with an excuse for thinking 'Perhaps her ex-husband should have got custody anyway'. I now think *Neaptide* would benefit from trimming, but once it was produced and published I felt it was somehow 'sealed'. Out of the plays included here it remains my favourite for reasons I shall not reveal for fear of being sensational, sentimental, or worse . . . melodramatic.

For *Byrthrite* I did, for me, an enormous amount of reading and research. I went several times to Mistley and Manningtree in Essex where Mathew Hopkins, the self-appointed 'Witch Finder General' (nicknamed 'the pricker') had based himself. I stood at the edge of the pond where women had had the 'choice' of drowning and proving they weren't witches, or floating, and proving they were. I shivered at the thought of it still being there. I wanted to write a play about the implications and dangers of reproductive technology for women. I thought that setting it in the seventeenth century – the time when the role of healer was taken out of the hands of women and established in the (male) profession of doctor – would give a poignancy to the ideas expressed in the play. With hindsight it might be accused of being too ambitious 'to be quite workable'.

Feminism is now, like panty-girdle, a very embarrassing word. Once seen as liberating, it is now considered to be restrictive, passé, and undesirable to wear. I didn't set out to further the cause of Feminism. However, I am proud if some of my plays have added to its influence.

Sarah Daniels
December 1990

RIPEN OUR DARKNESS

Ripen Our Darkness was first presented at the Royal Court Theatre Upstairs, London, on 7 September 1981, with the following cast:

MARY	Gwen Taylor
ANNA	
SUSAN	Cecily Hobbs
TARA	
DAPHNE	
RENE	Janette Legge
JULIE	Carole Harrison
DAVID	
ALF	David Calder
PAUL	
ROGER	John Gillett
MARSHALL	

Directed by Carole Hayman
Designed by Mary Moore
Lighting by Steve Whitson

Scene One

MARY's kitchen, Sunday morning. She has just made tea. Presently DAVID enters, wearing a dressing-gown over a shirt and tie.

DAVID. Good morning, dear, although that greeting seems almost inappropriate now, it being approximately nine fifty-five.

MARY (flustered). I can't believe it. Fancy sleeping through the alarm.

DAVID. Even if you had managed to wake up when it went, it was set for seven-thirty so we'd be half an hour behind already.

MARY (confused). But David, I'm sure that I set it for seven.

DAVID (kindly). Never mind. We've obviously both got to try and make up for lost time.

MARY. What would you like for breakfast?

DAVID. Oh, anything. (He crosses to the window. MARY gives him a cup of tea.) Thank you. Well, would you look at that. This is the day that the Lord hath made, and very beautiful it is too. The sort of day that makes you glad to be alive. And that reminds me, Mary, I don't like to mention it but it took me almost seven minutes to locate my underpants this morning.

MARY. Second drawer, dear. Will toast and cereal be all right?

DAVID. I know that now. Bacon and egg would go down well, but toast will suffice. And perhaps next time you reorganise the bedroom you would leave me a little plan or map as a guide, then I might be able to negotiate my way around the furniture, ha, ha. Maybe we could have a photo, ha, ha, then we'd be halfway to a National Trust booklet.

MARY. But, David, they've been in the second drawer for the last thirty years.

DAVID. While you're there a couple of tomatoes would be nice. I'm sure they could not have been there that long, dear.

MARY. I remember distinctly re-lining that chest of drawers on Remembrance Sunday, 1950.

DAVID. Goodness me, you mean to say that with the war still fresh in our memories, you spent its fifth anniversary sorting underwear?

MARY. I did stop for two minutes.

DAVID. I should hope so. Well, no matter, it's of very little consequence now. What I meant to say is, perhaps when you have a minute you could enlighten me as to the whereabouts of my trousers.

MARY (*not listening*). I wonder how many minutes' silence we'll have to observe after nuclear war . . .

DAVID. Really, dear, your sense of humour is quite macabre. But unfortunately it does not get me any further in the quest for my trousers.

MARY (*weary*). Where did you take them off?

DAVID. Ah ha, now that theory is good for as far as it goes. However, if I were to follow it through to its logical conclusion it would imply that they should be by the side of the bed where stepped out of them.

MARY. They're folded on the back of the chair.

DAVID. Far be it from me, dear, but if you persist in allowing yourself to indulge in this rather morbid train of thought, how do you hope to get lunch organised in time for church?

MARY. But David . . .

DAVID. We don't want to start the day off with 'buts', now do we?

MARY. I don't think I'll be able . . .

DAVID. Now please, let's not start that nonsense. It looks dreadful if you, of all people, aren't there. For goodness' sake, if the church warden's wife isn't able to come to church how do you expect us to reach the masses of Potter's Bar?

MARY. It's just that . . .

DAVID. And remember what we agreed, eh? What we worked out about being methodical, and getting things sorted out in a logical order so that it will give you more time to do things, to get important things fitted into the day. Especially Sunday.

MARY. Yes, David, I am trying.

DAVID. I know you are, I know. And this morning I'm going to help you out by getting the breakfast. How's that for men's lib, eh? Now, you sit down there. (MARY *sits absorbed.*) Well, you needn't look so grim about it.

MARY (*she has not heard*). Sorry, dear?

DAVID. I said, no need to be so glum.

MARY (*trying hard to please*). Oh no, it's very sweet of you. Thank you.

DAVID. And so to the gas.

DAVID *goes to the cooker.*

MARY. It's just that we're a bit behind anyway, and you've got a busy day ahead.

DAVID. That's precisely why I'm giving you a hand. Hmm, the gas doesn't seem to want to light.

MARY. Oh, no, I'm sorry, I forgot. You'll have to use the matches. The cooker's so old. I did ask . . .

DAVID. Don't tell me, it hasn't worked since the first Remembrance Sunday.

MARY. Strange really. I was always surprised that they didn't take it to turn into ammunition.

DAVID. Next step bacon. Where might that be?

MARY. In the fridge, dear.

DAVID. Ah ha, coming on in leaps and bounds. (*He looks in the fridge.*) Sorry, there appears to be no evidence of it here.

MARY. Second shelf, on the right, next to the half-eaten trifle.

DAVID (*removing the contents of the fridge item by item*). No, I'm sorry, dear, I'm prepared to say that it's not here.

MARY (*gets up slowly*). There, dear. (*She takes the bacon from the fridge and hands it to him.*)

DAVID. Now I was blowed if I could see it.

MARY (*cheerfully*). I'll do it, David . . . Please.

DAVID. The best-laid schemes and all that. Ah, well, don't say I didn't try.

MARY. Did you hear Simon come in last night?

DAVID. Considering the time, I think we should scrap the egg and bacon idea or I won't have room for lunch. A piece of toast, Mary.

MARY. Look at this mess. These plates. They come in at all hours, help themselves to something, I do wish they'd be a little more considerate.

DAVID. Boys will be boys, and they're not going to get any better if you persistently nag them, now are they?

MARY. I wouldn't mind, but Simon's twenty-three now.

DAVID. Goodness me, dear, we're not going to get very far if we keep nattering. Now, where's your pen and paper? I find things never seem so insurmountable if they're made into a list. For example, it will be easier to sort out the underwear drawer more than once in three decades, eh? Ha ha.

MARY. Pardon?

DAVID. Just a little joke, dear. Now, let me get those trousers on. What would Roger think if he knew his church warden was still prancing about in his dressing-gown at ten-thirty on a Sunday morning, that's what I'd like to know.

DAVID *goes out.*

MARY (*sits down, starts to write*). Sunday. One, Dinner. Pick mint from garden for peas. Take cheesecake out of freezer . . . (*She looks up at the clock.*) Too late, it will never thaw. (*She continues writing.*) Tinned fruit and ice cream for pudding, cheesecake for tea. (*She stops writing.*) What about supper? I must be getting old, running out of imagination. (*She recommences writing.*) Dear God, why have I come to dread Sunday?

PAUL *enters.*

PAUL. Morning, Mum.

MARY. (*startled*). Morning, dear. At least you're up.

PAUL. What's for breakfast?

MARY. Not long till lunchtime. Can't you hold out?

PAUL. Not really, no. How long's dinner anyway?

MARY (*brightly*). Four inches – it's a sausage.

PAUL. Please don't try to be funny, Mummy. It doesn't suit you.

MARY. Sorry. There's plenty of cereal in the cupboard.

PAUL. What sort?

MARY. Go and have a look.

PAUL. I won't bother then.

MARY *gets a bowl of cereal and gives it to* PAUL.

PAUL. Where's the milk?

MARY (*puts milk and sugar in the bowl of cereal*). There you are, dear.

PAUL. Ta, Ma.

MARY. Did you hear Simon come in last night?

PAUL (*stuffing his face*). Nope.

MARY. I don't think he came home last night. I haven't had a chance to look in his bedroom.

PAUL. He's a big boy now. A man of the world.

MARY. Even men of the world meet with fatal accidents. How would it look, 'Church warden's son run over and killed three days ago – his mother never even noticed'?

PAUL. Give it a rest, Mum.

MARY. I give up with you lot. Where's John?

PAUL. Judging by the sound of creaking bed springs coming from his room, I'd say he was reading magazines.

MARY. What on earth . . . Sometimes I can't follow a word you boys are saying. (*She shouts.*) John! Are you up? (*Then:*) Tut, they just ignore you. I don't know.

PAUL. Mum . . . I was wondering, could you see your way clear to lending me a fiver?

MARY. You mean give.

PAUL. It's difficult, Mum . . . I mean . . .

MARY. You go out to work. I lent you five pounds out of the housekeeping last week. What did you do with that?

PAUL. Oh, you know, I mean, it's not like the day when you could buy a pound of apples for a penny.

MARY. And when was the last time you bought a pound of apples? Here, you're not on drugs, are you?

PAUL (*laughing*). At a fiver a week, I couldn't even afford to be on Smarties.

MARY. There's five pounds in the drawer.

PAUL. Ta.

MARY. Don't you think you can get off that lightly. The washing-up, please.

PAUL. Ah . . . Mummy?

MARY. Who left all this out last night? That's what I'd like to know.

PAUL. Oh, Ma, give over. Stop going on for once, first thing in the morning, it's too much.

MARY. Perhaps next time you could wash up after yourself.

PAUL (already halfway through the door). Shut up, will you? You old bag.

MARY. PAUL!

PAUL goes out.

DAVID enters.

DAVID. Not nagging him already dear. (He shouts.) Morning, son!

PAUL (off). Wotcher, Dad.

DAVID. Mm, something smells good.

MARY. Well, I don't know what. I haven't had a chance to put anything in the oven yet.

DAVID. Not to worry. Plenty of time, eh? That's the idea. Now I hate to mention it, but (He points to his trousers.) that stain on the knee is still there.

MARY. Sorry. I couldn't get it out. I'll have to take them to the dry cleaner's.

DAVID. Don't be too rash, ha ha.

MARY. Pardon?

DAVID. I'm sure taking them to the dry cleaner's will be the great event of the week. Only a little quip. Hmm, yes well. Now, I really must be going. I suppose the car keys are in Paul's room. And you will make an effort to be at the service, won't you, dear?

DAVID *goes out.*

MARY (*shouts*). John, if you're not down here in one minute . . . please.

PAUL *enters.*

PAUL (*putting head round the door*). By the way, is it okay if I bring a bird home with me tonight?

MARY. I suppose you mean a girl.

PAUL. I don't mean a sparrow, do I?

MARY. You know your friends are always welcome here. Only I don't want you spending too much time in the bedroom. Whatever would people think?

PAUL. Okay. Okay.

MARY. Now just a minute . . . I want you to take these shirts upstairs for me. (*She counts the shirts.*) I must be going mad. Thirty-eight shirts for one week, between four men. Fancy wearing more than one shirt a day. (*She hands the shirts to PAUL.*) Daft. The whole lot of you.

PAUL. All right, Mum. I don't know whose is whose, so you'll have to sort them out later. I'll leave them on your bed.

MARY. Thank you, dear.

PAUL *goes out.*

DAVID *enters.*

DAVID. Mary, you'll have a word with that lad. I found something in his room which I am far from pleased about.

MARY. Oh.

DAVID. It's disgusting. Look!

He opens his hand just long enough for the audience to register that it is a used condom. MARY does not take it in.

On his floor. I'll not have it.

MARY. No, it is a bit much.

DAVID. A bit much?

MARY. What will you do with it?

DAVID. Burn it.

MARY. That's a bit cruel.

DAVID *gets an envelope out of the drawer, puts the condom in it, seals it and puts it in his pocket.*

DAVID. What do you suggest I do? Frame it? And while we're on about the sordid part of this family, you and I really must have a talk about Anna.

MARY. Oh, good. I'll drop her a line this evening if I get a chance. You know, I can't tell you how much I miss her.

DAVID. She's a disgrace.

MARY. David!

DAVID. We'll have a long chat about it later.

MARY. Yes.

DAVID. Oh, and there, I almost forgot to tell you. I've invited Roger and Daphne back after the morning service.

MARY. Oh, that's nice. (*Slight pause.*) They won't want anything to eat will they?

DAVID. No, just lunch and tea.

DAVID *goes out.*

MARY. Oh. (*She continues writing.*) Tell Paul – no slugs in the bedroom. Two extra for lunch. Peel more potatoes. More sausages, to make the chicken go further. (*Pause.*) Why does my life seem like a half-finished jigsaw while everybody else seems to have completed their pictures? What did he mean about Anna? Dear God, if our lives are predestined what's the point of prayer? (*Pause.*) Even if they are not, what's the point?

Blackout.

Scene Two

RENE's kitchen. ALF is drunk. SUSAN sits silently at the table. RENE buzzes around frantically, dusting and polishing the tatty furniture. She is a nervous, agitated woman with a frail, frightened voice, which seems to be about to break into a more hysterical pitch.

ALF (at SUSAN). Bleedin' slut. Cow. Little filthy fucker. See, yer know what this bleedin' is, eh? Retribution from God. All-bleedin' mighty. Mighty wrath of God lands you with a shitty, vegetating baby. Thank fuck Christ it's dead. (He lifts his hand to hit SUSAN.)

RENE (thin screech). Steady, Alf, there's no need. Your dinner's almost ready. Toad in the hole, your favourite. I've managed to get the sausages you like – plenty of pork. The butcher was only saying . . .

ALF. Shut your stupid fucking gob.

RENE. He doesn't mean it. He's just upset. He's hurt. It's upset him more than we'll ever know. He doesn't mean it.

ALF (shaking SUSAN). You cow. You fuckin' wretched whore. Blasted fuckin' bitch, you reduced the whole fuckin' family to humiliation, you stupid ignorant slut.

RENE. Please, Alf. All she's been through. I know . . . maybe they got the babies mixed up at the hospital. A mistake. These things can happen, yer know. That's probably it.

ALF. You bleedin' fuckin' stupid bitch. Can't you shut that fuckin' blabberin' cake-hole for one fuckin' minute before I shuts it permanently for you?

The doorbell rings.

RENE. My God, who can that be?

ALF (pokes SUSAN). Answer it, slut.

SUSAN goes to the door and comes back with ROGER.

RENE (tidying herself). Oh, hello, Vicar.

ROGER. Hello there . . .

ALF. 'lo Vicar.

ROGER (*smiles*). And you must be Susan.

RENE. Yes. Say hello to the vicar, Susan.

SUSAN. Hallo.

RENE. I know we haven't been to church recently like, Vicar, well ever. But we've had a lot on our plates and Alf here used to work nights, when he was employed like, and sometimes he had to work on a Sunday as well, I know that don't make it right, for one thing you're not supposed to work on the Sabbath . . .

ALF (*through gritted teeth*). Rene, my dear.

RENE. Sorry. Sorry. Ha! I do go on, don't I?

ROGER. I've come to offer my sincere sympathies about little Peter. I baptised him just before he was taken.

ALF. He needed more than that, with no disrespect, Vicar.

ROGER. I realise this must be a very difficult time for you all, especially for Susan, and sometimes there is simply no explanation for these things.

ALF. She's not married, Reverend, there's your answer. Sin of the flesh.

ROGER. I'm afraid that we don't believe God is that hard these days.

RENE. Can I offer you a cup of tea, Vicar, or something to eat? We was just about to 'ave dinner. There's plenty.

ROGER. Thanks, but I've already accepted an offer from my church warden. I really called round to say that if ever – and I don't believe in ramming religion down other people's throats – but if ever you feel that there is anything you'd like to discuss or if you need spiritual guidance, do pop round to the vicarage and if I'm not there my wife will always be willing to chat over a cup of tea. Or the church warden's wife, Mrs Johnson, is very homely.

SUSAN. You baptised Peter? . . . What does it mean? Did you try to bring him back to life?

ROGER. No, my dear, but it does mean that he will definitely partake of the life hereafter.

SUSAN. Oh.

ROGER. He will be in paradise. I can vouchsafe. Well, nice to see you all. I'm only sorry that it couldn't have been in happier circumstances.

RENE. Nice of you to call, Vicar, and we can't thank you enough. I'll see you out. (*They both go to the door.*) It was a terrible thing to happen. Tragic. But we're over the worst of it now. I hope.

ROGER. So do I. God be with you.

RENE. And you.

They both go out.

ALF (*to* SUSAN). Bring it back to life? You stupid, ungrateful cow.

RENE *enters.*

RENE. Well, it was nice of him to call.

ALF. Bleedin' irony of it. Poncing in here saying, 'I don't want to ram religion down other people's throats', well that, unfortunately, happens to be what he's bleedin' paid for. Soddin' git, don't know what a bleedin' day's work is anyway. Fuck it, I'm off out.

RENE. What about your dinner?

ALF. I'll have it when I get back.

RENE. It'll be spoilt.

ALF. It'd bleedin' better not be, and for fuck's sake woman, clear this place up a bit – it's like a fuckin' shit pit.

ALF *goes out.*

RENE. It ain't right, you know, Susan. I don't care what you say.

Naturally you're upset but we got to pick up the threads somewhere, and I for one ain't going to take this lying down. I'm so upset, we, we all are – oh, yes, even your father, although he'd never show it of course. We'll sue those doctors, and we'll start with that Dr Cart-bleedin' double-barrelled Wright-Smith. Probably his name was Smith, and he pinched the Cartwright bit off his wife. Well, it's the same the world over, men always pinch the best things off women, bleed 'em dry, and for another thing . . .

SUSAN (*quietly*). Please, Mum . . .

RENE. We never 'ad no handicap in this family, and as for completely . . . well so badly handicapped he died . . .

SUSAN. Totally fucked up.

RENE. Susan, don't say that. It's a something syndrome. I'm so sorry, love, but we knew it was going to happen and I s'pose it's better now than later, oh what am I saying? It's just too easy to go on blabbing about all for the best.

SUSAN. When the baby's funeral's over, you and me are going.

RENE. Where could I possibly go at my age? I know your father's not exactly gracious . . . downright hostile . . . but it's not his fault. . . . He's done his best by you he has.

SUSAN. So I noticed. Sorry. Perhaps we'd both better have a chat with the vicar's wife.

RENE. You've got to be joking. She's a real loony, she is. Mrs Wallanger from number forty-five can see their garden from her place. She told me that while the organ plays 'All things bright and beautiful' that vicar's lady wife tramps through the garden, ripping the heads off the snowdrops, shouting, 'Die damn you, die'.

SUSAN. Mum – Mrs Wallanger's hearing aid would have exploded if it was powerful enough to pick up that from the tenth floor – (*Slight pause.*) By the way, I'm going to see Julie next week.

RENE. What for? She didn't even know he existed.

SUSAN. There's no need to be so criticising.

RENE. You know what I think of that young lady – that's the wrong word – that young hermaphrodite more like, well I hope you don't pick up no bad habits, that's all I can say. Take it from me, Susan, women like that are never 'appy, how can they be?

SUSAN. Not like we are then, eh, Mum?

RENE. I thought it would be different when we was rehoused to Potter's Bar. (*She speaks more softly.*) It's my fault. I talked yer outta the abortion – mothers are supposed to know best – only this one's a complete bloody flop.

SUSAN. Mum, it's nobody's fault. If only for a few days Peter was alive.

RENE (*rising hysteria*). Alive! Alive my arse, he was like a bit of squashed fruit. (*She slaps herself.*) Oh, for Christ's sake, shut up, Rene.

SUSAN. Mum, I love you.

RENE (*getting out hanky*). Oh, shit. (*Pause.*) There's nothing to keep you here now, love. You go.

SUSAN. And leave you alone with him? No way.

RENE. What would I have done if you'd been a boy?

SUSAN. You'd 'ave ter have done the laundry yourself for starters. (*She picks up the laundry basket.*) See yer later.

RENE (*starts reading from the back page of* Woman's Own *aloud*). Dear Mary Grant, My wife and I make love about five times a week, which suits me down to the ground, but she will insist on watching telly over my shoulder. I don't mind this so much, but she will keep one hand free so she can switch stations with the remote control.

Pause.

RENE *puts down the magazine.*

Dear Mary Grant, I have a husband who drinks all my money away. I have two jobs to try to give him enough so he doesn't feel the need to slap me and my daughter around, but I usually fail. I have to lie in piss-soaked sheets, as my husband wets the bed every night. My daughter's severely handicapped baby has just died and I just can't stop fuckin' talking. I have dreams of doing myself in. Please don't reply as my husband rips up my mail regardless.

Blackout.

Scene Three

ANNA *and* JULIE's *kitchen*. ANNA *is knitting*. JULIE *is watching television*.

JULIE. What yer doing?

ANNA. Washing-up.

JULIE. Yer bleedin' knitting, ain't yer? Yer disgustin' pervert. Yer know what yer equivalent to, eh? A man exposin' himself in public.

ANNA. I'm not in public, but I'll go to the window and wave it out shouting, 'Get a load of this double ply', if you like.

JULIE. Same difference. Same crime.

ANNA. Be quiet, you're missing the programme.

JULIE. It's finished.

ANNA. Haven't you got an essay or something to write?

JULIE. Yeah. I've done it.

ANNA. Already?

JULIE. Here.

She hands ANNA *a postcard.*

ANNA (*reading*). Open University, Milton Keynes.

JULIE. Other side, Rubberhead.

ANNA (*turns it over, reads*). 'Dear madam, and if there is not a woman on the premises don't bother to read any further. I am writing to inform you that I cannot respond to any essay title with the word 'mankind' in it. Because it has the kind of alienating effect which really fucks me off.'

JULIE. What do you think?

ANNA. You can't start a sentence with 'because'.

JULIE. Do you think it's long enough?

ANNA. For you it's almost a thesis.

JULIE. Hey, that reminds me, what did your mother have to say this week?

ANNA. What did my mother have to say this week?

She hands JULIE *a letter.*

Here, read it for yourself.

JULIE (*reads*). 'Dear Anna, sorry I can't write much as I have to get on with the beds, love Mum.' (*She looks up.*) That's it? Blimey, the Post Office should've let her have a stamp half price fer that.

ANNA. I just don't know what to make of it.

JULIE. Are you sure you didn't upset her when you went home?

ANNA. Yes, at least, I don't think so. It's difficult to tell, he puts her on edge so much.

JULIE. Who?

ANNA. The old bastard.

JULIE. Oh, Flash Gordon, the church warden.

ANNA. Sometimes I feel my visits cause more trouble than they're worth.

JULIE. Did you get a chance to speak to her on her own?

ANNA. Yes, but she's . . . I don't know. I can't explain it.

JULIE. She's been bullied so long she don't know how to pick herself up again.

ANNA. Yes, but my father has never so much as raised his hand to her.

JULIE. So what exactly did you say to her?

ANNA. Nothing really. I thought it would make things about a million times worse if I told her about me and you.

JULIE. A cop out.

ANNA. Not altogether. I said I'd always preferred women to men.

JULIE. Not bad. What did she reckon to that?

ANNA. She gave me a long, wistful smile, 'Oh, do you, dear?', then, after a pause, she said, 'To tell you the truth, so have I. Half the time I don't know what men are on about.'

JULIE (shrugs). No one can say you didn't try.

ANNA. How can you explain to somebody whose whole life is centred around God and the family that our relationship is justifiable, let alone natural?

JULIE. It ain't up to us to tell her she's wrong.

ANNA. Hang on, is this the same person who had to be physically removed from the pub last night, screaming 'Off with their rocks!'?

JULIE. So? So?

ANNA. So? Half of my colleagues were there.

JULIE. Do you want to live a lie?

ANNA. That's not fair. They all know I'm gay.

JULIE. Gay? You're the most humourless, miserable fucker this side of the Blackwall Tunnel.

ANNA. All I know is that half the contents of the staffroom were making a valid point that all men go through the same shitty system as us, and your only positive contribution was to bang your fist on the table and shout, 'Off with their rocks.'

JULIE. Oh, yeah. I suppose, according to you, we should all go round cuddling rapists to make them more lovable human beings?

ANNA. No, but . . .

JULIE. Off with their rocks!

ANNA. I am honoured to have witnessed such a conversion in your personality. In the days when I first met you, you were a feminist with a few lesbian tendencies. Then you became a lesbian with a few feminist tendencies, to a radical revolutionary terrorist feminist, to a lesbian fuckwit.

JULIE. Am I still allowed to come to the school dance?

ANNA. Only if you can manage to keep from screeching out your obscenities. And this time you keep your lecherous thoughts to yourself.

JULIE. Bleedin' cheek, I ain't a man. Women don't feel lust.

ANNA. So what was the emotional force behind trying to get your leg over the secretary?

JULIE. Give over.

ANNA. Only you could fancy someone with seven kids and a husband in the police force.

JULIE. Fancy?

ANNA. Like 'be attracted to'.

JULIE. Oh, fuck me. What's a fancy got to do with anything? I don't try to look up women's skirts on escalators, or ogle the underwear ads, or shout 'Hello, darlin', what a nice pair you got', after women in the street. (*She kisses* ANNA *on the ear.*) Oh, Anna, stop this bloody boring knitting.

ANNA. We've only just got up! Women don't feel lust, my arse.

JULIE. This is my insatiable lesbian persona.

ANNA. Okay. Let me finish this row.

JULIE. Blimey, I hope that's not the equivalent of, 'Not just at the moment, darling, I've got a headache'. Can't you do it another time?

ANNA. Some of us work at other times, or had you forgotten?

JULIE. I do the Open University.

ANNA. What are you on about? Women do feel lust.

JULIE. Right, but there's one main difference – you don't find women wanking each other off under toilet doors.

ANNA. A fact I can't deny.

JULIE. So what's the reason why?

ANNA. Because they'd break their wrists on the partitions.

JULIE. Are you deliberately trying to misunderstand me? You find blokes going into toilets, sucking off other blokes and walking off without giving it another thought.

ANNA. Shut up, will you?

JULIE. What's the matter?

ANNA. I'm worried.

JULIE. I know you don't like the Open University. I suppose I did take on a bit much.

ANNA. You didn't have to do all 392 degrees. You'll end up in the bin.

JULIE. Well, I s'pose I could drop the extra-mural course in aesthetics.

ANNA. No, I'm a bit worried about my mum.

JULIE. Did you tell her she could come and stay here?

ANNA. Yes. She looked at me as though I'd just suggested that she cut her head off.

JULIE. Your spaghetti bolognese does leave something to be desired.

ANNA. When I suggested that she should go to a women's group she laughed.

JULIE. That all?

ANNA. No, she said, 'What do they do then? Put their hand on a toadstool and say, "I promise never to stir my husband's tea again!"'

JULIE. You just gotta wait till she realises it for herself.

ANNA. I can't see that she'll ever do that.

JULIE (*laughs*). You are a patronising big-head.

ANNA. What made your mum aware of male supremacy then?

JULIE. My dad.

ANNA. It's not as if she's read the right books.

JULIE (*explodes*). What?! Do all teachers reek of elitist arrogance? Whoever learnt anything from a book?

ANNA. All right, all right, but how . . .

JULIE. Life's experience don't count for nothing, I s'pose.

ANNA. Well you didn't do so well with the step-mother.

JULIE. Fuck off.

ANNA. Nor your half-sister.

JULIE. We still keep in touch.

ANNA. Come off it, the last time you heard from her was about a year ago.

JULIE. For your information I got a note from her yesterday suggesting that we go for a drink.

ANNA. That still doesn't excuse your unsisterliness in leaving home without her.

JULIE. Anna – I was sixteen. She was eight. Radical as I am, I never envisaged setting up an alternative Dr Barnados.

ANNA. Why do you always have the last word?

JULIE. Because I ain't read the right books, thank God.

Blackout.

Scene Four

MARY's *kitchen.* MARY, DAVID, DAPHNE *and* ROGER *are playing Monopoly.*

DAPHNE. Really, David. That's not fair.

ROGER. Come off it, darling. That is a jolly good offer.

DAPHNE. You're joking. David, you're practically giving it away.

DAVID. Nonsense. No one can ever win with that set. I'll swop you Leicester Square for Bond Street, plus five hundred pounds.

DAPHNE. Done.

DAVID. And, Mary, I'll give you five hundred pounds for Regent Street. Mary, dear? Are you with us?

MARY (*vacant*). Sorry? Sorry, dear, what did you say?

DAVID. I said I'll buy Regent Street from you for five hundred pounds.

MARY (*smiles*). That's all right, dear. You can have it.

DAPHNE. Mary, don't be daft.

DAVID. Try to play the game, dear. You'll never get anywhere unless you play to win.

MARY. Sorry, dear. It's just that I haven't caught up with the washing-up from lunch, and now the tea things . . .

DAVID. Don't worry about that, we'll all give a hand later. Now here's five hundred pounds.

MARY. Thank you.

DAVID. Besides, what were you doing while I was showing Daphne the rhododendrons?

MARY. Making the tea.

DAVID. I don't think we need contradict each other all of the time.

MARY. No, dear. I mean yes, dear.

ROGER. Where did you get all that money from, Daphne?

DAPHNE. From you landing on my property.

ROGER. You couldn't possibly have accumulated that lot.

DAPHNE. Some of us remember to collect two hundred pounds as we pass Go.

DAVID. Right. Now who wants houses?

ROGER. Six, please.

DAVID. Six houses at one hundred and fifty pounds each, that's . . .

ROGER. Nine hundred pounds. There you go, old boy.

DAPHNE. Is David always the banker?

ROGER. Whoever heard of an Anglican church warden cheating at Monopoly on a Sunday? What's got into you, Daphne?

DAVID. Well, you see, Mary's got no money sense.

MARY (*vague*). Pardon? The housekeeping's not out, is it?

DAVID. No, silly. I meant that you have no business sense.

DAPHNE. Well, three hotels for me please, David.

ROGER. See what I mean? Where did you get that cash?

DAPHNE. It's only Pentonville and Euston Road, for Christ's sake . . . er, I mean, for goodness' sake.

ROGER. I'll pretend that I didn't hear that.

DAPHNE. Hey, Mary, you haven't got a set.

DAVID. Don't worry, Daphne. Mary's never been much of a one for getting into the spirit of things. Hasn't got my drive for excitement. Now, whose turn?

ROGER. Mine. Now then, let's see . . . who's this on Fleet Street? David. Right, Fleet Street with two houses, that's six hundred pounds.

DAPHNE. If we'd have taken Mary's advice in the first place and played to the nearest ten pounds we wouldn't have spent nearly two hours getting to the buying stage.

DAVID. Playing to the nearest ten pounds! Have you ever heard the like, Roger? Sacrilege. I ask you. Pure sacrilege. Well, Roger, you have my sympathy if Daphne plays to the nearest ten pounds with the housekeeping. Ha ha.

ROGER. Sorry, Mary, it looks like you've landed on me. Let me see, Trafalgar Square with two houses . . . That's six hundred pounds.

MARY. Oh, dear. Well, it looks as though I'm cleared out.

DAVID. Wait a minute now, let's see. If you mortgage the stations and the gas works, plus the cash . . .

MARY. It's hardly worth it. I'll make a start on the washing-up.

DAVID. Mary, you have no sense of competition.

MARY. But, dear, I . . .

DAVID. Oh well, a cup of tea would be nice, while you're up.

DAPHNE. Do let me help.

DAVID (as MARY goes out). She hates anyone under her feet, don't you dear? (He sees her going off in the wrong direction.) Where are you going, Mary? What are you doing?

MARY (as she re-enters). I wanted to go to the lavatory first, David.

MARY goes out.

DAVID (embarrassed). Oh, sorry. There, see what I mean? Very absent-minded.

DAPHNE. Well, for the short time we've known you, Mary has always seemed a, well, a vague sort of person.

DAVID. It's not so much that as this 'couldn't care less' sort of attitude. I told her you were coming, but she didn't even have anything ready. Time and again it's been the same. Last week there was a twenty-minute gap between the first course and the pudding. Time and time again.

ROGER. Come on, old boy, don't be too hard on Mary. She needs a jolly good rest, and what we talked about seems just the thing.

DAVID. I'm glad you agree. But I don't want her to think anything's wrong. (*To* DAPHNE.) Daphne, perhaps after we've had a cup of tea, you two could have a little chat while you help her with the washing-up.

DAPHNE. What about you?

ROGER. Come off it, if he insists on doing the washing-up it will give the game away.

DAPHNE. You're the one to talk, darling.

ROGER. We have our work cut out on Sundays as it is, don't we David? And, in the separate occupation Our Lord has chosen for us, all the other days of the week as well. How are things at the office at the moment, old boy?

DAVID. Fine, fine. You know.

ROGER. Actually, I was going to ask you . . .

DAPHNE. I meant, why don't you talk to her first?

DAVID. Difficult to say that sort of thing, you know women. Ask them what's wrong and they get annoyed.

DAPHNE. How will you cope if she does go away for a week?

DAVID. Oh, the lady next door is very good.

ROGER. And I'm sure that plenty of the lady parishioners will rally round.

DAPHNE. Well, I must say she does look tired.

ROGER. And David, you must try and remember . . .

DAPHNE. Damn . . . I mean, blow. I've left my cigarettes in the car.

DAVID (*trying hard not to appear shocked*). I didn't know you smoked.

ROGER. She's trying to give up, aren't you, Daphne?

DAPHNE. Yes, Roger, I'm trying.

DAPHNE *goes out.*

DAVID. Oh dear. I hope it wasn't anything I said.

ROGER. Goodness me no. What were we saying? Oh yes . . . Now you mustn't be too hard on Mary. Her role is not to be undermined and routine can prove to be quite boring from time to time, so I've heard.

DAVID. But I . . .

ROGER. Even when they're used to it. I know it's sometimes hard to remember, I should know, I'm the world's worst. Take Daphne . . . though I must say she's much better since I gave her the go-ahead with the Youth Club. You know what Mary needs? A sense of responsibility. Maybe she could help out with the Mothers' Union . . . ?

DAVID. I don't think . . .

ROGER (*patronising*). And it's not really up to us to speak for them. Believe it or not women have minds of their own. Ha ha! You know sometimes I forget that Daphne has a degree.

DAVID. Has she?

ROGER. Yes. Mind, it's only a two:one.

DAVID (*unsure*). Ah, of course.

ROGER. But it all adds up to the fact that we do have to tread a bit carefully with the fairer sex these days.

DAVID. Yes, I suppose . . .

ROGER. And don't forget, I can always get Marshall Hutchinson to drop in.

DAVID. Marshall Hutchinson?

ROGER. That old college pal of mine. You know. Works as a psychiatrist at the Royal and General. Most of his work is

private, but I'm sure he'd make a home visit on the National
Health if I said it was for a friend of mine.

DAVID. That's very kind.

ROGER. Anyway, it might not come to that. I'm sure Daphne
will be able to cheer her up.

DAVID. Frankly, I'm beyond optimism.

ROGER. Nonsense. Women do each other a power of good.
There's nothing they enjoy more than a good chat about
depression.

DAVID. Believe me, Mary's about as alert as a ball of wool in the
fog.

MARY *re-enters.*

DAVID. By the way, how did things go with that family this
morning?

ROGER. Interesting. I'm very glad that estate is in the parish.
Working–class people are so genuine.

DAVID. Salt of the earth. (*He looks down.*) Where's my tank?

ROGER. Here, use the shoe, old boy.

DAVID. No, I always have the tank. It's been a tradition in this
family, from way back when we all used to play together as a
family. I've always been the tank. It reminds me of the Church
Army. Dear, have you seen the tank?

MARY. Where did you leave it?

DAPHNE *re-enters.*

DAPHNE. Your tank?

DAVID. On Fleet Street. Oh, dear me. It looks as if we'll have to
abandon the game.

DAPHNE. Oh no, what a shame.

MARY *pours out the tea, using the milk straight from the bottle.*

DAVID. Mary, don't we use the milk jug anymore, dear?

MARY. Sorry, I forgot to tell you. It broke last week.

While MARY's back is turned DAVID gives DAPHNE and ROGER a 'there-what-did-I-tell-you' look.

DAVID. Really, Mary. That was a wedding present.

MARY. I'm sorry.

DAVID. Well, don't worry, never mind. Can't be helped. Accidents will happen.

ROGER. Oh, yes, I've remembered what I wanted to ask you about. Perhaps, we could do a chat or something on 'Numbers in the Congregation'. I think, since my arrival, I've got them down to thirty-two.

DAPHNE. Haw haw, my Roger is really quite a card.

ROGER. That reminds me, did you hear the one about the Catholic priest who was arrested for practising celibacy in the street?

They all laugh, including MARY who doesn't understand it.

DAPHNE. Always find that one hilarious. (*She mutters through clenched teeth.*) Just as well, I hear it every blasted day.

DAVID (*drily*). Oh, very good.

MARY (*absently*). But how . . . I mean, he couldn't have been doing anything . . .

The others laugh at her but not unkindly.

ROGER. Never mind. How are the boys these days, Mary?

MARY. Oh, fine, fine. I think. I mean, aren't they David?

DAVID. Oh yes, all's well there.

MARY. Well, we've had one or two little traumas, haven't we?

DAVID. Not now, dear. We won't go into that.

ROGER. Sounds interesting. I'm in the wrong profession. It's only the clergy who think the phrase 'miserable as sin' is accurate.

DAPHNE. Now then, Roger.

MARY *resumes pouring the tea, without noticing that she is pouring it into the sugar basin.*

DAVID. My dear, are you aware that you are pouring tea into the sugar basin?

MARY (*flustered and embarrassed*). Tut, oh silly me.

DAPHNE. Come on, Mary, let me help you with the washing-up and leave these two to compare parochial notes.

DAVID *and* ROGER *go out, carrying cups of tea.*

DAVID. Come along, Roger.

ROGER (*off*). Oh Daphne? Could you give me Marshall's number? I've forgotten it at the moment.

DAPHNE (*finds address book in bag*). Coming! I won't be a second, Mary.

DAPHNE *goes out.*

Slowly MARY *clears up the game of Monopoly. When she has finished she finds the missing tank, but does not immediately put it into the box with the rest of the game. Instead she picks up a rolling pin from the washing-up and strikes the tank with it.*

MARY (*with aggression*). The (*Bang.*) Church (*Bang.*) Army (*Bang.*) drives (*Bang.*) you (*Bang.*) barmy! (*Bang.*)

DAPHNE *enters.* MARY *hastily puts the tank and rolling pin away.*

DAPHNE. Oh good. Now we can have a chat, just you and I.

MARY. Was it planned?

DAPHNE. Haw, haw, I don't think so. You and I never get the chance to chat together, just the two of us. (*Slight pause.*) Yes?

MARY (*suspicious*). Hmm. Well, it's nice anyway.

DAPHNE. Is there anything on your mind, Mary?

MARY. No. That's just it, my mind seems empty.

DAPHNE. I really do think you should try and get away, even if it's only for a few days.

MARY. You're not very subtle about coming to the point.

DAPHNE. Sorry, was it obvious? Believe me, Mary, you look like you need a rest.

MARY. But what would happen to all this?

DAPHNE. I'm sure the do-good lady parishioners can manage something . . .

MARY. Yes, plenty – all too willing to have a nose round the church warden's home and criticise his wife, I can just hear them now . . . Oh, I'm sorry.

DAPHNE (softly). Don't be. You don't have to apologise to me for your feelings.

MARY (pause). Actually, I would love to go and see Anna.

DAPHNE. Your daughter? She's a teacher, isn't she?

MARY. That's right. I can't see that David wants me to go.

DAPHNE. I think that he only wants what's best for you. How he arrives at the conclusion that he knows what's best is perhaps another matter. Goodness, all that washing-up!

MARY. Yes. All these years and the washing-up after Sunday lunch still not fitted into the routine.

DAPHNE. Do you have a tea-towel?

MARY. Second drawer. How do you think you're settling into Potter's Bar?

DAPHNE. Oh Mary, it's awful here.

MARY. How do you mean?

DAPHNE. Oh, you know, the people round here like to keep themselves so much to themselves . . . Even the dogs are too shy to shit.

MARY. No, I can see you're not liking it. David says that I've never tried to mix properly.

DAPHNE. What does he know – stupid bag of poop.

MARY. Daphne? Do you ever get cross?

DAPHNE (*cheerfully*). Oh, only about twice a year – and then it only lasts for six months at a time.

MARY. Do you think I'm mad?

DAPHNE. No more than the rest of us. Men are such bloody bastards.

MARY. Funny you should say that about men. When Anna was here she told me that she preferred women's company to men's.

DAPHNE. Don't we all, dear?

MARY. Only she seemed to think it was a big confession.

DAPHNE. Young people take themselves so seriously.

MARY. And I overheard Paul talking to her in the lounge . . . But I don't understand what anybody says any more.

DAPHNE. Well, what were they saying?

MARY. Paul said to Anna, 'You're a dyke'.

DAPHNE. What did Anna say?

MARY. Something about, 'It's been a long time since a little Dutch boy stuck his finger in me.'

DAPHNE. I see.

MARY. What?

DAPHNE. I think she meant that she prefers women's company in bed as well as out.

MARY. Oh. (*Then a long pause as she tries to digest this.*) Do you mean . . . I mean . . . Do they kiss?

DAPHNE. I should suppose so.

MARY. And touch each other?

DAPHNE. I would have thought so.

MARY. What on earth for?

DAPHNE. I don't know. (*She shrugs.*) Love?

MARY. No, she did say something, now I remember, about a political decision.

DAPHNE. Crumbs. I've heard of thinking about God, or the Queen, but the state of the economy? That's a bit hard to swallow. I would have assumed it was more of a biological thing.

MARY. Oh my. (*Pause.*) I always said that that antenatal care left a lot to be desired. (*Pause.*) Oh my. (*Pause.*) What a dreadful thing.

DAPHNE. Dreadful? Rubbish, it sounds jolly good fun.

MARY. Have you ever thought about it?

DAPHNE. Not as a rule. Certainly not when I'm fully clothed.

MARY. Daphne!

DAPHNE. Mary, how can it be wrong or dreadful if it just comes into your head naturally?

MARY. Well, sometimes, quite naturally, I have an idea that I want to kill someone.

DAPHNE (*shrugs*). We can't all be perfect, now can we? Now, I wonder what's happened to those frightfully hideous bores we married.

MARY. Daphne?

DAPHNE. Yes?

MARY. Have you . . . I mean, have you ever done it? With a woman?

DAPHNE. Goodness me, no. (*Slight pause.*) Not since I was at Millfield anyway.

DAVID and ROGER *enter.*

DAVID. Ha, there you are. (*He claps.*) Did you have a good chat?

DAPHNE. Yes, I think so. Mary was saying how much she'd enjoy a rest.

ROGER. Well it certainly seems to have brought the colour back to her cheeks.

MARY. I mean if it's not . . . if it won't be too much trouble.

DAVID. Nonsense, dear. I think it's a wonderful idea.

DAPHNE. Cheerio, and thanks for the lunch and the tea.

DAPHNE *goes to kiss* MARY *on the cheek.* MARY *visibly stiffens and turns away.*

ROGER. Yes, absolutely great. Bye.

ROGER *and* DAPHNE *go out.*

DAVID. I must say I do think you've made the right decision. I know that you won't take offence if I tell you that you've been looking so worn out lately.

MARY. It will be nice to see Anna on her own. I'll drop her a note this evening.

DAVID. Anna? Oh, no, my dear, the less we see of that young madam the better. I've arranged for you to go on a retreat. Didn't Daphne explain?

MARY. Daphne explain? A retreat? David, what are you on about?

DAVID. It's a special conference for those women who are married to men involved in the Church. An opportunity for you to meditate and re-dedicate your life to the Lord and His works.

MARY. But David, I am already!

DAVID. You've suffered a lapse in attitude. For example, I see Daphne had to help you with the washing-up which was still left over from lunch.

MARY. But David, you insisted that I play Monopoly.

DAVID. And that's another thing, your reluctance to take part in family activities.

MARY. But, David.

DAVID. Don't worry.

MARY. But, David . . .

DAVID. There you go again, dear. I think your epitaph could be 'But David'. Let's have some Horlicks.

MARY. Are you sure you'll be able to cope?

DAVID. I think we can manage until you get back, ha ha. And I'm going to see this doctor friend of Roger's while you're away and have a long chat with him.

MARY. Are you ill?

DAVID. No dear, about you. You see, you're just so disorientated.

MARY. Daphne was very strange this evening. Did you know that she hates men?

DAVID. Hates men? What a way for a vicar's wife to behave. Between ourselves she's not very popular. Even the bishop said she was unhinged.

MARY. Well, she swore.

DAVID. Good grief. I don't think you need repeat it.

MARY. Oh, I wouldn't repeat it, but she said all men are . . . blank, blanks.

DAVID. Great Scott! Did she? Do you think we should warn Roger?

MARY. No, don't do that.

DAVID. Hmm. Sure you haven't been hearing things again? Now, are you coming to bed? We've an early start tomorrow.

MARY. Soon. I've got too much to do at present.

DAVID (smiles). Well, don't be too long. See you in a minute.

DAVID goes out.

MARY. Monday, dinner – beefburger, chips and peas. Tuesday,

casserole, apple pie in freezer. Wednesday, fishcakes and . . . an
. . . oh God, I don't want to go tomorrow, everyone will know
I think rude words and that I'm decomposing from the inside
. . . (*Slower.*) Dear God, why do people kiss? On reflection it
seems so disgusting to put your mouth on somebody else's. Dea
God, where do other people get the motivation for living from?
(*She takes out the bible.*) Dear God, please give me some guidance
(*She opens the Bible, closes her eyes and sticks a pin in a passage at
random. She reads the passage.*) 'And Judas went out and hanged
himself.'

Blackout.

Scene Five

TARA. *Monologue.*

TARA. I don't believe you've met my husband, Marshall, yet.
He's a psychiatrist. Yes, quite a conversation stopper, isn't it?
People are always intrigued to know about the ins and outs of h
home life. You know, like the fascination we all have about
clergymen who embezzle the collection or policemen who
murder prostitutes, but unfortunately, Marshall's typically sane
Of course, he has his little routine and rituals. And as for sex,
well, my dear, you can imagine how paranoid psychiatrists are
about that. When we were first married we used to go to the
Greek islands for our holidays and I adored making love on the
beach but Marsh, poor love, was absolutely, obsessionally,
preoccupied with the fear of getting a grain of sand under his
foreskin. He thinks that magazines like *Forum* are where it's at.
That's where he got the idea to try and train me to relax my
throat muscles to perfect my fellatio performance. Don't
misunderstand me, it's not that I don't enjoy risking my life bu
do make it a little rule that I derive some pleasure from it. We'v
got two children and Marsh worked himself into a state of
psychosis in case they were born with one testis too few or too
many, but, despite all fears, they're terribly normal. Oh, yes,
they're both boys – pigs – don't tell me, darling, I've tried then

with the handicraft classes, cookery, the lot, until I've literally pulled my hair out – still, I must be fair, they're not all bad. The youngest, he's eight, burnt the Scout hut down last week, so there's hope yet.

Of course, we have someone who takes the tedium out of housework – you know, our little treasure – does that sound exploitative? Frankly, I'm bored out of my mind and if I had to do irksome grotto chores I'd go completely off my head.

I love going to the pictures in the afternoon – it's so common.

Marshall is still trying to sue Ken Russell because it was after I saw *Women in Love* I suffered my little bout of kleptomania. Anyway, you know that bit in the film where that other woman smashes a vase over that prick's head – are we still allowed to say 'prick'? Are we still allowed to say 'head'? God, this modifying of manmade linguistics has got us all confused. Anyhow, to cut a long story short, I lifted a Baccarat paperweight from Liberty's. Quite what I had in mind I don't know but one of our solicitor friends got me off the hook by saying I'd had a bad day.

Between you and I, Marsh has begged me to divorce him. Why should I? I don't want to live in some pokey little flat where some social worker might try and certify me for being batty. No thanks. I like being posh. Don't listen to this live without men rot. The way forward is to use them and have some fun.

Scene Six

The retreat.
    All the women sit in silence with cups of tea and Bibles on their laps.
WOMAN ONE discreetly tops up her tea with gin from a hipflask
which is concealed in her pocket. Presently a PRIEST enters dressed in a
cassock.

PRIEST. Good afternoon, ladies. I trust you enjoyed luncheon?
    (*There is a general response of smiles and nods.*) I would very much
    like to introduce you to Mrs Johnson who will be joining us this
    week. As you know we don't approve of the use of first names

here, just in case it puts any little temptations in the way of our vow of silence. So, when you have finished your tea perhaps you'd go to your room for your continual confession and purification in solitude. We shall reconvene at 9 p.m. for our daily service of Holy Communion, before retiring to bed . . . um, er, slumber . . . at nine-thirty.

The PRIEST *exits.*

Pause.

WOMAN ONE (*quietly, very slurred through excess of alcohol*). Holy Commune . . . Communion?

MARY (*leans over, confides in a whisper*). Eucharist.

WOMAN ONE. So would you be if you'd been here a frigging fortnight.

Gradually the women get up and go out in silence.

MARY (*to herself*). In all the time we've been married this is the first time I've spent a week away from David. I even had the last three children at home. I wonder if time on my own is what I need to find what is missing from my life. (*Pause.*) I wonder why I have always said 'not very well' instead of 'period'? And why . . . What am I saying? I am not here to indulge myself in obscene fantasies . . . Dear God, if you want me to recommit my life to your service please give me another, more appropriate sign. (*She opens her Bible, then looks up.*) But this is definitely the last chance you're getting. Otherwise there are going to be some drastic changes in this servant's life.

She shuts her eyes, puts her finger on a passage, then reads it aloud.

'Go thou and do likewise'.

Blackout.

Scene Seven

A week later, ANNA and JULIE's kitchen.

JULIE is surrounded by hundreds of cassettes which she appears to be relabelling. ANNA is looking through a pile of children's exercise books, occasionally tutting and ripping out a page.

JULIE. What are you doing?

ANNA (*absorbed in her own thoughts*). It's Open Day tomorrow.

JULIE. I know that, don't I? So what are you ripping up the books for?

ANNA. Because there are things in them that some of the parents aren't going to be overjoyed at seeing.

JULIE. What like? 'My teacher keeps a pin-up of Juliet Bravo on her desk lid'?

ANNA (*irritated*). Oh, you're so funny. (*She rips out another page.*)

JULIE. Let's have a look then.

She sits next to ANNA and they read through a book together.

ANNA. Here, look at this. (*Reading:*) 'Yesterday my Uncle Joe was drunk on the toilet floor and I had to step over him to have a shit.'

JULIE. Nice picture though . . . I wonder if they've really got a purple bathroom suite.

ANNA. This could be a good one. (*She looks at the cover and reads:*) 'Tracy Jones. News Book.' (*She continues reading:*) 'When my dad came home from the pub last night he smashed my mum up proper.' (*She says sarcastically:*) No, we don't say 'proper', Tracy, we say 'properly'. (*She rips out the page.*)

JULIE. Gawd, would you look at that picture. Wonder how much of our rates goes on red, black and blue felt-tips?

ANNA (*picking up another book*). 'Last night my daddy woke me up when he was doing things to my mummy.'

JULIE. Strange picture. Just a line?

ANNA. That's where I was looking over his shoulder and said in my best teacher's voice, 'No picture. Thank you, Darren.' And snatched the book away.

JULIE (*laughs*). That proves it, you are definitely prejudiced against heterosexuality, Miss Johnson. (*She writes on cassette cover.*) Wankers!

ANNA (*continuing to look through the exercise books*). Have you finished fucking up the OU cassette library?

JULIE. Yeah, I s'pose so.

ANNA. And what, dare I ask, did they think of your seminar?

JULIE. Which one?

ANNA. The one on birth control.

JULIE. They were bloody rude about it.

ANNA. Surprise, surprise.

JULIE. It was only s'posed to be a metaphorical piece, a point for discussion.

ANNA (*sarcastic*). I'm sure that your suggestion that birth control should be compulsory and used by men only went down a treat.

JULIE. Actually it did. Apart from that stupid reactionary woman who piped up from her Lentheric advert dream with, 'Oh, but I still enjoy men holding the door open for me.'

ANNA. Holding her legs open, more like.

JULIE. What's got into you?

ANNA. Nothing, sorry. So what went wrong?

JULIE. That hateful shit Nigel says, 'Oh yeah, and just what form might that take then, love?'

ANNA (*helpfully prompting*). So you said, 'A pill, to be taken by men'?

JULIE. No, I said, 'A hand grenade held firmly between the knees.'

ANNA. Perhaps you should write a book on how to put people's backs up, or how to get on with members of the opposite sex without losing your looks.

JULIE. You got any ideas on what I can do my thesis on? It's got to be something I'm interested in.

ANNA (*sarcastic*). Oh, that shouldn't be too hard, considering you hate everything.

JULIE. I do not. At most there are only five things I actually hate.

ANNA. Yes. Art, travel, society, anything manmade, or anything alive. Oh, sod it. What in hell's name are we doing? You with your cranky sabotage of the Open University. They're only ordinary people trying to get on as best they can – they weren't born into it.

JULIE. What do you suggest I do, become a housemother at Eton?

ANNA. And me. What in fuck's name am I doing? Priding myself on pioneering non-sexist literature for use in my classroom.

JULIE. You didn't get a letter from your mum this week, did you?

ANNA. No.

JULIE. Judging from the last one, she probably wrote 'very busy' on the back of a stamp. Have you phoned?

ANNA. Yes, no answer.

JULIE. She could have gone out.

ANNA. She only goes shopping. I've rung every break-time for the past three days.

JULIE. Well, ring now.

ANNA. They'll be at church now. I'll ring a bit later.

JULIE. There's nothing you can do till then, so stop worrying.

The doorbell rings.

ANNA. Who the hell can that be?

I hope it isn't that Nigel, with instructions of where to put your hand grenade.

JULIE. Oh, God, you go and answer it in your teacher's voice.

ANNA goes out.

JULIE picks up the exercise books and looks through them.

ANNA (*off*). Mum!

ANNA enters with MARY.

ANNA. What's happened? What are you doing? Are you all right?

MARY. Of course, I'm all right. I just thought I would come and visit my daughter, but I can't . . .

ANNA. Good, you've left him.

MARY. No, I haven't left him. Honestly, love, what a thing to infer. I can't stop, this is just a flying visit. I only wanted to see how you are. (*To* JULIE.) Hello, you must be Anna's friend.

JULIE. Hello, you must be her mum.

ANNA. Oh, sorry, Mum, this is Julie. Julie, this is my mum.

MARY. Nice to meet you, Julie. Anna tried to tell me about you last week.

Pause.

But it didn't sink in at first.

JULIE. Oh, really . . .

Pause.

MARY (*sighing*). Well, I can see that I'm going to have to wait a long time before you two insist that you're just flatmates.

Pause.

Now I really can't stop long.

ANNA. Perhaps long enough to sit down? (*Pause.*) So how did you get here?

MARY. Oh, yes. (*She sits.*) Right, well it's quite a long story, but your father – no, it started before that, really . . . You know I'd been feeling a bit under the weather . . . Well, anyhow, your father thought it would be a good idea if I went away for a rest, and he packed me off on this – I don't know quite how to describe it – this get together of women married to men working for the Church, only nobody was allowed to talk or communicate in any way, no phone, nothing. I couldn't even get hold of any paper to write a letter. Then it occurred to me that you were only a bus ride away.

ANNA. Thank God you've escaped.

MARY. I haven't escaped. I don't know why you have to be so dramatic all the time. (*She begins to get more agitated.*) Mind you, you always had to be different, didn't you? I don't know what else I could have expected. You always were odd. Everybody else marries a man, but not you. It looks as though I've got to resign myself to being the only mother in Acacia Avenue with three sons and four daughters-in-law.

ANNA. Mum, we are not married.

MARY. And why not, that's what I'd like to know. I wouldn't put it past you.

JULIE (*lightly*). I wouldn't have her, she can't iron a shirt to save her life.

MARY. I can quite believe it, Julie. I tried, oh yes, but Madam didn't want to know. I'm surprised she's not entirely defunct on the domestic front.

ANNA (*hurt*). Mum.

MARY. I wouldn't put anything past you. I'm still waiting to find out what was wrong with Kevin.

ANNA. Mum don't . . .

MARY. He was such a nice boy.

JULIE. Kevin?!

ANNA. He was training to be a butcher when I was doing my eleven-plus.

MARY. And he worked really hard at it as well. He's his own boss now, you know. (*To* ANNA.) If she'd played her cards right she could have been living over the Dewhurst shop in Camden by now.

ANNA. Am I ever going to win?

Pause.

MARY (*deep breath, then quietly*). Oh dear, I'm sorry, it's lovely to see you. Both of you. The last thing I meant to do was go ranting on. For ages now I've not felt quite right, must be the change of life, but I can't keep blaming that for everything. I became aware that something was definitely wrong when I started to beat the tank.

ANNA (*mouths at* JULIE). Beat the tank?

JULIE (*shrugs and mouths back*). A Potter's Bar expression for masturbation?

MARY. But now I've had the luxury of a whole week to myself and I've come to the conclusion that I don't really mind about it . . . umm, you. You two. Both of you. You know.

ANNA. I'm very pleased. Thanks.

MARY. To tell you the truth, in many ways it comes as a big relief.

ANNA. That's great.

MARY. From the day you were born I've dreaded the speech your father would make at your wedding.

ANNA. Now, in all honesty, I can't say that was one of my reasons.

MARY. I know, I know, I've come to the conclusion that I've worried about a lot of silly things. All my life I've dreaded being thought of as abnormal, while I've based my ideas of normality on David.

ANNA (*ruefully*). Fancy thinking Dad was normal.

MARY. Quite. Mind, you should meet the vicar. He's even more normal.

ANNA. So, you're going to leave him.

MARY. No.

JULIE. Er, I think I'll go and fix dinner. You will stay?

MARY. That's very kind, but I really haven't got time. I'll have to be back at two. David – that's my husband, Anna's father – is picking me up then.

JULIE. Won't they wonder where you've gone?

MARY. They'll wonder all right, but the irony of it is that they won't be able to say anything.

ANNA. How morbid.

MARY. I found it all rather intriguing. Agatha Christie fashion. I kept expecting to find a body in the linen cupboard, but no such luck. Although somebody had torn the last page of Revelation out of the Bible by my bedside.

JULIE. On that optimistic note I'll put the potatoes on.

JULIE *goes out.*

MARY. How nice, you can both make lunch.

ANNA. See, having one daughter-in-law too many could be advantageous.

MARY. Don't push me. Mind, it must be lovely not to have the whole day centred around mealtimes. You know, a lot of things you've said often to me have had a chance to sink in this week and I've made up my mind that when I get home things are going to be done on my terms. (*Pause.*) There, what do you think of that?

ANNA. I don't want to appear to be pouring cold water . . .

MARY. Then don't. I thought you would be pleased.

ANNA. Oh, I am. It's just that you might find it harder than you think. I mean, good intentions are one thing, but trying to put them into practice with Dad . . .

MARY. It's not as though he's a monster, now is it? *(Slight pause.)* Of course, he'll see reason.

ANNA. But . . .

MARY. He's a very reasonable man. He is. Your father is a very reasonable man. Believe it or not he is reasonable. Not quite reason itself, I grant you that, but . . .

ANNA. The words clash.

MARY. Pardon?

ANNA. 'Reasonable' and 'man'. You can't have them together in the same sentence.

MARY. I hope that's not a sample of what gets taught in the classroom today, that half of the population is unreasonable.

ANNA. No.

MARY. I suppose that if it was up to you, the male half of the human race would be cut up for dog food.

ANNA. Don't be daft.

MARY. Sorry. Look, I don't think what you're doing is wrong. I don't know what's right or wrong, but it can't be right for everyone. How can it be? Where would we all be then?

ANNA. Look, I'm not putting it very well. If any change is . . .

MARY. Change? Change? You can't change the weather. Some things you can't change.

ANNA. You just said that you were going to change things at home.

MARY. Quite, but it's one thing claiming to try and change nature, I'm only going to reorganise my kitchen, for goodness' sake.

ANNA. But you're not going to change Dad.

MARY. I don't know why you have to keep putting him down all the time.

ANNA. Because you've wasted the last thirty years of your life wading through the valley of the shadow of marriage.

MARY (*kindly*). Really, dear, there's no need to take that tone. Goodness me, you make it sound like a living death. You might think that they've been wasted, but let me remind you that you are a direct product of them. I don't think you realise what you're saying half of the time.

ANNA (*snaps*). That's right, I'm mad.

MARY. I'm sorry.

ANNA. No, it's me. It's just that Dad's so set in his ways – still, that's not for me to say. You know him better than I do.

MARY. At least we're agreed on that. (MARY *gets up*.) Well, I'd better be . . .

ANNA. I was so worried about you.

MARY. It's me that's supposed to worry about you. It's been lovely to see you. (*She turns to go, then says as an afterthought.*) I've often wondered, if anything happened to me, would you ever consider going home to look after them?

ANNA. Let's not end on a sour note.

MARY. Good, I'm very glad of that.

JULIE *enters*.

MARY. Thanks. Bye love.

MARY *goes out*.

JULIE. Better?

ANNA. I don't know.

JULIE. She didn't seem very vague to me.

ANNA. Bloody hell.

JULIE. Shall I run a hot bath?

ANNA. I hope she's all right.

JULIE. Here, do you want to come with me this evening?

ANNA. Where?

JULIE. I'm meeting Susan, remember? Oh, I don't know, perhaps I better see her on my own, she might be in trouble.

ANNA. Do you mean 'in trouble' trouble or in trouble, trouble in general?

JULIE (sarcastic). I really wish I was as well read as you and then I might be able to express myself with such articulate coherence. (Slight pause.) I didn't particularly mean pregnant but anyway, if she needs to, she could come here.

ANNA. What, come here to live?

JULIE. Yes, it would be a great idea, me and her can . . .

ANNA. Look, why would she want to live here?

JULIE. You saying she can't?

ANNA. No, well, yes.

JULIE. What, why not? Don't tell me, let me guess. You read it in a book. The law according to Sheila Rowbotham. 'Thou shalt not take thy lover's half-sister into your flat.'

ANNA. Our flat.

JULIE. Well then. She'd really enjoy it and the two of us could step up Operation 'Bugger the Open University'.

ANNA. While muggins here goes to work.

JULIE. I can't help your self-righteous fetish for always having to be in the minority.

ANNA (exasperated). Oh, I give up.

She slams an exercise book on the table and goes out.

JULIE (shrugs). Just a joke.

Blackout.

Scene Eight

SUSAN *sits in the pub, an orange juice in front of her. She is nervous, intensely absorbed in the pattern of her skirt.* A YOUNG MAN *stands at the bar.*

Presently he comes over to her.

YOUNG MAN. Quiet in here tonight innit? I don't think I've seen yer in here before. (*He finishes his drink.*) I was jus' about ter git meself another drink, can I git you one?

SUSAN *shakes her head but doesn't look up.*

Not very talkative are yer? I was wondering like, I know this great disco up the road and like it . . .

JULIE *bursts in.*

JULIE (*oblivious of man*). Hello, sorry I'm late.

SUSAN (*looking up relieved*). That's okay.

YOUNG MAN. You two on yer own? I was just explaining ter yer mate, if yer wanted ter come ter this disco . . . it wouldn't cost yer anything on account of . . .

JULIE (*turns to him*). Fuck off.

YOUNG MAN. Like I know the bloke on the door, don't I?

JULIE. Bloody well piss off.

YOUNG MAN (*moving closer*). What about yer friend? Ain't yer goin' ter let 'er speak fer 'erself?

JULIE. Make one more move, and I'll slit yer throat.

YOUNG MAN. Okay, okay, love. Point taken. (*To SUSAN.*) A real vicious piece of skirt, her. Yer didn't let on you 'ad a bloody guard.

Pause.

Slags.

He goes out.

JULIE (*sits down*). You haven't been here long? Have you?

SUSAN. Nope.

JULIE. Come on, let's get a drink.

Pause.

JULIE. How's things?

SUSAN. Okay. (*Pause.*) You know, awful.

She starts to cry.

JULIE. Hey, I mean, look, I wouldn't have really slit that bloke's throat, would I? I mean if you'd have wanted ter . . .

SUSAN. Christ, no, not that . . .

An OLD MAN *sits next to them, staring into a half-empty pint glass*

OLD MAN (*looking up*). Here, you two aren't punks, are you?

SUSAN (*to* OLD MAN). Pardon?

JULIE. Take no notice.

OLD MAN. This used to be a nice pub, till those noisy green-haired punks got in.

SUSAN (*to* JULIE). It's just that I want ter talk ter somebody and you're . . .

OLD MAN. What they need is National Service. We need another war. Wouldn't worry about 'ow many earrings they 'ad then, if they was trying not to get their balls shot off.

JULIE. A man after my own heart.

OLD MAN. I was at Dunkirk, y'know, I've got the VC. We saved thousands of men that day. So frantic to get in the boats, they was paddlin' with rifle butts. I bin' in the trenches too, y'know. My best mate got shot to bits. Lay next to me for a fortnight in canvas bag.

JULIE. All right, mate, what do you want to drink?

OLD MAN. That's very kind of you. A pint of bitter, please.

JULIE *goes to the bar.*

OLD MAN. Not all that bad, you youngsters. What sort of life you got here, eh? This country's all full of lazy jobless scroungers.

JULIE *returns with a pint and a brandy.*

JULIE. On yer bike, action man.

OLD MAN. Why, ta very much, son.

SUSAN (*hisses to* JULIE). Why d'yer do that? He's a fascist.

JULIE. No, he's just a bloody old fool. They all bloody well are. Don't look like we're going ter be able ter git much talkin' done 'ere. Let's go somewhere, an 'ave something ter eat.

SUSAN. Yeh.

Both go out.

Blackout.

Scene Nine

RENE*'s kitchen. One o'clock in the morning.*
RENE *sits in a chair reading* Woman's Own.
ALF, *purple-faced, is slumped over the table with a currant bun in his mouth.*
SUSAN *enters.*
Silence.

RENE (*looks up. Then flatly*). Your father's choked to death on a scone.

Blackout.

Scene Ten

ANNA *and* JULIE*'s kitchen. Two o'clock in the morning.*
JULIE *enters, slumps in a chair, head in hands.*
Pause.

ANNA *enters wearing a dressing-gown.*

ANNA (*forced*). Hi, did you have a good time?

JULIE (*quietly, aggressively*). Barrel of laughs.

Pause.

ANNA (*sarcastic*). Oh good. It's nice to know that you weren't being raped. (*She explodes.*) Where in fuck's name have you been? The pubs shut hours ago. I've been worried sick. Christ, I thought . . .

JULIE. That I'd run off with the bus conductress on the number ninety-eight.

ANNA. You could have phoned.

JULIE. We went for a meal. (*She sighs.*) Do you ever git the feeling that all happiness is at someone else's expense?

ANNA. What did you do? Eat the waiter?

JULIE (*angry*). You want to know something, you can be such a patronising bleedin' . . . bloody . . .

ANNA. Who's stuck for an expletive which isn't exploitative, then?

JULIE. You bleedin' thick dickhead!

ANNA. Well, where is she?

JULIE. What d'you mean, 'Where is she?' You bleedin' well told me she weren't to stay here.

ANNA. When did that ever stop you? Your idea of democratic reasoning can be likened to the chances of a blind cat running in front of a speeding juggernaut.

JULIE. Oh dear me, we've been trying to read Muggeridge again.

ANNA. But of course, once it got out that you were looking for someone to live with she got killed in the crush.

JULIE (*quieter*). She won't leave her mum in the shit, will she?

Pause.

ANNA (*relieved*). That's settled then.

JULIE. Yeah. Want ter know something, eh? You're positively repulsive when you're smug.

The phone rings. Both exchange puzzled glances.

JULIE *picks up the receiver.*

JULIE. 'Lo. Christ, hello. What's happened? Did the old git try and lay inter yer when . . . (*Slight pause.*) Well, what? (*Long pause.*) Yes, love. Right, see yer. Ta taa. Oh, was it a scone or a scon? (*Pause.*)

She replaces the receiver. To ANNA:

My father's dead.

ANNA (*amazed*). God Almighty.

JULIE (*flatly*). No, my father, Alf.

ANNA. How? I mean . . .

JULIE. Drunken sod. Choked to death.

ANNA. Hell . . . what do you feel?

JULIE (*thinks*). Relieved . . . glad.

ANNA. But, Ju, he's dead. I mean it wasn't all his fault.

JULIE (*lightly*). Look love, don't try and spring your ideological unsound criticism crap on me.

ANNA. But . . .

JULIE (*quietly, angry*). You can theorise about anything else you fucking want but don't ever say that to me, not until you've been smashed from one side of the fucking room to the other.

ANNA. Sorry.

Pause.

JULIE. Does that mean Susan can . . .

ANNA. But why should she want to, now?

JULIE. Oh, fuck off!

She goes out.

ANNA. Ju?

Blackout.

Scene Eleven

Monday morning. MARY's kitchen. MARY is mopping the floor.
Presently DAVID enters, fully dressed with the exception of his
trousers.

MARY (*softly singing*).
'Glorious things of thee are spoken,
Zion, City of our God,
Heaven and earth . . .'

DAVID. Good morning, dear. It's so nice to have you back and in
such good spirits. A change is as good as a rest. Now you
haven't forgotten that Dr Hutchinson, although he may prefer
you to call him Marshall – no side to these professionals – is due
in a few minutes?

MARY (*pleasantly*). No, dear.

DAVID. I know you're fine, but it's just a check-up, a safety valve.
And he's a very useful person to know. I must say that we've all
been at sixes and sevens in your absence. Simon tried to iron a
shirt but soon found that he had bitten off more than he could
chew, ha ha.

MARY (*kindly*). Did he, dear?

DAVID. Still, Mrs Roberts has been a tower of strength, an
absolute gem. But it appears that the same old problem has
returned, namely that my suit trousers are missing. (*Pause.*) I
wonder if you could shed any light on the problem?

MARY *mops and sings with an edge of venom.*

I can hardly greet a psychiatrist in my underpants, now can I dear?

MARY (*genially*). They're in the garden.

DAVID (*crosses to window*). What, may I presume to ask, are they doing out there? Mary, I can not believe my eyes. My trousers are on the lawn, with a garden roller on top of them.

MARY. Getting a damp press.

DAVID (*anxious not to aggravate her 'problem'*). Curiouser and curiouser.

MARY. Saves pounds on dry cleaning.

DAVID. Would you please bring them in from the garden and I'll be prepared to turn a blind eye.

MARY. David, you are about to hear something which has never been uttered in this kitchen before.

DAVID. Which happens to be what?

MARY (*firmly*). Do – it – yourself.

DAVID (*becoming impatient*). Just how much longer are you going to keep this 'dog in the manger' facade up, eh? Marshall's visit hasn't come a moment too soon. Let me assure you that immediate steps will have to be taken to get you cured. That will knock this stuff and nonsense out of your sails. (*Pause.*) Mary, I can't go out into the garden in my underwear. Please.

MARY (*sighs*). Don't go away.

She goes out.

DAVID (*mutters*). Why couldn't you take a leaf out of Daphne's book? She's always so sophisticated.

MARY *enters with the trousers.*

The doorbell rings.

DAVID (*hastily putting on his trousers*). That'll be him now.

DAVID *goes out to open the front door and enters with* MARSHALL HUTCHINSON.

DAVID. Hello, Dr Hutchinson.

MARSHALL. Hello, David. Do call me Marshall.

DAVID (*squirming slightly in his very damp trousers*). Marshall, this is Mary. Mary, this is Dr Hutchinson.

MARSHALL. Good morning, Mrs Johnson.

MARY (*pleasantly*). Good morning, Doctor.

MARSHALL. Do call me Marshall.

DAVID. Nice to see you again, Marshall. How is Mrs Hutchinson?

MARSHALL. She's fairly well, I think. Thank you, David.

DAVID. Well, I'm sorry, but I'm afraid that I really must be off, I'm late for work already. I'm sure you two don't need me anyway, but of course you have the number if you do need to be in touch.

MARSHALL. Right, perhaps I'll do that, and don't forget what we talked about.

DAVID. Yes, right. Fine. (*He kisses* MARY, *who seems startled by this.*) Bye dear. Goodbye, Marshall.

DAVID *goes out.*

MARY (*calmly*). Please, do sit down.

MARSHALL (*sits at the table*). Thank you.

MARY. Would you like a coffee?

MARSHALL. That would be very nice, thank you.

MARY (*makes coffee, gives cup to* MARSHALL, *and continues to tidy kitchen*). Sugar?

MARSHALL. No thanks.

MARY. I suppose you'd have that thick brown sugar that tastes like sand.

MARSHALL. No, I've never had sugar.

MARY. Oh good, as long as you're not one of those brown rice and yoga fanatics.

MARSHALL. Do I look like a brown rice and yoga fanatic?

MARY (*still wiping cups, etc*). No, you look like a bored middle-aged man.

MARSHALL. Would you consider yourself fastidious, fanatical about cleanliness?

MARY. No, I'm sexually frustrated.

Pause.

MARSHALL. And why do you think that is?

MARY. Because I'm married to an emotional eunuch. (*Pause.*) No one ever taught me about sex. I had to learn the hard way.

MARSHALL. Which way was that?

MARY. A lifetime of misery.

MARSHALL. Quite. Look, Mrs Johnson, I am here to try to help you.

MARY. In that case you could have a go at cleaning my cooker.

MARSHALL. I really don't think that would get us very far or solve anything much.

He takes a fountain pen out of his breast pocket, and flicks some ink on to a piece of paper, which he folds in half and presents to MARY.

Now, Mary, what does that represent to you?

MARY (*still wiping round the table, etc*). A piece of paper with an ink blot on it, folded in half. I hope you haven't come here to flick ink all over my kitchen.

MARSHALL (*sighs*). Do you think you transmitted your disgust of sex to your daughter?

MARY. I never told her anything about it except to screech in a state of semi-hysteria that it was a very beautiful thing in marriage.

MARSHALL. Do you concede that this has undoubtedly been responsible for her immature, perverted and inadequate sexual behaviour in adult life?

MARY. I'm sorry, I don't know about her private affairs. Certainly she never told me of . . .

MARSHALL. You were not aware that she was living with another person of the same sex?

MARY. Oh yes. She's in love with a woman named Julie, oh yes.

MARSHALL. You don't feel that her so-called choice of bed partner has anything to do with your non-communication in her formative years?

MARY. Well, she was breast-fed.

MARSHALL. Mrs Johnson, are you aware of the nature of a sexual relationship between two women, of the insufficiency of human response?

MARY. No.

MARSHALL. Well, a lot of research has been carried out on the subject of female homosexuality, by very learned men. And if you want I'll précis down some of the relevant facts for you.

MARY. Please do. I'm very interested.

MARSHALL. Really, it's a dead loss, and very frustrating too.

MARY. Is that so?

MARSHALL. Yes, these people can only rarely achieve any degree of satisfaction, unless one of the two partners has unusually well-defined physical attributes. For example, occasionally a woman may have an unusually large clitoris, maybe two or even more inches in length.

MARSHALL *holds up his finger and thumb to show the size.*

Now then, if the woman concerned happens to be a lesbian and her partner spreads her legs as wide as she can, well, they may just be able to attain some degree of penetration. Of course, this type of woman is hardly the average, and the normally endowed woman may turn to the dildoe, which in reality is no more than a sponge, rubber or plastic penis.

MARY. But I . . .

MARSHALL. Please let me finish. You must understand that this forever will be the curse of the homosexual, no matter how their tastes are developed, or the success rate they may claim – basically they all end up involved in some parody of normal heterosexual intercourse. The ancient Far East is a common place to look for solutions to problems of this nature, and true to form there is a Japanese device, known as a harigata. Basically a dildoe as I have already described, but designed to be the two-headed member of the family, one head per vagina. Once inserted the partners go through the motions of heterosexual intercourse. I always end up asking myself at this point why they don't just snip it in half, both go home and enjoy themselves at their own leisure.

MARY. Are you sure about this? They seemed so happy to me?

MARSHALL. True happiness depends on a lasting relationship, an option usually denied to homosexuals. Relationships between women do tend to last longer than they do for men – possibly this stems from the male's obsession with anal activities – but they are still full of unhappiness. But male or female, their eventual problem is common to both sexes. They are all looking for satisfaction where there can be no lasting satisfaction. They are all looking for love in a world where there can be no love.

MARY (*very softly*). I think he's talking shit.

MARSHALL. Pardon?

MARY. I think you are talking shit.

MARSHALL (*pause*). Were you aware that you wanted to cannibalise your son's penis?

MARY. I beg your pardon?

MARSHALL. Your husband told me that when your youngest son – Paul, is that right?

MARY. That's right.

MARSHALL. When he quite innocently asked, 'How long's dinner?', you snapped back, 'Four inches, it's a sausage'. Were you aware that you wanted to undermine his sexuality and render him impotent by alluding to the fact that his penis was four inches long and edible?

MARY. I don't know quite how to say this, but I think perhaps you should see a doctor.

MARSHALL. Now that we've got that into the open, it still leaves us with the question of why I'm here and, more to the point, why you are here.

MARY (firmly). I am not . . .

MARSHALL. Metaphysically, I'm afraid, the evidence is indisputable.

MARY. I am not mental.

MARSHALL. That's a very old-fashioned word that we no longer like to use these days. Instead we have a less crude, more specifically defined vocabulary of terminology.

MARY. In that case, I'm not psychopathic, hysteric, neurotic, psychotic, paranoic, schizophrenic, manic depressive, hypochondriac, a raving lunatic or a screwball.

MARSHALL. Quite, but we prefer to think of it as an illness. Just as the body can fall sick for no apparent reason so can the mind.

MARY (louder). I am not mental.

MARSHALL. Mrs Johnson, I'm afraid . . .

MARY (screams). I AM NOT MENTAL.

MARSHALL (shouts). YES YOU FUCKING WELL ARE! (Slight pause.) Oops, sorry . . . overworked . . . (Gently.) Look, why else would I be here? And look at these letters your husband gave me.

He takes some letters from his pockets and starts to read one:

'Dear God, if I have three grown sons, how can it be that I cannot bear to see my husband undressed? Penis running dry. I'm afraid I can't go on.'

MARY (*puzzled, looks at the letter he holds out to her*). No, my 'pen is running dry', i.e. it contains no ink. Therefore . . . I couldn't write anything else after that . . . You seem to be penis-mad. I haven't given the things a second thought in years.

MARSHALL. Do you think that is the evidence of a sane woman?

MARY. How would you know?

MARSHALL. We are supposed to be trained in these matters.

MARY. In being a woman? Impossible. All you're trained in is a load of men's mumbo jumbo garbage. Oh yes, by your values I'm nuts, but by my values I was – but I am no longer. I've wasted my life in a bitter compromise. I've bitten my lip and said nothing when inside I've been screaming. And when I've practically wanted to wring his neck I've said 'Yes, dear' or 'Whatever you think, dear'. Yes, you win. I was no longer alive, and now I am insane. It's great to feel things, it's just great to be mental. Take any prize you want. Now bum off.

MARSHALL. Let me tell you, it's you with the anal fixation, not me.

Good day.

MARY. Goodbye.

MARSHALL *goes out*.

MARY (*starts to write*). Dearest Anna . . .

Lights fade on MARY.

Lights up on ANNA, *reading a letter she has just finished writing*.

ANNA. Dear Mum, I am writing to tell you how much strength I have gained from our conversation on Sunday, and how much your supportive feelings have meant to me. I think you will probably find things harder than you expected this week, and hopefully I will drop in next Sunday when the old bastard (*She crosses this out.*) when Dad is at church. Take care of yourself, much love Anna.

Lights fade down on ANNA and fade back up on MARY, still writing.

MARY. . . . and so, dearest Anna . . .

PAUL *enters.*

PAUL. Wotcher, Ma.

MARY. Wotcher, you little grass.

PAUL. Ma?

MARY. Grassing me up about my one and only joke.

PAUL. The 'Four inches, it's a sausage' one?

MARY. What else? You're always so full of what a humourless cow I am. What other joke could I possibly mean?

PAUL. Gawd, do you have to go on so much?

MARY. What are you doing home this time of day anyway?

PAUL. Sick. Said I was sick.

MARY. Which roughly translated means you've got a bird lined up.

PAUL. Got it in one. But I'm going to watch *Crown Court* first. Okay?

MARY (*gently*). Do you care about me, Paul?

PAUL. Course I do. Bleedin' hell, last week it was bedlam. Blimey, if I didn't care about you would I still be living here? Any chance of something to eat?

MARY. What would you like to eat?

PAUL. We got any toast?

MARY. We've got bread and a toaster. I'm sure it's a simple enough equation for someone with an HND in mechanical engineering.

PAUL. Can't yer give it a bleeding rest?

MARY. Why do you have to talk to me like that?

PAUL. Because I want to, right? Why do you talk like you do?

MARY. Like what?

PAUL. That pathetic simpering.

MARY. I'm sorry.

PAUL. You really get on my nerves. I'll be in my room if you deign to change your mind about the toast.

PAUL goes out.

DAVID enters.

DAVID. Hello, dear, I came as quickly as I could.

MARY. Why, what's happened?

DAVID. Marshall rang me, he says you definitely qualify for a bed. Can you imagine, a National Health bed? I just popped home to tell you that you can be admitted this evening. It's all right, I'll take you, of course.

MARY. But David . . .

DAVID. Now, Mary, it must be a voluntary admission, for your own good. Once it becomes a Mental Health Section it becomes legally binding. Now I really have to be getting back to the office.

MARY. But David . . .

DAVID. Don't worry about a thing, we'll manage, I'll pick you up. Bye dear, see you later.

DAVID goes out.

MARY. And so, dearest Anna . . .

Long pause while she writes first paragraph, then:

MARY. . . . and so I ask you nothing except for one thing – is that what they call a double bind? – please don't confront the boys or your father over this, but keep quiet. Don't waste any time trying to live up to what you thought my expectations of you were – you have already fulfilled them. I couldn't have loved you more if I'd understood you less, Mum.

She puts ANNA's letter in an envelope, which she seals and addresses.

MARY (*writing new letter*). Dear David, your dinner and my head are in the oven.

She crosses to the cooker, finds a comfortable position, turns on the gas and puts her head in the oven.

Fade. Blackout.

Scene Twelve

RENE. *Monologue.*

RENE. It's bin ages since I seen a show. I don't rightly see the point of 'em myself. With my life I 'aven't 'ad no room for dramatic art – know what I mean? What I call good entertainment is the royal wedding – no, it might surprise you to know that I don't love 'em and, to be honest with you, I do feel if we've paid for it, and let's face it, we have – they could have all made the effort to look nice. For my money the Queen looked a frump, well, didn't she? Mind, I say that but I wouldn't 'ave her job fer the world, but if the truth be known when Mountbatten copped his lot I didn't feel anything. If you want to know something, I almost breathed a sigh of relief when I heard the Pope had bin shot. Would you trust a man who vowed never to have sex? I don't mean to be funny but if God hadn't meant us to do it, he'd 'ave put pollen on our plates, wouldn't he? Don't get me wrong, I'm not saying I wished him dead but when I saw him sitting up in hospital I felt me hopes had been dashed. I know it's wrong. It was wrong. It's just like with Alf passing on so suddenly I seem to have death on the brain. Police come round, didn't they, insinuating that it was mighty peculiar that the body was cold before the doctor was called but even they have to accept the coroner's verdict of death by misadventure, not before they'd turned the whole place upside down, I might add.

And terday, y'know, I woke up and I felt different – everything seemed to have changed. Susan and me had breakfast together and we didn't have to whisper or try frantically to hush the Rice Krispies up. I was an old nag I was, I used to rabbit on and on and yesterday evening, coming home from the bus stop on me own I started to get that nervy feeling again but I ain't never bin beaten up or raped outside me own home. For twenty-four hours a day I lived with that fear . . . Oh Gawd, don't start me off. When Susan was in hospital she met this woman who used to go on all the time you know, she was a bit like that Julie nutter except for . . . Don't try and tell me – career or family or both, it don't seem to make no difference – still moaning. I said ter her, I said, that's the trouble with us, we don't seem ter know what we want. We 'ad this long conversation, really nice girl she was, but I can't fathom some of them words and I don't want nothing what I can't understand. But I do understand one thing now. Like even if in the future I met a nice respectable man and even if I was to marry him – he nor any man wouldn't mean that much in comparison to what my daughter means to me.

cene Thirteen

hospital room.
MARY *in bed, semi-conscious.*
Presently THREE WOMEN *enter.*

1ARY (*mumbles*). What? Where? Oh, er. What's . . .

)LD WOMAN. It's all right, dear, you're perfectly okay. You're safe.

1ARY. How? How did I get here? What happened? Who are you?

)LD WOMAN. Gently now. Try and give yourself room to think.

1ARY. Oh, no. I feel so ashamed. It must be a month since I cleaned my cooker. Smell my hair.

OLD WOMAN. Mmm. Roast beef. Hadn't you been converted to North Sea Gas. It's not poisonous, so I am told.

MARY. No, the cooker was too old.

She smiles.

Oh dear, fancy talking about the state of my cooker the minute I come round from . . . well.

OLD WOMAN. I don't worry. I'm usually greeted with, 'How many calories are there in a hundred valium?'

MARY (*to herself*). Funny matron.

OLD WOMAN (*gently*). I am here to tell you that I love you and have done so all your life. I am ahead of myself. Introductions first. I am the deity.

MARY (*confused, to* TALL WOMAN). I suppose she means the day-ity shift as opposed to the night-y.

OLD WOMAN (*gesturing to* TALL WOMAN). This is the Holy Hostess with the mostest and this (*She gestures to* YOUNG WOMAN) is my daughter who bled in a shed for you – and for many.

Silence.

MARY (*panics*). Now hold on a minute, what sort of hospital is this? It's a loony bin, isn't it? He's had me committed to the bin.

She is frightened.

OLD WOMAN (*takes hold of* MARY's *hand*). No, Mary, you're in paradise.

MARY (*shouts*). Christ alive. I'm dead!

YOUNG WOMAN (*smiles*). No need to call up false images.

MARY. But I mean, I never got the feeling that God approved of me.

OLD WOMAN (*shrugs*). That's just as well. He doesn't exist.

MARY. But I, oh . . .

OLD WOMAN (*kindly*). You are here, like other women, because your life was at best monotonous, and at worst unbearably painful. But you have the choice to go back to where you left off.

MARY. Go back?

OLD WOMAN. Yes. To that awful existence you call life. I can assure you that you won't have to do anything you don't want to.

MARY. Excuse me, but what happens to men? In the Bible it says . . .

TALL WOMAN (*shrieks*). That libellous load of crap!

OLD WOMAN. That is a myth created by men in their fear. Men don't have eternal life. How could they? They have no souls. You must have noticed. They're all two-dimensional.

YOUNG WOMAN. Just bloody bores . . . excuse my menstrual jargon.

MARY. So you can beam me back to Earth? Like on *Star Trek*?

TALL WOMAN. That libellous load of crap.

OLD WOMAN (*smiles*). What sort of hostess are you? Honestly, you'd think she'd learnt only one colloquial expression from the world of man. (*All three shudder.*) Mary, you are in a twilight zone. The choice is yours.

MARY. But my daughter . . .

OLD WOMAN. Remember, I am with you. If you go back I will do all I can to help you stand against that war-ridden shit heap men call earth.

MARY. Who'd have thought the deity would say shit?

Slight pause.

I must go back.

OLD WOMAN. As you wish.

MARY. At least until she's happily married.

Thunder roars, lightning flashes.

What am I saying?

TALL WOMAN. Take it from me, Mary. She's found something better than that load of crap.

OLD WOMAN. There you go again.

TALL WOMAN. Well you said shit.

MARY. If I decide to go back, can you give me the power to put the fear of God – I beg your pardon – into those men.

OLD WOMAN (*shakes her head and smiles*). I'm sorry, Mary, but we simply know no fear.

MARY. In that case . . .

I'm home.

Immediate blackout.

From the complete darkness we hear ROGER *in his official capacity.*

ROGER. Forasmuch as it hath pleased Almighty God of his great mercy to take unto himself the soul of our dear sister here departed: we therefore commit her body to the ground, earth to earth, ashes to ashes, dust to dust;

Lights up on MARY's *kitchen.*

DAPHNE *is at the table making cucumber sandwiches. There is a tray of full sherry glasses on the table.*

ROGER *and* DAVID *are drinking tea.*

DAVID. I really can't thank you enough. It was a very moving service.

ROGER. That's quite all right, old boy. It was the very least I could do in the circumstances.

DAVID. I only have ten years left before I retire.

ROGER. Rotten. Rotten bad luck.

DAPHNE (*screams*). Rotten bad luck. (*She checks herself quietly.*) Roger, she reached despair, she killed herself.

DAVID. I'll thank you to keep a civil tongue in your head. Mary was always very careless about leaving the oven door open. It is my opinion that she tripped up and fell asleep before she had time to get up.

ROGER (*nods*). All part of God's rich plan.

DAPHNE. God has a wondrous philosophy, you know what it is, eh?

ROGER. Come along, Daphners, old girl.

DAPHNE. Do you want to know what it is, eh, David? Yes, of course you do. It is this. No sooner does one door shut than the whole fucking house falls in.

ROGER (*pats DAVID on the back*). Rest assured we're all in God's hands.

DAPHNE (*screams, for she has now lost her head*). What's he doing then? Having a jolly good wank with us all?

DAPHNE goes out.

ROGER. I'm going to have to get on to Marshall over this. Do you mind if I use the phone?

DAVID. Please do. She is obviously very sick.

ROGER. Her guilt has turned inwards and consumed her. Shan't be a mo.

Both go out.

Blackout.

ANNA *and* JULIE *enter.*

ANNA *wears a black skirt and tee-shirt.* JULIE *has probably conformed to a pair of black dungarees.*

ANNA (*looks round kitchen picking up things and putting them down*). What didn't I do?

JULIE. I don't know.

ANNA. Was I too arrogant? Did I give her enough room to say what she wanted?

JULIE. I don't know.

ANNA (*smiles*). And I thought you knew everything. C'mon, let's go home.

Both hug each other to be interrupted by DAPHNE – kicking the furniture as she re-enters.

DAPHNE. Bastards. Gits. I'm going to kill them, I am. I'm going to strangle them with a cheese wire and I'll not be satisfied until I see their severed heads bobbing up and down in a washing-up bowl.

ANNA (*gently*). Please . . .

DAPHNE. Why did she want to keep quiet, look where it got her. (*Louder.*) Look where it got her. She's dead. For Chrissakes! She's dead.

She pulls two knobs off the cooker and gives them one each.

There, I have metaphorically castrated your mother's murderer, pulled the knobs off the cooker, ha ha!

JULIE. Daphne? Please.

DAPHNE. I'm not mad. For Christ's sake. I'm angry. (*She smiles.*) Don't worry. I'll sabotage tonight's salad – rinse the lettuce in Dettol.

Blackout.

Scene Fourteen

MARY's *kitchen*.
ROGER *and* DAVID *begin to set out the game of Monopoly.*

DAVID. Shall we play to the nearest ten pounds?

ROGER. That's not a bad idea. I'll have to be going at three if I'm to get to see Daphne.

DAVID. How is she these days?

MARY (*voice off, softly*). David . . .

DAVID is mildly disconcerted as though he has heard something far away.

ROGER. They've done wonders since she first went in. When I managed to speak to the top bod he said that in all his years of psychiatric care he'd never seen anyone in such mental anguish.

DAVID. Despite the fanatical support for Church unity one can't help feeling that those Christian Scientists are definitely barking up the wrong tree. If the Lord hadn't intended Largactil to be invented he wouldn't have given men such marvellous minds.

MARY (*voice off*). But David . . .

DAVID seems slightly irritated but dismisses it.

ROGER. True. Mind, Monopoly isn't the same without her.

DAVID. No. In fact it's never been the same since I lost my tank.

ROGER. Here, use the gun. The curate in my last parish told me that when Runcie was a canon he always used to play with the gun.

MARY (*off*). You know where you can poke the gun.

Tank drops from height to the table.

ROGER. Talk of the devil. Here it is.

DAVID. Mrs Roberts has been stupendous. I can't imagine what we'd have done without her.

MARY (*off*). Mother Almighty, what, tell me, is the point?

Blackout.

THE DEVIL'S GATEWAY

The Devil's Gateway was first presented at the Royal Court Theatre Upstairs, London, on 24 August 1983 with the following cast:

BETTY	Pam Ferris
IVY	Rita Triesman
CAROL	} Lizzie Queen
FIONA	
ENID	Susan Porrett
LINDA	Chrissie Cotterill
JIM	} Roger Frost
MR GARDNER	
SOCIAL SECURITY OFFICER	
POLICEMAN	

Directed by Annie Castledine
Designed by Annie Smart
Lighting designed by Val Claus

Scene One

Second-floor flat in Bethnal Green. BETTY's *living-room which incorporates kitchen area. Although the furniture is old everything is spotlessly clean. The room is brightened by several 'cheap' ornaments, i.e. a brandy glass with a china cat up the side, a bright orange luminous ashtray on a stand.*

JIM *and* CAROL *are watching* Nationwide, *having finished their meal,* IVY *is still eating hers.* BETTY *is washing-up.*

BETTY. Sometimes I feel like a washing-up machine on legs. I don't know why we don't get paper plates. (*Nobody is listening.*) Oh Betty, talk to yourself then.

JIM. Bet, Bet, come on, Lady Diana's on next.

CAROL. You already told us, Dad.

JIM. I know but you know what she's like, faffing about.

BETTY. Who's she? Thank you very much.

JIM. And if you miss it, who'll get the blame? Me, that's who. Come and sit down Bet or you'll miss it.

BETTY. Keep your hair on. (*She dries her hands and crosses to the telly.*) I can't see her.

JIM. That's because they're still talking to that bunch of headcases. I told you, she's on after this.

CAROL. Is Joe-Joe all right, Mum?

JIM. Stop calling him that cissy name, Carol. He's named after his grandad, Big Jim and Little Jim.

BETTY (*crosses to the window and looks out*). They seem to be playing happily. (*Pause.*) Whoops.

CAROL. What's happened? (*She gets up.*)

BETTY. Don't worry, a little misunderstanding about whose trike it was but Joe-Joe has left them in no confusion.

CAROL. Shall I call him in?

BETTY. No, no, it's all okay now. (*She comes back to the telly and sits down.*)

JIM. Gawd, this is going on a bit. I reckon you've got time to put the kettle on. (BETTY *pretends not to hear this.*) Just look at them, would yer. Mad, mad as hatters. They should be interviewing the blokes that work there.

CAROL. Dad, nuclear power isn't news, it's a fact of life and those women because they're weird make news. Darrel reckons soon it will all be forgotten and we'll have a spate of Alsatian dogs biting children next week.

JIM. Huh, you wait till we get this cable TV. God only knows what sort of Russian infiltration we'll get then.

CAROL. Don't be daft, it's just a silly stunt.

JIM. Just look at it. Look at the state of it. I'm surprised those kids haven't been taken into care.

BETTY. What is it?

IVY. This potato's got lumps in.

BETTY. It can't have, Mum, it's Smash.

IVY. Well, the water couldn't have been hot enough. It's cracking round me dentures.

BETTY. D'you want some more?

IVY. No, ta, look, can I turn over for *Crossroads* now?

JIM. We haven't seen Lady Diana yet.

IVY. Who wants to see her? Traipsing round another nursery looking very embarrassed.

JIM. With the baby, you daft bat.

IVY. Another mouth to feed.

BETTY. Go on, Mum, turn over. (BETTY *gets up to make the tea.*)

IVY (*switches channels by using the remote control which is on the arm of her chair*). Ta Betty.

JIM. Turn it down for the adverts – just look at that would yer, Carol? Would you look at that? Modern technology, that is, just point it at the set. No wires, no nothing. Only put one pound fifty on the rental. Can you credit that, one pound fifty for something that brilliant. You should get Darrel to invest in one.

CAROL. He won't have anything on HP or rental. He says (*She tries to recall his exact words.*) 'It's immediate gratification for people who live from day to day.' (*Then:*) It took us a year to save for our telly but it's worth it 'cos it's ours.

BETTY (*from the washing-up bowl*). Oh yeah, madam. For your information this is not like on the knock yer know, 'cos shall I tell you something, if anything goes wrong with our set they come out and replace it the same day. Now, if your big valve goes, that's going to set you back another three hundred quid and that will probably mean you put your brass toilet holders in hock.

CAROL. Gold-plated dolphin toilet-*roll* holders. And anyway, you'll have paid for that set twenty times over before you're finished, Darrel says.

BETTY. Well, you tell Darrel, how comes he's got a whacking great mortgage 'cos you'll have paid fifty times over for that rabbit hutch when you've finished. Tell him to put that up his panatella and smoke it.

JIM. You hoovered in here today, Bet?

BETTY. You know full well that I do the hoovering on Wednesdays and Fridays.

JIM. Even so it's looking a bit grubby.

BETTY. Maybe if we all concentrated on getting the food from our plate into our mouths instead of studying what was on the carpet we wouldn't have time to drop it there in the first place.

JIM. Okay, I was only asking.

BETTY. Sorry, it's just if I do it now, it'll be grubby again by Friday.

IVY. Don't do it now. We won't hear *Crossroads*.

CAROL. Nanny, do you think we could turn over to *Star Trek* at quarter to? It's Joe-Joe's favourite.

IVY. He doesn't seem too bothered to me.

CAROL. Nanny, please.

IVY. Fair enough. (*She shouts in the direction of the window.*) Son, do you want to see *Star Trek*? If you don't speak up, you want *Crossroads*.

CAROL. Nan! He can't hear you.

IVY. Nan nothing. Manners maketh man, Nan, that's what he's trying to say. Really he's as anxious as me to know what happened to Diane and Mr Paul.

CAROL. Darrel says *Crossroads* is bad television.

BETTY. Lucky then that Darrel is a solicitor's clerk and not the Controller of ITV.

CAROL. He's a solicitor, not a clerk.

BETTY. I thought he was doing his columns.

CAROL. His articles.

JIM (*to* BETTY). So what have you bin doing today?

BETTY. Well, I did the bedrooms, took the washing to the launderette.

JIM. Yeah, you spend all week there, gassing if you ask me.

BETTY. Then I came home. Me and mum 'ad dinner. Then we went shopping. We had to wait half hour for the bus to Stratford and half hour coming back.

JIM (*winks at* CAROL). Is that all? What else did you do?

BETTY. Cooked your bloody tea. I haven't sat down for five minutes.

JIM. I s'pose you and her had your dinner on the bus.

IVY. Go on, tell big mouth what you nearly did today. That'll show him, tiresome bugger.

CAROL. Nanny!

BETTY. Shut up Mum, you're a real stirrer you are. As Enid would say, a real devil's avocado.

JIM. I might have guessed Enid was behind it.

BETTY. I never did nothing. Mum, I could kill you. I never did it.

JIM. Did what? Well, what Betty . . . ? I'm waiting.

BETTY. It's nothing to get het up over. I was only thinking mind, that maybe I should go to Carol's old school and ask if they needed a dinner lady, like, to help out.

JIM. Have you gone stark staring crackers, woman?

BETTY. Now Jim, Jim, now Jim, Jim. I was only thinking about it.

JIM. How many times have I told you, Betty? For God's sake, woman, listen once and for all. I am worried every day that the Social Security are going to catch up with me, every day. You don't want to start going out to work and all, otherwise we'll all be in jail and anyway, the money you'd earn would be like a piss in the ocean.

IVY. Shut it, Brian Clough. I can't hear the telly.

CAROL. He's right, Mummy, it wouldn't be fair.

BETTY. Yes, I only thought about it. I didn't do anything.

JIM. And you won't, will ya?

BETTY. No. (*Pause.*) Where on earth is John? This is the third time I've had to throw his tea away this week.

JIM. He can look after hisself, Bet, don't worry. When I was his age, perhaps a bit older, I was doing my National Service.

BETTY. Yeah, so is he, on a YOP's-flops course.

JIM. Now you're being silly.

BETTY. Say what you like but I wouldn't want him over in the Falklands, thank you very much.

JIM. Nor would I Betty, nor would I, but someone had to go.

BETTY. Why?

JIM. What do you mean, why? Because the people of this country are not going to be pushed around.

IVY. Since when?

JIM. Are you watching *Crossroads* or not?

CAROL. I'll make the tea, Mum. (*She gets up to pour the tea.*)

BETTY. I don't see why they couldn't have played a football match over them.

JIM. You are being totally ridiculous, Betty.

CAROL. It's more complex than that, Mummy.

IVY. For a start, two Argentinians play for Spurs.

BETTY. Huh, load of silly boys' games if you ask me, but then they never grow up, do they, Carol?

CAROL. I hope you're not including Darrel in that? He supports Women's Lib. Won't hear a word against Mrs T. and let's face it she gave the orders.

BETTY. Well, I never liked her much.

JIM. No one in their right mind does.

BETTY. The only nice thing about her is her hairdo.

JIM. That's right, you stick to something you know about. You know something, my wife's so outta touch with the world she thought the handbrake in the car was the clutch because you clutched it in your hand. It wasn't until I paid out for a driving instructor and he asked her to put her foot on the clutch that she learned her lesson.

BETTY. Bloody sprained my ankle trying to stamp on that stick from a sitting position.

CAROL. I've heard all this one hundred times.

IVY. You'll hear it a hundred times more and all. It's a real bone of contention between them.

JIM. Complete waste of money more like.

BETTY. They were your idea.

JIM. Only 'cos you kept moaning.

BETTY. Anyhow, we had to get rid of the car so where's the point in going on about it?

JIM. See this, Carol, and take note not to get like this at her age. Nothing suits her, and course to get out of it, she reckons men, who let's face it, run the world without fussing about hairdos, are little boys. I ask you.

BETTY. Don't you remember, Jim, when you worked on the print and found out how close this country came to it in that Cuban crisis? You were only little at the time, Carol, and that night we stood over your bed and cried, didn't we, Jim?

JIM. You did, Betty. I had a bad cold if you remember.

BETTY. And we said what sort of world had we brought her into.

CAROL. Better watch out, Dad, or we'll be seeing mum chained to the railings in some windswept corner of the woods.

JIM. Huh, she can't even find her way to the launderette, let alone Newbury bog.

BETTY. What is? What are you talking about?

JIM. Those women on the telly.

BETTY. What? What's he on about?

CAROL. Where've you been? There are a group of women living rough on some common as a protest.

BETTY. What protest? What common?

CAROL. They don't like the idea of nuclear weapons.

BETTY. Oh. (*Pause.*) Does anyone?

CAROL. But it's a bit naive, not to say daft.

BETTY. But why live on a common? Why not sit in the Houses of Parliament?

JIM (*exasperated*). Because the common is where the government is hoping to put the missiles.

BETTY. Oh.

JIM. It's silly because they think they'll stop them. Ha ha ha. Bunch of lunatics.

CAROL. But if misguided people did sit up and take notice, then we'd be in a worse mess. Just because we get rid of weapons, the Russians won't, and we'll have cut our own throats, literally. Darrel says.

BETTY (*innocently*). I don't see why anyone's got to have them.

JIM (*weary*). You silly born bitch. How stupid can you get – know all, know nothing. You'd have us all dancing about with bows and arrows, charging through the bushes, you would. Betty, we are living in a highly civilised age of technology, thank God.

BETTY. Thank God? Well, I wouldn't be thanking God if I was sitting under a table with you lot, four cans of baked beans and a plastic rubbish bag to put the dead bodies in.

JIM. We wouldn't have time, Betty, so don't worry about it.

BETTY (*sarcastic*). Oh that's nice. What a relief, I'll stop worrying then.

CAROL. Actually, Darrel was talking about the possibility of getting a mortgage for a fall-out shelter.

IVY. Oh that's good, we'll all come round on the big day.

CAROL. Well, Nanny, we haven't got a very big garden as you know.

BETTY. What have we got?

IVY. There'll be a riot if the lift's out of order.

CAROL. Anyway, you only get a four-minute warning.

BETTY. Oh, console us. Interesting to see what everyone will do with the last four minutes on earth.

CAROL. Darrel says, ironically it would make a very interesting study of human nature.

JIM. Maybe all those sociologist people could arrange a trial run.

BETTY. And what are you planning to do in those four minutes Lord Jim?

JIM (considers this). A bit of hanky panky with my wife.

BETTY. And then what?

CAROL. Mummy!

BETTY. Well, that's only two minutes gone. I tell you, Carol, I just have time to say, 'You've left your socks on again', and it's all over.

IVY laughs.

JIM. What are you laughing at?

IVY. David Hunter forgot his lines.

CAROL. Mummy! Really!

BETTY. What's with this, 'Mummy' malarky bit? You'll be saying 'my husband and I' next. You might have the lifestyle of Princess Margaret but let me remind you, you're not related to royalty.

CAROL. I don't need any reminding, you're so flippin' crude.

BETTY. Crude? Flippin'?? What sort of word is that, can you believe this, Mum, your granddaughter?

IVY (*flatly – still watching the telly*). I told you Bet, I thought it was a miracle her getting up the club. Reminds me of the old song about God Almighty lifting up her nighty.

CAROL. Do you have to be so vulgar, Nanny? Think of Joe-Joe.

IVY. I was.

BETTY (*to* CAROL). Oh and just where do you think you came from?

JIM. Do you mind?! I've just eaten.

BETTY (*to* CAROL). I suppose you think Harrods flew you here in a Tupperware picnic basket with gold-plated shark handles.

CAROL. Frankly, sometimes I'd prefer to think that. Anyway, how many more times, it's gold-plated dolphin toilet-roll holders. I think it's time I was going. Darrel will be home soon and we're going out tonight.

BETTY (*pleased*). Oh Joe-Joe can stay here.

CAROL. It's okay. Thanks, but we've arranged for next door to babysit. Darrel says it's reciprocal. They do it for us and I do it for them.

BETTY. I'm not good enough then?

CAROL. Don't be like that, Mum. Mind you, I'm glad he's playing outside. God alone knows how his vocabulary would be improved if he'd have picked up any of the conversation in here.

BETTY. He's got to know the facts of life, you can't bring him up on a load of rubbish.

CAROL. That's a laugh coming from you. I had to leave home before I discovered Tampax doesn't ruin your married life.

BETTY. They can do if you keep them in.

JIM. Just leave it out will ya?

IVY. Don't you bring your sanitary towel talk in here, madam, not in mixed company. Where are you off tonight, a husband-swapping party?

CAROL. Theatre actually.

IVY (*disappointed*). Oh. (*Then.*) What is it, *No Sex Please We're British*?

CAROL. No, *The Importance of Being Earnest*.

IVY. You'll like that. He was born in a handbag.

CAROL. See you next week then.

BETTY. I'll come and say goodbye to Joe-Joe.

CAROL. Oh Dad, when you see John, would you tell him that Darrel has found that old air rifle if he would like to call round for it.

BETTY. He'll do no such thing. Jim, do you hear me? Jim, I am not having that thing in the flat.

IVY. Certainly not. Before I know where I am, I'll have a jacksee full of lead. I'm a sitting target.

JIM. Bit of luck he'll aim fer yer boat. That'll shut a few gobs round here.

CAROL. Bye Dad, Nanny.

CAROL *and* BETTY *move out of the earshot of* JIM *and* IVY.

BETTY. You and Darrel haven't decided yet on whether or not to go in for another little brother or sister for Joe-Joe?

CAROL. Oh Mum, Darrel was really torn, so he tossed a coin and the Mini Metro came up heads.

BETTY. Huh, as if British Leyland hasn't got enough to answer for. Besides, I don't think much of that as an idea to enforce population control.

CAROL. Anyhow, Joe-Joe's still young and we've got to get on our feet.

BETTY. Can't you arrange for an accident?

CAROL. What on earth for? We can't afford a fully comp. insurance policy.

BETTY. Not to the car – to you. You know . . .

CAROL. No, I couldn't. God, Mum, that's more than my life's worth. Besides, there's something to be said for taking responsibility.

BETTY. For what?

CAROL. For thinking what sort of world you're bringing a child into.

BETTY. Gawd help us, if everyone carried on like that there'd be more dodos running about than humans. (*Pause.*) Take care, love.

CAROL. And you. (*She kisses her.*) See you soon.

CAROL *goes out.* BETTY *returns to the others.*

JIM. What was all that about?

BETTY. Women's talk.

JIM. Oh Gawd, that only means one thing – trouble.

BETTY. D'you think she's okay?

JIM. Yes. She's fine. You always fuss too much.

IVY (*without looking up*). She's okay. It's the bleedin' chinless wonder she married what's a pain in the bum.

JIM. The fact that you don't like him is enough recommendation for me.

BETTY. Do you think she's ashamed of us?

JIM. Look, Betty, she wanted to better herself. You can't blame her for that and she's done all right by him. I for one am proud of that.

BETTY. Umm . . .

JIM. Darrel's an all right bloke as it happens, he is. Think back, Betty, some of the potential son-in-laws we could've got landed wiv, it's a wonder we ain't on our knees thanking God every day.

BETTY. Well, I wouldn't go that far, Jim.

JIM. Huh, one thing's for sure, if she'd ave married that dead-head Ted she'd ave bin up Pentonville visiting him every other week. (*Pause.*) Come to think, that's where I'll be an all if the Social catch on about me job.

BETTY. Don't say that, Jim. Anyhow they can't send you away for that; there'd be more in than out.

JIM. At one time, Betty, I used to reckon the scrounging sods deserved all they got.

BETTY. I remember.

JIM. Makes you think don't it.

IVY (*sighs*). Can't be all bad then.

Scene Two

FIONA *and* LINDA's *squat in Hackney.* FIONA *is ironing a dress.* LINDA *enters.*

LINDA. You're early.

FIONA. Yeah, but I've got to go to another bloody boring meeting in a minute.

LINDA (*noticing the dress*). Oh no, not again.

FIONA. 'Fraid so. I won't have time to do it tomorrow morning.

LINDA (*picks up the dress by the sleeve and sniffs the armpits*). Phew, when was the last time you washed it? It could stand up by itself. All you do is throw it in the bottom of the wardrobe and iron it when duty calls.

FIONA. Who cares?

LINDA. I thought the whole point of social workers wearing a dress in court was to create a good impression.

FIONA. Yeah.

LINDA. Can't imagine it going down too well you standing there stinking like a three-week-old meat pie.

FIONA (*laughs*). There are no rules about what you smell like.

LINDA. Just as well there's no law against it. Although there probably will be one day.

FIONA. I bloody hate it. Every time it's such an ordeal.

LINDA. Not half the ordeal it is for the poor bugger in the dock.

FIONA (*agreeing*). Okay, but what difference should it make what I wear? Oh, moan, moan, moan. How was your day?

LINDA. Bag of laughs.

FIONA. You don't stink none too healthy yourself.

LINDA (*sending FIONA up*). Being the chief fish fryer at Littlewoods canteen is not without ordeal or responsibilities you know.

FIONA. What responsibilities?

LINDA. Making sure the oil's hot enough, the batter's thick enough, and that mad Annie doesn't dice the fish and put them in the trifles.

FIONA. She sounds wonderful.

LINDA. Gets beyond a joke sometimes. Today right, she gets all the dish cloths, dips 'em in batter and they only get sent down as cod. (*They both laugh.*) I don't know why I'm laughing, I nearly got the bleedin' sack over it.

FIONA. Gawd, how did you explain that away?

LINDA. With a lot of difficulty. Still, certainly breaks the monotony working with someone with a run amok brain. Lucky she lives in this borough, otherwise you'd be her social worker.

FIONA. Oh, that reminds me, I've got to see a family who live in the same block as your mum.

LINDA. Never was a problem estate until our lot moved in, we set a trend.

FIONA. No real derangements. The son was fast becoming a hardened glue-sniffer till we got him on a YOP's course.

LINDA. You fraud, pushing kids into those.

FIONA (*agreeing*). Umm. (*Then.*) At least it keeps 'em off the streets and I s'pose carpentry is a practical skill.

LINDA. Right. Now he can cement his nostrils together with Plasticwood to his lungs' content.

FIONA. I think they must live on the floor above yours.

LINDA. The mother's name's not Betty?

FIONA. I'm not sure. I think the grandmother's name's Ivy.

LINDA. Gordon Bennett, I went to school with her daughter.

FIONA. Don't be daft, she must be pushing fifty.

LINDA. Not Ivy's, Betty's, Carol.

FIONA. Who?

LINDA. Carol's Mum is Betty. Betty's Mum is Ivy. Carol is Betty's daughter. Betty is . . .

FIONA. Okay, Okay . . . but I don't think the youngest, Carol? right? is living at home.

LINDA. Na, she went through a very unfortunate phase at school and ended up marrying him.

FIONA. Shame. Suburban maisonette job?

LINDA. Worse. Stripped pine Islington job.

FIONA. She'd know your mum then.

LINDA. Doubt it. Betty does.

FIONA. You haven't told her you're living with me?

LINDA. No, I told her I was living with the Olympic women's caber-tossing champion.

FIONA. I mean where I work and that?

LINDA. Don't worry, I said you was the personnel manageress at Littlewoods.

FIONA. Trust you.

LINDA. Well, it pleased her that I had illusions of upward mobility. She worked her way up from knickers you know.

FIONA. Pardon?

LINDA. She started on the knicker counter and worked her way up.

FIONA (*laughs*). Charming. (*She has finished ironing and starts to throw things into a rucksack.*)

LINDA. You should be flattered, it's a good job, lots of responsibility. You can determine how long someone can stay in the sick room if they have a period pain.

FIONA. Power.

LINDA. If she likes you, you can get anything up to four hours. If she don't, ten minutes.

FIONA. How long do you get?

LINDA. I keep a bottle of Paracetamol in my locker just in case.

FIONA (*looking up from rucksack*). You sure you can't take tomorrow off?

LINDA. Sorry. No.

FIONA. You don't want to go anyway though, do you?

LINDA. What for?

FIONA. Little thing like an interest in life.

LINDA. Boring. (*Pause.*) The way I see it, there are more important things to get excited about.

FIONA. Nothing will matter in the event of a nuclear war, I'm sure even NATO don't care if sex shops go up.

LINDA. Oh yeah? You try explaining that to the woman who's raped and killed out there tonight. Shame you couldn't stick around, love, and see the war what might or might not have bin.

FIONA. So we sort it all out – then get blown sky high?

LINDA. Oh, and so by some miracle we do stop it. Then we can all go back and not worry about anything ever again. Yip, yip, yippee.

FIONA. Perhaps you start at the worse end of the scale.

LINDA. But anyway, what has it got to do with women? That's what I want ter know?

FIONA. Apart from the fact that we're fifty-two per cent of the population. Besides, it's a way of reaching women.

LINDA. Huh.

FIONA. Huh? Huh nothing. It's a household word.

LINDA. Huh? Huh is a household word?

FIONA. Greenham Common (*She looks at her watch.*) Shit is that the time? I must go.

LINDA. You find me one woman that you see in your job who knows about it . . .

FIONA. And you'll go . . . (*She crosses to the door.*)

LINDA. Who doesn't think they're a bunch of lunatics, then I might go . . .

FIONA. Deal.

LINDA. For a picnic.

FIONA *goes out.* LINDA *finishes ironing the dress.*

Scene Three

ENID *and* BETTY. BETTY *is ironing.*

BETTY. Took the best part of yesterday morning to do all this stuff. I had to lug it up to Cambridge Heath and all.

ENID. What about the one round the corner?

BETTY. You should see the two and eight it's in. Nothing works.

You can feel the tension between putting your money in and waiting for the light to come on.

ENID. Gawd, I couldn't have lugged that lot up there.

BETTY (*not nastily*). Last time you did your washing in public was with a bar of soap and a scrubbing board.

ENID. I've told you often enough you can use my machine.

BETTY. Jim won't hear of it. Anyhow the exercise done me good. I've put on about seven pounds in the last couple of months.

ENID. Well, I didn't like to say nothing but you really should start coming to Weightwatchers again.

BETTY. No thanks, I can't cope with it.

ENID. It does work Betty, it does. You know together we give each other strength.

BETTY. Enid, there are three things I believe you should do in private. Breast-feeding, going to the toilet and weighing yourself.

ENID. Don't be such a paradon of virtue, weighing yourself isn't dirty.

BETTY. No, but it's embarrassing.

ENID. That's what gives you the insensitive though, don't it? Besides, going there on Thursday means I'm out when money-grabbing Molly comes round with the poxy catalogue.

BETTY. Here, John told me a joke about that.

ENID. Think about it, Betty, you know you always tell the punchline first.

BETTY. What lies in the grass and goes ding dong?

ENID. A snake with a bell on its prick.

BETTY. No, no, a dead Avon lady.

ENID. Gawd, is that it? My answer was better than that.

BETTY. Just count yerself lucky I didn't say, 'Heard about the dead Avon lady lying in the grass going ding dong'.

ENID. I can just picture Molly rolling about in her petunias gasping her last breath. (*She laughs; then:*) We mustn't be nasty though.

BETTY. They're not petunias, they're gladioli.

ENID. Are they?

BETTY. I only know 'cos my Carol told me.

ENID. It's all right for some, Molly got a ground-floor place and she hasn't got no kids, or disabled in the family.

BETTY. She always seems to know how to get everything.

ENID. Got a lot of mouth, Betty. Where's Ivy by the way?

BETTY. Up Florrie's. She's making a special effort this time. Florrie's got something to help her hear the telly better from the Social Services and Mum wants one.

ENID. What? Nanny-radar-ears-Taylor, her hearing's more sensitive than a bat's.

BETTY. It means you can still hear the telly when other people are talking in the room so I gather.

ENID. I wouldn't fancy them nosey do-gooders sniffing around.

BETTY. Mum can handle them.

ENID. Well, my Bob won't stand for it. He won't. I don't know exactly what he earns so he ain't going to relish the thought of blabbing it to someone else.

BETTY. Now I don't agree with that, Enid. We're living in modern times, bin years since we got the vote.

ENID. Oh he's never kept me short, Betty, you know that. I'm sure if I really knew, it would only make for unpleasantness.

BETTY. And they earn it. You can't expect a man to flog his guts out for nothing, I s'pose. They're entitled to their pleasure.

ENID. Not that that costs them anything. Not now. Mind, was a time when a packet of three meant going without tea.

BETTY. Don't I know, risks I've taken.

ENID. Me too.

BETTY. For the pleasure of one tea and one F in the same evening, I have a sixteen-year-old son.

ENID. Could've bin worse like me and had five kids.

BETTY. Now that was bad luck.

ENID. Bad luck?! I can tell you, Betty, if I'd 'ad me wits about me I'd 'ave sued Durex, I would. Featherweight and Gossamer my arse. I'd rather they were made outta bloody inner tube – safer.

BETTY. Maybe Bob didn't get the air outta them properly.

ENID. Didn't get the air outta them? Betty, they split so many times I threatened to take a pumice stone to his dong.

BETTY. Enid! Really!

ENID. Betty, it don't matter, no one can hear us. You know how they was invented, don't you? That John Wand used sheeps' innards.

BETTY. Load of tripe.

ENID. No, it's true.

BETTY. I was making a joke.

ENID. I know, so was I.

BETTY. Oh. (*She picks up TV remote control.*) See this? Do you see this?

ENID. Oh we've had one of them for ages, what about it?

BETTY. Look at it, just look at it, and think about contraceptives.

ENID. Do what? (*Pause.*) You mean hold it between your knees while he tries to get on top of you.

BETTY. They can make these two a penny but they can't make nothing better than johnnies.

ENID. Well, they can't apply electronics to sheaths. You can't have a silicone chip in a condom, you daft apeth.

BETTY (*looking at the blank screen*). Hey, Enid, have you ever heard of the Common?

ENID. What are you insinuating?

BETTY. I mean, land, like park, common.

ENID. What, Clapham Common, Ealing Common, Wanstead Flats.

BETTY. No, on the telly. Some women living in caravans and tents and that because they don't want the bomb.

ENID Oh yeah. It's called Greenham Common.

BETTY. What do you think of it?

ENID *pulls a face and puts her forefinger to her head in order to indicate that someone is mad.*

BETTY. Who is?

ENID. Those women, who else?

BETTY. That's the same face you pull at the thought of the government.

ENID. Who cares?

BETTY. But what was it about?

ENID. Betty this is boring.

BETTY. Tell me?

ENID. You should have heard my Bob going off about it.

BETTY. About what?

ENID. They desecrated the local war memorial. Bob was raging, carrying on about who was they to shit on our war dead, reckons people have had their throats cut for less.

BETTY. What you mean, desecrated it. Smashed it up?

ENID. No, I could have understood that. It was more spooky.

BETTY. Go on then.

ENID. Oh Betty, I don't know why you're so interested, they put little stones all over it.

BETTY. How d'you mean? Threw them at it?

ENID. No, just put them there.

BETTY. What on earth for?

ENID. According to them to remember all the people what copped it in Hiroshima but as Bob reckoned it puts a new meaning to getting stoned.

BETTY. Well I never.

ENID. I was just thankful he found his humour before he blew 'is gasket.

BETTY. But a lot of people must have died in Hiroshima.

ENID. Yeah, and if you'd have seen the telly you'd 'ave known. They collected a hundred thousand or something.

BETTY. Jesus Christ.

ENID. I think they left him out of it. Anyhow, come to think, just shows how outta touch they are, everyone has Japanese tellies.

BETTY. Don't you care, Enid?

ENID. What about, war memorial? Stones? Japanese tellies?

BETTY. No, about the bomb.

ENID (shrugs). S'pose so.

BETTY. Then we should be grateful for what those women are doing.

ENID (aggressive). Should we? Should we? Should we really Betty?

BETTY. I only . . . I mean, don't take on, Enid.

ENID (crossly). How many bombs have we had dropped in our lives, Betty?

BETTY. We was only kids.

ENID (*angry*). Not that, how many times have we been at our wits' end? Eh? What about when you was evicted, when your Carol was a baby and me with Linda – when she was really ill and the bloody doctor thought I was neurotic. In the end she had an operation which left a ruddy great hole in her back and it meant keeping her clean, which meant washing her in the sink in a freezing cold kitchen. No hot water, nothing.

BETTY. All right, all right, we've had it tough. I didn't say we hadn't.

ENID. Do you want to know something, Betty, I'm glad, I'm really glad. They're all running scared with about as much direction as a chicken with its head cut off. Where were they when we were fighting for our kids' lives? If this is the only thing that threatens their lives then I'm glad.

BETTY. Enid, don't be so bitter. They might have had it rough and all.

ENID. Oh yeah, well I ain't joining in because I ain't protesting next to some posh woman so she can make sure her cut glass and Capo da Monte flowerpots are still intact.

BETTY. I thought you didn't care.

ENID. Huh. (*Pause.*) All I care about is having a laugh. I'm going back to me cooking, laughing all the way to teatime.

She goes out.

BETTY *opens her mouth to say something, sees the paper, picks it up but it's too late.* ENID *has gone.* BETTY *opens the paper to read an article.* IVY *enters.*

IVY. Blimey, just saw my Bob Big Gob flying across the balcony like a vulture outta hell.

BETTY. She only popped in for five minutes.

IVY. Giving it plenty of the bunny no doubt. Wonder she ain't got lockjaw.

BETTY. How was Florrie?

IVY. Pathetic. It's pathetic, Bet. If I ever get like that I'll drown meself in my commode.

BETTY. Well, you was with her long enough.

IVY. Made sure I ad a good butchers at that telly thing. I know what to say to the welfare now.

BETTY. Charming.

IVY. Oh, Florrie's okay, I feel sorry for her but once people start feeling sorry for you you've had it.

BETTY (*sarcastically*). What are you coming as, Ludovic Kennedy?

IVY. Enid upset you?

BETTY. No, we was talking.

IVY. She bragging about 'My Bob's antics' again?'

BETTY. No.

IVY. Come on, I'll take a turn at that.

BETTY *puts a chair next to the ironing board and lowers it so IVY ca sit and iron. Then she puts the kettle on.*

BETTY. Actually, we were talking about the bomb.

IVY. Oh, cheerful. Funny though, so was me and Florrie.

BETTY. Was you?

IVY. Florrie watches all the news every day. Well, she watches everything, can hardly get out of the chair. She puts on a big ac when the social worker comes cause she don't want to go into a home.

BETTY. She'd be better off.

IVY. Course she wouldn't. Talk sense.

BETTY. What did she have to say?

IVY. She reckons if she had an address she'd send a quid a week outta her pension to those women at that place, whatsit Common.

BETTY. Surely she don't approve of them?

IVY. It ain't that unbelievable, there ain't that many buggers who want to go up in a puff of smoke.

BETTY. But seems odd.

IVY. Got death in common ain't they? Florrie spends a lot of time worrying about death. State she's in it's hardly surprising.

BETTY. Enid reckons they was all worried about their china.

IVY. What does Enid know? She's never met them.

BETTY. I think she thought they were worried about their nice lives, so they could go back and still have homes.

IVY. If they was worried about their lives they'd build a fall-out shelter. Anyhow they've left their homes – daft twit Enid is –

BETTY. But Enid . . .

IVY. Oh Enid, Enid, where has Enid bin all her life? Nowhere. Sometimes I think she just stepped out of Emmerdale Farm.

There is the sound of an outer door shutting.

BETTY. Hello? Jim? Jim? Is that you? Jim?

JIM enters.

JIM. Who do you think it was, King Kong?

IVY (*mutters*). Take your gorilla suit off then.

JIM. What did she say?

BETTY. Nothing, nothing. Take no notice, Florrie upset her.

JIM. Florrie upset her? That's a laugh. She usually takes her do-it-yourself euthanasia kit round to upset Florrie.

BETTY. What?

JIM. Failing that, her mouth.

IVY (*who is ironing a shirt of JIM's, uses the iron with a vengeance*). I think I'll take these through.

IVY *gets up and exits with a pile of ironed clothes.*

BETTY. Jim, can't you be a bit more civil to Mum?

JIM. She's your mother. She doesn't have to live here.

BETTY. Now, Jim.

JIM. All right, Betty, but I always get the impression she's taking the rise outta me.

BETTY. I know she can be difficult.

JIM (*sees the paper*). What you got the *Sun* for?

BETTY. I didn't. Enid dropped in to return a fag she'd borrowed. She dropped it.

JIM. I do wish you wouldn't encourage her to come flapping round here every ten minutes.

BETTY. I didn't. I don't.

JIM. Anyway, listen, I've got some good news. I reckon I might b in with a chance of a full-time job at the garage.

BETTY. That is good news. Oh, that's wonderful.

JIM. Be a relief from all that cash in hand business. Mind, won't b for a couple of months. Don't bloody let it slip to that welfare officer.

BETTY. Course not. I am pleased, Jim.

JIM. Yeah well.

BETTY. Aren't you?

JIM. Oh yeah, I'm pleased. It's better than nothing, a lot better, but you know I spent seven years as a lad doing an apprenticeship. All my mates thought I was mad. They were earning much more than me. But it was worth it. Bet, I got a skill, I was proud of work, at the end of the day, I'd achieved something. I know I had ups and downs, changes of jobs, but I still felt something of worth. I was worth something. D'you understand what I mean?

BETTY. Yes. Yes I do.

JIM *goes out, to hang his coat up.*

JIM (*off*). And now what am I doing? Changing tyres – filling up cars with petrol. I tell you, Betty, even you could do that.

BETTY. Even me? Even me, who's mopped up after redundancies, unemployment, put you back on your feet again. Even me, who's done nothing of any worth except cook and clean and keep everything bloody together. Aren't I allowed to consider meself even a bit important?

JIM (*off*). What's that you say? Bet?

BETTY. Nothing.

Scene Four

Monday afternoon. FIONA *is at work. Interview room. Mud-splattered rucksack in the corner. She is on 'duty'.*
MR GARDNER, *a client, sits opposite her. The desk is between them.*

MR GARDNER. I know one thing, I've just about had enough. Darling, I'm telling yer, don't sit there all smug wiv me girl cos that's exactly how the other one, that wimpy geezer, started wiv me and he ended up wiv a chair over his head.

FIONA. I did not make your wife do anything, she did it of her own accord.

MR GARDNER. How come she never done it before then?

FIONA. She did go and stay with her mother once didn't she?

MR GARDNER. But she came back like a bloody shot.

FIONA (*pause*). Mr Gardner, you broke all the windows.

MR GARDNER. But she came back didn't she? That old cow always hated me, they bloody ganged up on me. Now stop beating about the bush and tell me where she is. I know my rights, she's my wife.

FIONA. I'm afraid I don't have the right to tell you. She knows where you are so I suggest you go home and wait for her to contact you.

MR GARDNER. Do yer? (*He becomes extremely angry.*) Do yer, darling, well I suggest you start to tell me where she is right this minute or . . .

MR GARDNER *leans across the desk.* LINDA *enters.*

LINDA. Christ, sorry . . . I thought you were on your own..

FIONA (*gives* LINDA *a look of panic so* LINDA *remains where she is*). Mr Gardner, I'm sorry but I've got other people to see . . . If you don't mind . . . (*She gestures towards the door.*)

MR GARDNER (*looks between them both, pause*). You haven't heard the end of this yet. I'll git you . . . You can't git one over on me, love, and don't think you will neither.

FIONA. Good afternoon, Mr Gardner.

MR GARDNER *goes out.*

LINDA. Rewarding afternoon?

FIONA (*sighs*). How lovely to see you.

LINDA. They told me you were on duty but they reckoned you'd be on your own.

FIONA. For a moment there so did I. (*Slight pause.*) What, you've been up to the office?

LINDA. Yeah, how d'you think I knew where you was?

FIONA. You didn't go up there with that badge on I hope.

LINDA. Unlike some I could mention I don't have two personas you know. If it's okay to go and hold hands down Greenham Common, then it's okay to hold hands up the Mile End Road far as I'm concerned. How was it by the way?

FIONA. God, it seems like a million light years away, day I've had.

LINDA. Have you had time to find any disarming converts yet?

FIONA. It's not that easy you know, go marching into people's homes, saying, 'Date of birth, any problems? No? Good. By the way, what are your views on peace camps?'

LINDA. I always told yer Social Services got a lot in common with the Gestapo, that's why they got the same initials.

FIONA. Don't start that up again. At least I don't work for a capitalist industry.

LINDA. Huh, I don't have the bloody choice, I wasn't lucky enough to get an education to escape my roots.

FIONA. Mine wasn't exactly handed me on a plate as you full well know.

LINDA. Granted. What was you saying about the converts?

FIONA. Only that it's difficult with all the shit that's going down in some people's lives for them to muster what's happening out there.

LINDA. Told yer. Anyway you haven't told me how you got on.

FIONA. I'm glad I went. Quite cold though. I missed you. What about you?

LINDA. Great time, didn't get up till six o'clock yesterday evening – then had breakfast in bed. It was really warm an' all.

FIONA. By the way your left wellie boot leaks.

LINDA. Really?

FIONA. And so I left them there.

LINDA. That's useful.

FIONA. This woman's right wellie boot leaked so I thought I'd donate them, is that okay?

LINDA (agreeing). Fine, now I've done my bit I can rest easy.

FIONA. Ah good, I'm glad I've caught you in an activist mood.

LINDA. Oh dear.

FIONA. I want you to come down with me, for the anniversary, before the eviction.

LINDA (*lightly*). What about all the people what get evicted round here? Who's fighting for them? I ain't going all the way down there for a bundle.

FIONA. You'll like it, I know.

LINDA. Why?

FIONA. Well . . . umm . . . because . . . because it's there . . . the space . . .

LINDA. I know it's an open space, so is Victoria Park.

FIONA. Naw, the space for . . . creativity . . .

LINDA. Creativity?! Ha, Bourgeois crap.

FIONA. It's not, not altogether, well I liked it.

LINDA (*teasing*). Creativity? You? Your whole career is about control. What a load of rubbish.

FIONA. You can't be cynical all your life you know.

LINDA (*playing around*). Oh, goddess of creativity come down an cleanse my cynicism.

FIONA (*laughs*). Okay, okay point taken.

LINDA. It's just that I want it to change more than war.

FIONA. Course it will. It's women only.

LINDA. Even so . . .

FIONA (*takes leaflet out of her jacket pocket*). Listen to this then. (*She reads.*) Apart from everything else . . .

LINDA. What's this? A bloody poetry reading?

FIONA. If I give it to you you won't bother to read it.

LINDA. I hope you ain't going to read the whole thing. I thought we were going out fer a meal.

FIONA. I'm only going to read two sentences.

LINDA (*lightly*). Okay wake me up when you've finished . . .

FIONA. Apart from everything else . . .

LINDA. You've said that once.

FIONA. Apart from everything else, authority, which is male oriented, is confused, bemused and deeply threatened by the growth and the assertion of women working together in a different way. The women's peace camp is dealing with the tip of the iceberg . . . Cruise missiles, and at the same time, the base – patriarchy. (*She looks up.*) Well?

LINDA. I ain't going dancing naked through no woods painting myself with menstrual blood.

FIONA. But where's your creativity?

LINDA. In the bloody fish fryer. Come on, let's get out of here before another one of the Patriarchy's henchmen bursts in.

Scene Five

BETTY and ENID. *A month later.*

BETTY. I begun to think you'd emigrated.

ENID. Sorry, I've had a lot on me plate.

BETTY. I thought it was something I said.

ENID. Don't start up that war-mongering again.

BETTY. I wasn't.

ENID. We got enough bleedin' trials and tribulations of our own without taking on the world's.

BETTY. All right. I'm not going to say anything.

ENID. Well, aren't you going to ask what's wrong?

BETTY. Not if you don't want to talk about it.

ENID. Well, if you must know, our Kim got herself in the club again.

BETTY. Oh, Enid, I am sorry.

ENID. I don't see why any of us should be. She's not. Bob took on alarming about it.

BETTY. I can imagine.

ENID. I doubt that, Betty, I doubt if you can. Bob bellowing at her that she's always been a disgrace to the family since the day she got herself in trouble for the first time.

BETTY. Oh dear.

ENID. It weren't Bob though, it was her. She started screaming at him, 'How could I have get *meself* in trouble unless you're suggesting I'm the Virgin fucking Mary.'

BETTY. Enid!!

ENID. I'm only telling you what she said. Christ, I'd never say the Virgin fucking Mary in case I was struck down with lightning through the noonar, and Linda, she's even worse than her you know. Oh yes. Three boys no trouble to me at all. Two daughters what are headstrong crackpots. Our Linda's barmy. Bob hates her.

BETTY. Oh Enid, she can't be that bad. She used to be such a wisecracker, takes after her mum.

ENID. Not anymore. I'm telling you, she's a po-face now. She's only got to see a bit of thigh on the telly and she goes mad, starts screaming, 'Sexist rubbish', and hitting the set with her garlic press thing. I tell yer. Cracked. I told her, I said to her straight, I haven't lived through a world war to think the naked body's wicked.

BETTY. What she say to that?

ENID. Told me not to go over the top with the Alf Garnett act.

BETTY. She's not married yet then?

ENID. You're joking. Goes round wrecking marriages more like. tell you, she's probably been more responsible for the divorce rate in this country than the Marriage Guidance Council. I haven't seen her since Christmas. Takes me six months to calm Bob down after she's bin. Just get him settled and what happens? The other one starts up. Anyhow what's bin going on with you?

BETTY. Nothing, nothing. Jim might be getting a proper job but otherwise nothing.

ENID. I wish our Dennis would do that. Gawd knows what he does but he gets paid a lot.

BETTY. Haven't you any idea?

ENID. Well, seems to be something to do with rollies.

BETTY. Cigarettes?

ENID. Yeah, every now and then he gives me a few and reckons save it and give yerself a treat. I kept 'em in me bag.

BETTY. You'd think if he earned that much he could buy his mum some decent cigarettes.

ENID. They're all right, as it happens. (ENID *takes out a couple of fags from an otherwise empty pocket – they are joints.*) Here, try one.

BETTY. No thanks. Let's have a look.

ENID. Smell a bit funny and they really ketch the back of your throat, but yer know beggars can't be choosers.

BETTY. Enid, I think these are drugs.

ENID. Naw, ther's no harm in them.

BETTY. I think this is pot.

ENID. No, Dennis wouldn't have nothing to do with that. He fainted when he had his smallpox injection.

BETTY. These are illegal.

ENID. Oh Gawd, I smoked one in the doctor's surgery.

BETTY. Enid, I can't believe this. You've really let yourself go.

ENID. Oh I have, Betty, I have. These last few weeks.

She lights a joint.

BETTY. 'Ere you not going to smoke that in here?

ENID. Why not?

BETTY. S'pose the police bust in?

ENID. Betty, in all the years you've been alive have the police ever bust in to your front-room?

BETTY. But it's drugs.

ENID. It's nothing – try it, one puff.

BETTY. I think I should watch you in case you see purple elephants, or try to fly out of the window.

ENID. Don't be ridiculous. If I could cook tea the day after me youngest was born, still shot through the eyeballs with pethidine, then a few dried tea leaves in a Rizla paper ain't going to bother me none. Come off it, Betty. Dennis would rip his own mother off. Sure as hell if it was proper drugs he wouldn't give me any. Try it.

BETTY. I'd rather not.

ENID. All right, don't. Never taken a risk in your life, Betty. Why start now?

BETTY (*grudgingly takes it*). You'd lead me to the gallows, you would.

ENID. Well?

BETTY. Don't feel any different.

ENID. Told you.

BETTY. What's that?

ENID. Where?

BETTY. I can see a big spider.

ENID. That's cos there is one. (*She bangs it with fag packet.*) Daft bat.

BETTY. Shame, I s'pose I wanted it to work and all.

ENID. Have you got anything to drink?

BETTY. Only some ginger wine left over from Christmas.

ENID. Get it out. Leave all the chores. Let's 'ave a game of cards, turn this place into a real den of Equity.

Lights change. There is a time lapse of about one hour.

BETTY and ENID are playing cards. Although they don't realise it they are slightly stoned.

BETTY. I bet you my electric cake knife.

ENID. You haven't got one.

BETTY. Well, I'm not going to lose.

ENID. Let's not play any more.

BETTY (*pushes cards aside*). Boring. Enid?

ENID. Come in Betty, I hear you.

BETTY. Enid, I want to tell you something.

ENID (*face lights up*). You've never had an organism.

BETTY. No. Something important.

ENID. Go on Betty. I'm receiving you loud and clear. Over.

BETTY. I'm bored.

ENID. Thanks a bundle. You don't exactly qualify as this estate's answer to Chas and Dave.

BETTY. Not you. I'm bored with my life, everything.

ENID. Buck up, wrestling on Saturday.

BETTY. That makes me more bored. Sometimes I don't feel I've done nothing with my life.

ENID. You haven't done nothing, you've taken drugs.

BETTY. As John would say 'big fucking deal'.

ENID. Yeah, no wonder Dennis is in so much trouble, selling things under false pretences. If I'd paid for this I'd sue him.

BETTY. I s'pose I feel a bit dizzy.

ENID. Same as smoking your first Woodbine. Let's face it, we've been spoilt by the filter tip.

BETTY. D'you think our mothers was bored?

ENID. 'Course not. Never had time. I blame machines, we got it easy, we got time to think . . .

BETTY. How bored we are.

ENID. Anyhow, we've done a lot. At least your kids are normal, look at me, my daughters seem to have lost their trollies years ago and we moved from crappy Freedaman Street to modern places, that's not nothing.

BETTY. I wish we'd stayed now.

ENID. What, standing in a pile of rubble?

BETTY. No, like Beryl fought with the others in their street and they kept their places. Council put in all mod cons and all.

ENID. Spent years without hot water though, when we had that, and baths and indoor lavs.

BETTY. And every day, every day, what have we got to show, eh? Just different foods to wash off the plates.

ENID. Get paper plates?

BETTY. Enid, sometimes I give up on you.

ENID (sarcastic). Oh hello, Bob.

BETTY (stands up). Can I show you something?

ENID. Well? As long as it's not your operation scar.

BETTY (gets out old cereal packet and spills its contents of news cuttings on the table). I'm collecting them.

ENID. What are they? Blimey, don't tell me you're the secretary to Errol Flynn's fan club all these years?

BETTY. No, look at them.

ENID (*glances at a couple*). Betty? These are about those silly women.

BETTY. I don't think it's that silly. Look, look, one woman has left her husband and five kids.

ENID. That's news?

BETTY. Says here, somewhere, that we're used to seeing men go off to war but we should get used to women going off for peace. Makes you think, doesn't it?

ENID. Does it?

BETTY (*collects them up, puts them back in the box*). Well, it made me think. If we're not going to use these weapons what's the point of having them?

ENID. They're a detergent against those who got 'em.

BETTY. Enid, you know the difference between a deterrent and a detergent.

ENID. In someone's face it would amount to the same thing.

BETTY. Aren't you worried at all?

ENID. Ain't bothered.

BETTY. Enid, sometimes you strike me as being as interesting as a piece of wet fish.

ENID. Oh do I? do I? Really? Well, I could tell you things that would make your hair curl.

BETTY. Oh yeah, you couldn't make a corkscrew curl.

ENID. Oh couldn't I? I'll show you, I tell you. I could make the hair in your nostrils curl.

BETTY. Go on then.

ENID. Oh no, you ain't getting anything to use on me.

BETTY. That's because the most daring thing you ever did was pinch a packet of fish fingers.

ENID. They was in a Hotpoint multi-freeze at the time though, don't forget. Tell you what we'll do – a phisological experiment.

BETTY. Pardon?

ENID. I saw it on telly just before *Maidenhead Unvisited*. Give us here that bit of that paper. Now, write down on it something you've never told no one.

BETTY. Enid, there was always something about your brain I couldn't fathom. That's because there's no depth to it.

ENID. Piss off and write it down. Go on.

Both write something on a bit of paper.

ENID. Now swap. (BETTY *looks at her paper again.*) What's the matter?

BETTY. Just checking the spelling. Okay.

They swap and read.

ENID. Betty!!

BETTY. Enid!!

ENID. God Almighty, I'll never be able to look her in the face again.

BETTY. Come to think, he don't look like the rest.

Both look at the papers again and start roaring with laughter.

JIM enters.

BETTY. Jim? Jim? Is that you Jim? Oh hello, Jim? Mum with you Jim?

JIM. She's hanging her coat up, Bet. Bet. What's for tea?

ENID. Hot pot. (*She laughs.*)

JIM. If I was going to employ an au pair, Enid, you missed the boat by about forty years.

BETTY. Don't be ridiculous, Jim, child labour is against the law.

IVY enters.

ENID (*who, like* BETTY, *has been trying to control her giggles, bursts into laughter*). Oh hello, Mrs Taylor.

IVY. What's the matter, Enid, you just laid an egg?

She sits down and switches the telly on.

ENID. I ain't laid nothing lately except the table.

BETTY (*hisses*). Enid, Enid.

JIM. You're half cut.

BETTY. No, Jim, no we just finished off the bottle of Stones Ginger Wine, wasn't even half, was it, Enid?

ENID. Quarter, if that.

BETTY. Not even that, eggcup full, thimble.

ENID. It was off but it was a pity to waste it.

JIM. You never touch drink, what's the matter with you?

ENID. Celebration, Jim, anniversary, my Walter was divorced ten years ago today.

JIM. You celebrating that?

ENID. Celebration? Did I say celebration? I mean commiseration, you know me, always getting words wrong.

JIM. Silly great mare.

ENID. Broke my heart, we was drowning our sorrows.

Both women giggle.

JIM. You don't look too miserable to me. (*Pause.*) What's that smell?

BETTY. Shush.

JIM. Like burnt compost.

ENID. Indoor fireworks. I had them left over from Christmas.

JIM. Oh great, let's have a look. Is there a little gun?

BETTY. Chute.

JIM. Well they usually go puff puff. I haven't seen those since I was a boy.

BETTY. They're down the chute.

JIM. Betty, my dearest wife, the chute has been blocked for the past eighteen months.

ENID. Bin. They're in. The bin.

JIM. Hey, let's have a look, we can get 'em to work again with a couple of matches. John and I saw it on *Magpie*.

BETTY. No, no. Don't go rooting around in the bin, they're dead.

JIM. State you're in I'm surprised you can tell. (*He makes for the door.*)

BETTY. No, no, you wouldn't want to go down there. I emptied the commode in it.

JIM. You silly born bitch. What a stewpid thing to do. What you want to go and do a thing like that for? We'll have to treat the dustmen to take it away.

ENID. It will be a treat and all.

JIM. Are you going home or what?

ENID. On my way. Now remember Betty, you mustn't empty the pot in the bin again.

BETTY. You don't mind if I don't get up, do you?

ENID. No dear, you've had a nasty shock.

ENID *goes out.*

JIM. Shock? Pot? Crackpot? She is. Living with her must be like hell with the lid off.

BETTY. Jim, I've bin thinking.

JIM. State you're in, I find that a bit hard to swallow.

BETTY. Maybe I'll go down the chippy and get us tea.

JIM. Have you lost your head, it's not Friday.

BETTY. Make a change. Now what d'you want?

JIM. You're not going in that state.

BETTY. Mum, pop down the chip shop, will ya, I'll have a pie, saveloy and chips and an apple pie and perhaps a Mars Bar.

IVY. How can I? I'm housebound.

BETTY. Housebound? You're out so much you're practically a claustrophobic.

IVY. Yeah, well I might meet the social worker down there.

BETTY. Didn't see her playing bingo then?

CAROL enters.

JIM. I'll go but for goodness' sakes, pull yourself together woman. (To CAROL:) Hello love, I'm just going down the chip shop, d'you want anything?

CAROL. No thanks, Dad, I can't stop long, I've left Joe-Joe with Darrel.

JIM. Plaice for you, Nan?

IVY. And chips.

BETTY. You can't have chips, you know full well they play havoc with your tracts.

JIM. Won't be long. (He goes out.)

CAROL. Hello, Nanny, Mummy.

BETTY. How many times do I have to tell you, I'm not bloody Tutankhamun reincarnated.

CAROL. Sorry, Mum.

BETTY. Nan, come on. You better have your bath while *Blue Peter* is on otherwise you'll leave it once you get stuck in front of the telly.

IVY. I hope you never get old, Carol. (She gets up.) Just as you look forward to a bit of peace and quiet the whole world gangs up and closes in on you.

IVY *goes out.* CAROL *sits next to* BETTY *who is staring out of the window. Silence.*

BETTY. Doesn't the sky look beautiful.

CAROL (*unnerved*). Yes, very pleasing to the eye, Mum, I'm sure.

BETTY. You know something a Sunday School teacher once told us?

CAROL. I never knew you went to Sunday School.

BETTY. Oh yes, your nan wanted us kids outta the house on Sunday afternoons. She had no more dignity or respect for the day of rest than a common streetwalker.

CAROL. Is that what the Sunday School teacher told you?

BETTY. No. Although it wouldn't surprise me if he was knocking her off.

CAROL. Mummy! Sorry, Mum! but really!

BETTY. No. This. Now tell me, can you imagine perfection?

CAROL (*pause*). Er, yes.

BETTY. What?

CAROL. Darrel's prize roses.

BETTY. Now can you imagine a man being able to make something perfect like a rose?

CAROL. No.

BETTY. Well, that's the theory. That logically there must be a God or at least something more capable than man.

CAROL. Must there? (*Silence.*) Well, if you say so.

BETTY. Though all these years I've bin thinking that there's got to be a flaw in it somewhere. If yer Nan had let me stay on and do my matric I was going to try and suss it out. (*Silence.*) Mind you, sometimes I look at the sky and think it's boring.

CAROL. Sometimes I look at Darrel's prize roses and think they're boring.

BETTY. Are you bored?

CAROL. 'Course not. I've got a beautiful home and little boy and a lovely husband.

BETTY. Huh, lovely husband. Which one is the little boy? I never forget when you came crying to me the first week back from your honeymoon, when Darrel had thrown a tin of tomatoes at your head.

CAROL. Well they didn't actually hit my head, and it was my fault. I didn't know he hated tinned tomatoes. And you were right. You sent me straight back and told me to make it work and I have but I'll always be grateful to you for that.

BETTY. 'No use crying over spilt milk Betty', that's what they should call me.

CAROL. Don't be silly. From that day to this, he's never so much as thrown a tin of baby food at me. Well, not so long ago, he threw a hair brush, but that was when McEnroe lost the Men's Open to Connors, and there again I shouldn't have left it lying around on the settee.

BETTY. I mean some things get patched up and patched up but maybe we're all terrified of admitting that they're useless.

CAROL. Mum, what is the matter with you? I can't follow your train.

BETTY. Like you don't see old cars today that were around twenty years ago. Why? Because they don't work.

CAROL. Ah, but like you said, cars are manmade. Marriages are made in heaven.

BETTY. Marriages are made uneven.

CAROL. Don't say that, Mum.

BETTY. We don't even talk any more like we used to.

CAROL. What am I doing then? Singing La Traviata?

BETTY. And you try and speak posh all the time.

CAROL. Well, you know Darrel and his friends . . .

BETTY. Matter more than we do.

CAROL. No, but a silly thing of how you talk matters more to them than it does to you.

BETTY. And all those stupid parties you go to, Carol. They're just so boring and rubbishy.

CAROL. Oh, coming from you. They're no more boring than looking after Nanny, or scheming with Enid all day on how to avoid the Avon lady. Sorry, sorry!

BETTY (kindly). Okay, nuff said. I'll put the kettle on. (She gets up.)

CAROL. Good idea. (She picks up the notes on the table and proceeds to read them aloud whilst BETTY tries to conceal her panic.) Dennis's real father is Mick the Masher of Bow Common Lane who's now serving time with the Kray Twins (?) (Then:) I married Jim on the rebound after I discovered my fiancé in bed with mum (?) Mother! What's this?

BETTY. Ah, not what you think. Ah, it was a silly game and not what you think at all. No. Enid and I were just saying how silly those stories were in *Woman's Weekly* and how we could write something better. Then we realised that we had such boring lives we couldn't. So we made up the most unlikely totally ridiculous thing possible. Pathetic, isn't it pathetic?

CAROL. Pathetic? It's macabre.

BETTY. It was dreadful, sick, fancy writing such a slanderous thing against your nan, even though it was a joke. If anything happens to her now I'll never forgive myself.

JIM enters.

BETTY. Ah, you're back. There you are, Jim. Nice to see you.

JIM (sarcastic). It's been so long my darling, have you missed me? Where's the old rooster?

BETTY. In the bath. Here, I'll put hers in the oven.

CAROL. Mum was just saying how fed up she is.

BETTY. Not now, Carol.

JIM. Should think she is. Sat on her arse all day yakking to Bible-basher Enid.

BETTY. Huh, Enid ain't as holy as you imagine.

JIM. No, she's a . . .

CAROL. Dad, you don't understand. Housework, same thing day in, day out, gets monotonous.

JIM. Yeah, so does working.

CAROL. Apart from anything else, she can't go out to work because of Nanny.

JIM. Nanny, my armpit. She ain't exactly decrepit, you know. I'm sure if she can watch *Grange Hill* and still make the six-thirty bingo session she could probably get a job training Sebastian Coe.

BETTY. Oh I don't know. I just want something that matters to me.

JIM. Your husband and son don't matter of course.

BETTY. Yes they do. Where is John by the way?

JIM. Probably gone for a drink with the lads.

BETTY. Oh I don't know.

JIM. That's right. You don't know what you want, you're like the old lady who lived in the vinegar bottle.

BETTY. I want something to believe in.

JIM. Something to believe in. Hear that, Carol eh? That's a laugh. Coming from her. Someone who believes that you get pneumonia if your underwear isn't aired, that you mustn't walk under a ladder, or drop a knife, or that you can get dirty diseases off a bog chain.

CAROL. Dad!

JIM (*thinking he's being funny*). I suppose God and the Labour Party aren't enough to believe in, eh, Bet?

CAROL. Mum?

BETTY. I feel a bit dizzy. I think I'll lie down for half an hour.

JIM. What about your dinner?

BETTY. I don't feel too good. I won't be long.

She goes out.

JIM. Gawd, she's never done that before.

CAROL. Dad, you know about, I mean, Mum, time of life, the change.

JIM. Carol, I know all about women's troubles.

CAROL. I think, I think, now don't get cross. Sometimes Mum doesn't understand when you're making a joke.

JIM. She's out of practice, we haven't exactly 'ad a lot to laugh at lately.

CAROL. It's bin hard on her, you know.

JIM. Look, Carol, I might be able to get another job on the side, but don't mention that to Darrel mind, although it shouldn't be long before I get a full-time job. Then it'll be different, mark my words, I'll make it up to her. I'll see her all right.

Scene Six

BETTY's kitchen. *Several weeks later.* JIM *has been as good as his word. The kitchen is now sporting an electric toaster, liquidiser, microwave oven etc.* ENID *enters with a sheaf of daily papers.*

ENID. Blimey, it's getting to look like a regular Argos showroom in here.

BETTY. Yes.

ENID. Soon you'll be able to sit in a chair and press a button and everything will be done.

BETTY. Hasn't made much difference except now the toast pops up automatically burnt.

ENID. How can you be so ungrateful?

BETTY. I don't mean to be. I've tried talking to him, Enid, half these gadgets frighten me.

ENID. But he's trying, Betty. Gawd if I start saying I'm unhappy to my Bob he'd say count meself lucky or I will give yer something to be unhappy about. I'd be over the moon at all this, isn't even as if he's got a proper job yet.

BETTY. Enid, if you say to someone I'm cold and they set light to you, do you think that's the answer?

ENID. Betty, I think you're a bit loola, otherwise you bin listening to too much Radio Four. Anyway cheer up, I've got all the papers.

BETTY. Good, you know even Jim's had to think about it after seeing the Labour Party Conference on telly.

ENID. Well, I didn't half feel a twit asking for *The Times*, *Telegraph* and *Guardian*. Right, are we going to cut them up?

BETTY. It'll have to be later. Social worker's coming this morning.

ENID. I'll get out the way then. Don't want her analysing me, thanks very much. Where's Ivy?

BETTY. Trying to make herself helpless as possible.

ENID. Trying to undo the habit of a lifetime, must be some task. See you later then. (*She goes out.*)

IVY *enters.*

IVY. My Bob Big Gob done?

BETTY. Yes. Now, don't be rude to the social worker, we want something, remember?

IVY. Don't teach your grandmother to suck eggs. Anyone can fool that snipetty-jig of a young do-gooder girl.

BETTY. Don't be so sure. I reckon they got as much power as the police if they got a mind – Jim calls them the caring branch of the SPG.

IVY. Ha, him. He couldn't control a fart in a bottle.

BETTY. Maybe not, but don't go telling her you got paralysed from the waist down in a bomb scare 'cos they might be stupid but they got access to doctors' records.

IVY. Na, they don't understand arthritis either, to them it's just another word what means old.

The doorbell rings.

BETTY. Remember when in doubt keep stum. (*She opens the door.*

FIONA. Hello, my name's Fiona, I'm from the Social Services. I wrote and told you I was coming.

BETTY. Yes, do come in. Would you like a cup of tea?

FIONA. No, thanks very much.

BETTY. Well do sit down.

FIONA (*sits, so does* BETTY). Thanks, how are things?

BETTY. You know, mustn't grumble but mother's not getting any better.

FIONA. I'm sorry to hear that. Hello, Mrs Taylor, how are you feeling today?

Silence.

BETTY. Hearing's not so hot.

FIONA. Really? There wasn't anything on the file.

BETTY. Ears like everything else don't improve none with age.

FIONA (*stands in front of* NANNY *mouthing and shouting*). Mrs Clayton was saying your hearing has deteriorated.

IVY (to BETTY). What she say?

BETTY (gesturing). She said you're a bit deaf. Worried about deaf.

IVY. Death, of course I am. Nobody wants to die, do they, dear?

BETTY. Not death. Deaf, deaf.

FIONA. Have you seen your GP for a hearing aid?

BETTY. Oh no, she don't have one. Never bin one for human conversation, you might say. What she misses most is hearing the telly.

FIONA. We do have a special device, I might . . .

BETTY. Works like headphones?

FIONA. I think that's right.

IVY. Like Mrs Appleton's got at number seven?

FIONA turns round.

IVY. I've got the same trouble in me back as Mrs Appleton. We was comparing ourselves other day. Very bad legs.

FIONA. That's nice. How do you manage to see her? She's housebound like yourself.

BETTY. Er, my husband if he's not 'ad too 'ard a day carries her up the road.

IVY. What you say?

FIONA (shouting). She said her husband often takes you.

IVY. Keep your filthy assanations to yerself.

BETTY. Nice company for her them both being in the same boat – deaf like.

FIONA. Now, I was wondering about the possibility of a day centre.

BETTY. I don't think she'd like that.

FIONA (mouthing, shouting). Would you like to try going to a day centre?

IVY. I ain't setting foot in no play school for geriatrics.

FIONA. They do some lovely things, light factory work, basket weaving.

IVY. I ain't bloody blind.

BETTY. What she's trying to say is that she'd miss *Afternoon Plus* too much.

IVY. At least I don't shit meself like that load of cabbages up at the play centre.

BETTY. Mother. (*To* FIONA:) She's rambling. She gets like this. Take no notice.

FIONA. But she is usually quite lucid?

BETTY. Oh no. Her bowels are her strongest point.

IVY. When I was in hospital, the Sister says to her, your mother is marvellous. There's not a blemish up her back passage, didn't she, Bet, what did . . .

BETTY. Mum.

FIONA. That's nice, well it seems like we've got to the bottom of the matter, ha ha, yes. How, how is John these days? Is he enjoying the YOPS course?

BETTY. Seems to be, we don't see much of him. You know, out and about, but they're like that when they're young, aren't they?

FIONA. And is your husband still out of work?

BETTY. Er yes, but he's not here at the moment because he's doing the shopping. Gets on men's nerves hanging about the house all day.

FIONA. Can get on women's nerves as well. No troubles with the DHSS?

BETTY. Not so far. I mean, giros arrive on time and that.

FIONA. That's one thing.

BETTY. You ain't the same as them are you?

FIONA. No way. We call them the Department of Stealth and Total Obscurity.

BETTY (*unaware that this is a joke*). Oh really, we call it the Social.

FIONA. Well. (*She gets up.*) No other worries?

BETTY (*lightly*). Except the bomb.

FIONA. Not much Social Services can offer there.

BETTY (*trying to be casual*). Er, have you ever heard of that err peace camp thing in the south?

FIONA. Greenham Common?

BETTY. Yes. I expect you think those kids should be in care. What with them going to prison and that.

FIONA. No, I don't think that at all.

BETTY. You don't think they're mad?

FIONA. No, what do you think about it?

BETTY. I've bin trying to follow it.

FIONA. Have you?

BETTY. Well, you know, what I've seen on the telly and that. Do you know anyone what's actually bin there?

FIONA. I have, as a matter of fact.

BETTY. What's it like?

FIONA. Like it is on the telly only colder.

BETTY. You know all the other women?

FIONA. Not really, no.

BETTY. Are they all well off and that?

FIONA. No, all sorts of backgrounds.

BETTY. I read in the paper that one woman was a doctor.

FIONA. That's true.

BETTY. But I s'pose that's the sort of thing the papers would pick up on.

FIONA. Yes, I s'pose it is.

BETTY. Still, I can't keep you standing chatting all day, you must be busy.

FIONA. That's okay. (*She takes what is now a crumpled piece of paper from her pocket.*) This is a sort of handout leaflet. D'you want it?

BETTY. Are you sure?

FIONA. Of course.

BETTY (*takes it*). Thanks . . . I've been sort of saving news cuttings.

FIONA (*searches her bag*). Hang on – there's something about it in this magazine. You can have it, I've read it.

BETTY. That's very kind.

FIONA. I'm very pleased that you're interested.

BETTY. So am I. Pleased that you are I mean.

FIONA. I've got some other stuff at home, I'll bring it with the gadget for the telly.

BETTY. Thanks very much.

FIONA. Nice to meet you. (*She goes out.*) Bye.

BETTY. And you. Bye.

IVY. What was that all about?

BETTY. You know full well. You won't go telling Jim now, will you?

IVY. Betty, you've got to stick up for yourself. Look at the way he creates about me going to Bingo but there's nothing he can do about it. What should it matter to him what you talk about – to her or for that matter to that silly born banana Enid.

BETTY. She can't help getting her words mixed up.

VY. She can. She does it for a laugh. She just ain't grasped the fact that you're s'posed to take the Michael outta someone else not yourself.

There is the sound of a door shutting.

BETTY (*hides the magazine and slips the piece of paper inside a copy of* Woman's Realm). Jim? Jim? Is that you, Jim?

JIM *enters.*

JIM. No, it's Omar Sharif returning to his harem.

BETTY. You just missed the social worker.

JIM. Did she want to know where I was?

BETTY. I told her you was shopping.

JIM. Did she believe you?

BETTY. Yes, she didn't take no notice and we fooled her and got one of those things for the telly.

Silence. JIM *switches on the telly.* BETTY *reads the piece of paper* FIONA *gave her, between the covers of* Woman's Realm. *A long pause.*

BETTY (*without thinking*). Jim, what's patriarchy mean?

JIM. Do what?

BETTY. What's patriarchy?

JIM. Who? What are you reading?

BETTY. Nothing. It's in this magazine.

JIM. Let's have a look. What's the sentence?

BETTY. It's a recipe for a patriarchy cake.

JIM. A patriarchy cake? What in hell's name . . . ?

BETTY. What does it mean?

JIM. No idea. (*Pause.*) Hang on. Hierarchy is like boss at the top – then the deputy's under him, then under them, then at the bottom the workers.

BETTY. How d'you mean?

JIM. Like a triangle with the boss at the top and all the workers along the bottom, but funny name to call a cake.

BETTY. Maybe it's in the shape of a triangle.

JIM. Well, I'm certainly looking forward to eating it.

IVY (*looks up*). So am I.

.

Scene Seven

The next day. BETTY *is sitting at the table with both the October edition of* Sanity *magazine and the paper.* ENID *enters. There are three jam-centred swiss rolls on the table.*

ENID. Coast clear? Where's Nanny?

BETTY. Cutting her toenails, chiropody's non-existent round here now. Enid? What does patriarchy mean?

ENID. A sort of parrot disease.

BETTY. I don't know why I bothered to ask.

ENID. What on earth d'you want to know that for?

BETTY. I haven't got time to go into it all. But you know that welfare worker that came yesterday?

ENID. Not personally no.

BETTY. She gave me this paper all about it.

ENID. About welfare workers.

BETTY. No. The women's peace camp.

ENID. Social Services are telling people about that, blimey, as if they haven't got enough work to do.

BETTY (*impatient*). No, like it just cropped up in the conversation

ENID. I reckon they must be real lonely, wanting to spend the whole day inflicting themselves on folk and bending their ears off.

BETTY. Listen, anyway I asked her, but then I asked Jim what it meant by mistake because then he asked where I read it, so I told him it was a cake recipe, so now he wants to eat patriarchy cake.

ENID. Oh I see, clear as mud.

BETTY. Are you going to help me or not?

ENID. I don't see how I can, I can't understand a word you're on about.

BETTY. It's this bit. (*She reads.*) We are dealing with the tip of the iceberg. Cruise missiles and at the same time the broad base patriarchy.

ENID. I don't see what I can help with. I s'pose Cruise missiles are the bomb, broad base – like a flan case I suppose.

BETTY (*tracing a line with her finger*). This is a tip.

ENID (*looks round*). Well, could do with a hoover.

BETTY. No, look. (*She traces another line.*) This is the base. Jim reckoned it must be like hierarchy which is like a triangle. Now it's a case of sticking these Swiss rolls together and cutting the edges in the triangle.

ENID *picks one of the Swiss rolls up and gives an impression of Groucho Marx.*

Can't you ever be serious?

ENID. Me? Me? Here you are, making a God-knows-what cake.

BETTY. Patriarchy.

ENID. And you don't even know the meaning of the word. Me, me. You know something, Betty, if anyone's losing their marbles, it's you.

BETTY. Wait a minute.

ENID. What, for the men in the white coats?

BETTY. What did Steptoe call his father?

ENID. A dirty old man.

BETTY. No, when he was trying to be posh.

ENID. Dirty old basket.

BETTY. Pater.

ENID. Oh yeah, always thought that was funny, his name was Albert.

BETTY. Tut. It means father.

ENID (*sarcastic*). Oh what a relief. There, you've solved it. Father triangle, that's what it means. Father Christmas, Father Time and Father Triangle. Christianity, Timearchy and Patriarchy.

BETTY. Maybe that's it. God the Father, he's at the top.

ENID. I thought you reckoned the bomb was at the top.

BETTY. I just don't . . .

ENID. I believe in one God, God the Father, God the Bomb and God the Holy Patriarchy Cake.

BETTY. Enid, don't say that.

ENID. Anyhow, three Swiss rolls stuck together aren't going to fool Jim.

BETTY. I'll cover it with icing, he won't know.

ENID. I bin thinking.

BETTY. Don't strain yourself.

ENID. You know when I got the papers this morning, Betty, they'd had another brick through the window.

BETTY. Not again. Poor souls.

ENID. And I was sort of thinking like, what would they think about all this peace camp business. Petrol through the letter box every other night. Never knowing if they'll all be burnt in their beds. What are they going to worry about a bloody missile for, probably welcome it dropping on them bastards, I would.

ETTY. I thought you weren't bothered about them.

NID. Got me thinking, Bet, we think we've 'ad it hard.

ETTY. We don't know the half.

NID. Maybe like those women have got nothing really to do with us.

ETTY. Oh no. Then look at this. (*She points to* Sanity *magazine.*)

NID. Sanity? At least you recognised your problem, Betty, you ain't got any. Where d'you get it?

ETTY. Social worker gave it to me.

NID. She thought you was insane as well.

ETTY. No, no, it's about . . .

NID (*picks it up, opens it*). The Church and the bomb. We weren't wrong, Betty, it's in here.

ETTY. No look here. Here. Those women went to prison for what they believed.

NID. Well, my Dennis bin sent down fer what he believed in, just so happens that the judge's beliefs was not in accordance wiv 'is.

TTY. And one of them reckons she was the sort of person who ust made the tea for other people, before she got involved.

NID. Well?

TTY. I've made lots of tea.

NID. She means at meetings, you don't do that.

TTY. But I could describe my life as making tea for others.

NID. This thing's obsessed you, you're obsessed. You'll be naking tea for others in the nuthouse the way you're carrying n. Either that or Holloway bloody prison.

BETTY. Did you see in the evening paper about them lying down in the road up Westminster?

ENID. I said to Bob I said. They're asking for it. Pretending to be dead, then a bloody great bus will run 'em over and nobody will know the difference.

BETTY. Everybody thought the suffragettes were mad at the time.

ENID. Oh no, you ain't bin to see another boring exhibition down the library?

BETTY. I bin thinking about it. Remember them letters, from the Labour MPs? Even they thought it was disgusting that women should 'ave the vote.

ENID. Yeah well, it didn't change much.

BETTY. Maybe 'cos people forgot about it, what with the war an that.

ENID. Anyway, you'd better get on with this daft cake. One thing they never forget in a hurry is their stomachs.

BETTY. You going to give me a hand?

ENID. Don't worry, if it turns out okay I'll make Bob one. Never know, eating patriarchy cake could become like Pancake Day.

    IVY enters.

ENID. Hello Mrs Taylor, are your feet any better?

IVY. Yeah, I'm just off to audition for the Sugar Plum Fairy.

ENID. Second thoughts I think I'd better get along.

    The doorbell rings.

BETTY. Who can that be?

ENID. I'll get it. (*She opens the door to a man.*)

MR SMITH. Good morning, madam, I'm from the Department Health and Social Security.

ENID. Hello and goodbye.

MR SMITH. Actually I wanted a word with your husband.

ENID. He don't live here.

MR SMITH. Oh, this is . . . (*He looks at his file.*)

BETTY. Please come in, this is a friend of mine who was just leaving.

ENID. Like I said, hello and goodbye.

MR SMITH. Oh . . . Hello Mrs Clayton, is your husband at home?

BETTY. No, who are you?

MR SMITH. I'm from the Department of Health and Social Security.

IVY. We had a visit from you lot yesterday.

MR SMITH. Really, I wasn't informed.

BETTY. About an aid for the TV.

MR SMITH. That must have been Social Services, I'm from Social Security.

BETTY. Oh it is good of you to come, we only put in for a heating allowance for Mum a few weeks ago.

MR SMITH. It's not about that I'm afraid. Could you tell me where your husband is.

IVY. He's babysitting for his daughter.

MR SMITH. When will he be back?

IVY. Not sure. She had a hospital appointment, you know what they're like. Why?

MR SMITH. We have reason to believe that he is in fact working.

IVY. Whatever gave you that idea?

MR SMITH. We received a letter stating details.

BETTY (*shocked*). From who?

MR SMITH. We're not permitted to divulge its source even if we knew it.

IVY. No and you won't be got at whatever you say 'cos that

MR SMITH. I would remind you that to investigate a possible fraud by th

BETTY. You mean to say someone wrote you a poisonous pen letter and you believed them?

MR SMITH. You'd be surprised how reliable they are.

BETTY. Well, that's funny, 'cos if anyone gets one in the post, the police usually advise you to throw it away, but I s'pose they tell you to believe it.

MR SMITH. Not exactly but we have to check these things out.

IVY. Well, he ain't working and that't that. Now what about my heating allowance?

MR SMITH. I'm not sure if this family is entitled to Social Security. I'm afraid I can't apply for a heating allowance until I find out definitely whether your son-in-law is working.

IVY. By which time it'll be the middle of December and I'll have kicked the bucket with hypothermia.

BETTY. Mum.

MR SMITH. I'll make a note of it. Now, you're Mrs Taylor, Mrs Clayton's mother?

IVY. No I'm her pet snake.

MR SMITH. And what makes you think you're entitled to a heating allowance?

IVY. You wily bastard.

BETTY. Mum! (*To* MR SMITH:) She don't know what she's saying.

IVY. Oh yes she does. She knows what he's saying and all, he means we have to make a guess at what would qualify us for a heating allowance and if we guess right we can have it. Well have I got news for you mate – this ain't family fortunes. For one thing, I'm always cold. I have to have a fire on even in the summer and all night in my room in the winter. I've got chronic arthritis and I'm very weak – for Chrissake, I'm a dying woman.

MR SMITH. We're none of us getting any younger, ha ha.

IVY. No and you won't be getting any older if you don't take that sneer off your mush.

MR SMITH. I would remind you I'm here to investigate a possible fraud by the claimant of this household. I do not take kindly to being threatened within inches of my life. I will look into the heating allowance but, mark my words, not until we've investigated the other matter thoroughly.

BETTY. Thank you for coming.

MR SMITH. Good day, Mrs Clayton.

BETTY. Umm, have you heard of Greenham Common as well?

MR SMITH (*thinks by now the whole household is mad*). As well as what? What about it?

BETTY. I just wondered what you thought.

MR SMITH. It's nothing to do with me I'm sure, but no doubt some of them are extracting state benefits under false pretences. We're probably having a field day down there. Good day.

He goes out.

BETTY. Oh dear.

IVY. To think people died in the war for the likes of that cretin to breed.

BETTY. You realise you went too far I s'pose, Bette Davis. Well, you're not going to get an Oscar for that performance.

IVY. What are you going to get 'It was nice to meet you' Betty, when are you going to stand up for yourself, eh? People like that are scum of the earth, they don't deserve the time of day.

BETTY. No, Mother, people what wrote that letter are the scum of the earth. Mind, he didn't like the idea of Greenham Common much.

IVY. I hope it drops on the bloody lot of 'em, put pay to the likes of him. That'll teach him a lesson he'll never forget.

JIM *enters.*

BETTY. Oh Jim, something terrible's happened.

JIM. Nanny's dentures fallen down the bog again?

BETTY. No, sit down, sit down. Man from Social Security's been round, they know you're working.

JIM. Know? They can't know.

BETTY. Well, someone's s'posed to have written a letter ain't they?

JIM. What? What bastard?

BETTY. I don't know. What are we going to do?

JIM. You didn't tell them nothing?

IVY. We never. We carried on about we thought it was for the heating allowance.

BETTY. Who could have done that?

JIM. Nobody knew about it. Wait a minute, I know who it was, Enid, that's who.

BETTY. No, Jim, no. She wouldn't.

JIM. Want a bet, I never want her in here again.

IVY. Jim, I ain't never had a lot of time for the woman but I don't think it could've bin.

JIM. We'll see if she has the audacity to show her boat again, but my bet is she'll lay low for a couple of weeks and, as far as I'm concerned, for ever.

Scene Eight

LINDA *and* FIONA's *squat.* LINDA *is cutting up pieces of card so that it makes a stencil. (We can't see what it reads.)* FIONA *enters with shopping bag.*

LINDA. Hi.

FIONA. Hi, got the paint.

LINDA. Great. Did you remember the spaghetti?

FIONA. What do we need that for?

LINDA. Tea?

FIONA. Oh hell, sorry I forgot.

LINDA. Don't matter. No problem.

FIONA. Sorry.

LINDA. S'okay. Are you all right?

FIONA (*flatly*). Yeah. Went to see Betty today.

LINDA. Thought you were pleased about that. Certainly proved me wrong.

FIONA. She seemed . . . well . . .

LINDA. She gone off the idea of going down there, then eh?

FIONA. Not exactly. Have you?

LINDA (*smiles*). A deal's a deal. So what was Betty pissed off about?

FIONA. She seemed more preoccupied with some sort of misunderstanding she'd had with your mum.

LINDA. Perhaps we should get together and form a club. Non-effective direct discussions we've had with Enid.

FIONA. It seems to have really got to her.

LINDA. Did you manage to get out of her what it was all about?

FIONA. The fraud squad have been round there. And Betty's old man thinks your mum grassed them up.

LINDA. My mum, whatever else she might or might not do, would never do that, not in a million years, never.

FIONA. Apparently she hasn't been round there since.

LINDA. Why ever not?

FIONA (*shrugs*). They assume guilty conscience.

LINDA. Didn't you go and talk to Enid?

FIONA. How could I? Apart from the fact that my job description doesn't involve peace-making between neighbours, I find the whole concept fraught with Freudian tension.

LINDA. What you on about?

FIONA. I don't relish the thought of case work with your mother.

LINDA. Oh dear. It looks like I'll have to do a mother–daughter reunion number.

FIONA. It wouldn't come amiss. You haven't been home for months.

LINDA. Paternal problem patterns.

FIONA. Do what?

LINDA. Uses his kids as a target practice against life's frustrations. Kicked me down three flights of stairs once.

FIONA. My mum used to belt us when we were kids.

LINDA. Yeah, I s'pose I was only twenty-three at the time.

FIONA. How does Enid get on with him?

LINDA. She gets on my nerves. Basically, she weaves a web of complete fabrication round everything. She refers to the stair episode as that time your father was helping you down the stairs.

FIONA. Surely she doesn't believe it.

LINDA. Well as time goes on they get even more modified. Till every action he does becomes bloody saintly.

FIONA. Don't you ever get to talk to her on her own?

LINDA. Rarely, then she's on edge in case he comes through the door. Oh, she won't have a word said against him. The most that ever gets admitted, is that they've had their ups and downs but that's followed immediately by, if she ever had her life again she'd marry him again. Mind you she does say it parrot fashion and at breakneck speed like she might be struck dead at any moment for such an enormous lie.

Silence.

FIONA. What d'you think it would take for Betty and Enid to change their lives?

LINDA (*pause. Smiles*). A bomb?

Scene Nine

VY. *Monologue.*

VY. When you see old people on the telly in those comedy programmes what are made by morons and aren't at all funny, all they ever seem to open and shut their traps about is the war. Everybody's fed up to the back teeth with the bloody boring war. You know all that British Legion stuff about, 'I died in the war for you' and being proud that half their relatives got splattered all over the shop for a better nation and once in a while you gets round to thinking that this is the better nation and it's the sort of thought that's so depressing you don't want to get round to thinking it again for a few years.

We had a great time round here in the war. Yeah, I know you're thinking, 'And the silly old crow's going to tell us it brought us all together'. Course it brought us together. Half the bloody streets disappeared. Every Saturday there was a party 'cos you didn't know which house would be flattened next. One day we'd be having a knees-up and the next the place would be a pile of dust. Women became strong. We had to be. We ran the country and when it was over we could see the way things were going and that it was a bit late for us but we invested our dreams and hopes and plans in our daughters, only to see them evaporate like pee in the lift on a hot day. Having kids is important, but having a washing-machine, a television and a car became more important. And a husband with a steady job was set up as number one main aim. Bloody silly values for a country what was s'posed to be embarking on freedom, that's all I can say. The war's so bloody boring because what did it change for the better? For us, seems like sod all.

Scene Ten

CAROL *and* BETTY.

CAROL. All this time, I can't believe it.

BETTY. We walked past each other on the stairs, never said a word.

CAROL. Is the lift broken again?

BETTY. On and off, I won't get in it in case I get stuck.

CAROL. Forget it, Mum, if Enid wants to act like that let her, you've got enough worries and I'm sorry to say, but it proves it must have been her.

BETTY. No Carol not Enid. Anyhow your dad's been employed properly, well three days a week with tax and insurance is better than nothing.

CAROL. It's a pity you had to get rid of all those things to pay back the Social Security.

BETTY. I didn't want them in the first place.

CAROL. But Dad cares, he could have spent the money on himself.

BETTY. He doesn't listen, he's never listened to me or what I want.

CAROL. What do you want?

BETTY. I don't know.

CAROL. How can he understand that if you don't?

BETTY. Anyway, that's enough of me moaning on, how are you and Darrel?

CAROL. Oh, fine. (*Pause.*) Listen, Mum, you remember before I was married?

BETTY. When you was courting.

CAROL. As you'd put it, yes. You know we used to come back here when you and Dad had gone to bed.

BETTY. Carol, love, there's no need to go into that. I know, I know young people these days well, like to make sure they're well suited before . . . (*Then she adds quickly.*) they get married.

CAROL (*laughs*). No, Mum, not that.

BETTY. Oh, well that's a relief.

CAROL. We used to have a real laugh. Darrel used to line up all your ornaments on the floor and describe them as though it was an auction – go into detail – orange plastic ashtray.

BETTY. It was that funny?

CAROL. I used to laugh, Mum, but inside I was sad, I used to think, I still do, this collection of trinkets is all my mum's got to show for her life. I swore I'd never be like you.

BETTY (*quietly angry*). Carol, I never wanted posh things, I didn't want anything else. I know this place might seem like a pile of tawdry crap to you and your friends but that's their problem. I don't want to have to go tripping round antique china, or freeze to death with pine-stripped floorboards for that matter.

CAROL. I didn't mean to upset you. I was trying to explain.

BETTY. A lot of this stuff was bought for me by you and John when you were kids, surely that's more important than a Rembrandt painting?

CAROL. Yes, but it boils down to nothing.

BETTY. Is that what you wanted? A posh home, posh car, posh husband, because that's exactly what you got. What does that boil down to, eternal bliss, eh? Cos you don't seem none too ecstatic to me.

CAROL. I didn't want to be like you. I wanted a husband with prospects, a home with a garden and kids, kids who would grow up with all the things I never had, but no I'm not happy.

BETTY. You and me ended up the same – we both don't know what we want.

CAROL. What else is there?

The doorbell rings.

BETTY. The doorbell. (*She gets up and answers it.*) Hello.

LINDA. Hello, I don't know if you remember me, I'm Linda, Enid's daughter.

LINDA enters.

BETTY. You remember Carol, you used to go to school together.

CAROL (*forced smile*). Linda, how are you these days?

LINDA. Okay thanks and you?

CAROL (*rather abrupt*). I'm married now.

LINDA. I'm not.

BETTY (*pleased*). You always got on so well together.

LINDA. Umm, look I've come round because I think there's been a misunderstanding. Mum was a bit afraid to come.

BETTY. Huh, I don't believe Enid's afraid of anything.

LINDA. It seems that someone tipped the DHSS off about your husband working and you thought it was Mum.

BETTY. Actually, no. Jim thought it was.

LINDA. Well, it appears the same day someone came round to investigate my brother Dennis's illegal working habits and my dad thought it was you.

BETTY. Why didn't Enid tell me?

LINDA. Because you've been avoiding her. What was she to think?

BETTY. Where is she?

LINDA. Pacing the balcony like something out of a John Wayne movie.

BETTY. Hang on a second. (*She goes out.*)

CAROL *and* LINDA *are left alone. There is an awkward silence.*

CAROL. I've got a little boy now.

LINDA. That's nice.

CAROL. I don't s'pose you really think that.

LINDA. Why not?

CAROL. I remember the things you used to say at school.

LINDA. I remember the things you used to say.

CAROL. You were always getting me into trouble.

LINDA. Really? I thought that was Darrel.

CAROL. Well, I've changed.

LINDA. So I see. What d'you mean me? You were the one. It was me who took the rap because you looked as though butter wouldn't melt in your mouth.

CAROL. I suppose you're one of those lot at Greenham Common.

LINDA. Actually, I'm the chief fish fryer at Littlewood's canteen. I would have thought women's peace camps were more your bag than mine.

CAROL. You're joking.

LINDA. Don't you want a world for your little boy to grow up in?

CAROL. Actually we're thinking of emigrating to Australia.

LINDA. Oh, that's nice.

CAROL. I know you don't think that for one moment.

LINDA (*shrugs*). Been some good Australian films on the telly recently.

CAROL. And I suppose you're a vegetarian.

LINDA. 'Fraid so.

CAROL. Huh, I remember the time you pulled the tail off the mouse in the biology lab.

LINDA. That was an accident. I remember you told me not to worry, it would grow another one, and you believed it.

Both laugh. Then there is an embarrassed pause.

CAROL. Don't mention anything about cross-country running.

LINDA. What cross-country running? We spent the whole time . . .

CAROL. I said don't mention it.

LINDA. Mum's the word.

BETTY *and* ENID *enter.*

CAROL (*to* LINDA. *Put down*). Funny how we haven't got anything in common any more. (*Then to* BETTY:) Hello Mum, everything all right?

ENID. Bleedin' stupid nanas we've been.

BETTY. Yes, we sorted it out.

ENID. Take me the rest of my life to sort Bob out though. Thanks to you, madam.

LINDA. He started it.

ENID. And you, you had to retaliate didn't you, couldn't keep your trap shut.

LINDA. When someone bellows in your lughole, 'You filthy bleedin' perverted . . .'

ENID (*cuts her short*). Yes well, your father's tolerance of you has been stretched to the limits.

LINDA. So has mine.

BETTY. Let's all have a cup of tea.

ENID. You're on the road, Bet, it starts with cups of tea at meetings.

LINDA. What you on about, Mum?

ENID. Never you mind.

BETTY. Tell her, Enid, she might know something about it.

ENID. Here we go. Have you heard of the women's peace camp at Greenham Common?

LINDA. No, what's it about?

ENID. You must have. Everyone has.

BETTY. Been on the telly, everything.

LINDA. Yes, I have.

ENID. See, that's typical of her, contradiction is her middle name.

LINDA. I wouldn't choose a middle name with dick in it, thank you.

ENID. Well, what did you say no for then?

BETTY. Enid, don't carry on at her.

ENID. Typical Betty that is. (*To* LINDA:) Well you know something, Betty's possessed by it.

BETTY. I'm only interested.

ENID. And I became the research worker. In fact, I reckon I should apply to the GLC for a grant.

BETTY. Oh, Enid.

ENID. What that means, is, I went to get the high class papers. What Betty was too embarrassed to.

LINDA. What do you think about it?

ENID. Me? Well, you know me, Linda, I think people what value their lives are worthless.

LINDA. I weren't aware you thought your life was insignificant.

BETTY. Take no notice, Linda. Even Enid's admitted to thinking.

CAROL. What I want to know is why there are no men there?

BETTY. Oh, I'd never thought about that.

CAROL. Why does it have to be women only? That's a bit sexist isn't it, Linda?

ENID. Oh, the men would only spoil it.

LINDA. It was set up on women's initiatives, Carol. There are very few things women can call their own in this society.

BETTY. Because of the patriarchy.

CAROL. The what?

ENID. Ah, don't you know what that means?

CAROL. Do you?

ENID. We know all about it and we know what the opposite is an all; matriarchy, and even though that's been extinct for a few thousand years, me and Betty is raising it from the dead.

BETTY. I wouldn't say that, Enid.

ENID. What would yer say then?

BETTY. Well, it's certainly buried round 'ere, but it ain't exactly dead.

LINDA (*interested*). What do you know about . . .

ENID. All I know is, if I don't get Atilla the Hun's tea within the next two seconds I'm going to be a gonner meself. Now listen girl, don't go leaving it another few thousand years before you condescend ter drop in again.

LINDA. Mum, how can I wiv him? Why don't you come and see me?

ENID. I ain't setting foot in no commie squat.

BETTY. Oh, Enid . . .

LINDA. Well, I'd sooner set foot in a piranha-infested swamp . .

BETTY. Hey, why don't you two meet round here when Jim's working late?

ENID. Look at this eh, Carol. See what this lark's set off. Betty's now into bloody communes. Where will it end?

LINDA. Sounds like a good idea to me.

BETTY. Trouble is with you, Enid. You're afraid of change.

ENID. See! She's even talking like one of them. Next we know she'll be wearing an afghan.

LINDA (*eyebrows raised*). Mum.

ENID (*smiles*). It's a dog's life.

BETTY. Wednesday evenings, Jim always works late.

LINDA. What d'you say?

ENID. I reckon it's like a bloody James Bond film just ter see me own daughter. Shall we wear a red carnation?

LINDA (*gets up to go*). Meet you by the lift at seven . . . I've got to go now.

CAROL. How are you getting home?

LINDA. Bus. (*Slight pause. She smiles.*) It's a bit cold for a cross-country run.

CAROL. I'll give you a lift if you want.

LINDA. Ta. See yer . . .

ENID. Take care, love.

CAROL. Bye Mum, Enid.

LINDA *and* CAROL *go out.*

BETTY. Listen, Enid, we ain't ever going to get in this sort of mess again, right?

ENID. From now on whatever spills outta Jim or Bob's mouth we take no notice.

BETTY. We make up our own minds.

ENID (*pause*). Your Carol seemed a bit quiet.

BETTY. I don't really think she's very happy.

ENID. But she's got everything she wanted. She thinks she's got problems, could've turned out like our Linda.

BETTY. It was strange seeing them both together. Linda seems so much younger, so full of life . . . I don't know . . .

ENID (*pause*). God, sometimes I could kill Bob.

BETTY. Huh, you're always claiming that when they made him they broke the mould.

ENID. It was obviously cracked already, if you ask me. It don't do going on about it but today, Betty, he was out of order . . . really out of order.

BETTY. They must really rub each other up the wrong way.

ENID. He's only got ter ketch sight of her and he starts up. An' yer know something, Betty, it was really good of her ter come over here, Christ knows how long this carry-on would have lasted. (*Pause.*) Come to think, how the hell did she know about it?

BETTY. Well, don't look at me.

ENID. An' Bob wouldn't 'ave told her, that's fer sure.

BETTY. Strange like, the bond between mother and daughter, yer know, Enid.

ENID. Oh Gawd, Betty, don't go all psychic on me an' all. That's all I need.

Scene Eleven

12 December 1982. Four a.m. LINDA and FIONA dressed in dark clothing have just completed spraying a sex shop.

LINDA (*stands back to admire her work. Makes a gesture with her hand*). Bellissimo.

FIONA. Come on let's get outta here.

LINDA. What do you think of it?

FIONA. Wonderful. Come on, make sure you've not left any evidence.

LINDA. Oh yeah, didn't I tell you? I've sprayed, 'I did it really' on your back.

FIONA. Very funny. Leave the can and let's get out.

They start walking.

LINDA. Just as well you let me do it. We'd have been here till the bloody shop opened, the polemic you wanted to inscribe.

FIONA. Save your breath. We might get a few hours' kip if we're lucky.

LINDA. You know something, your spelling is a discredit to your sex.

FIONA. As long as that's the only thing, I'm laughing.

Both smile and FIONA puts her arm round LINDA.

FIONA. Er, oh. (*She lets her arm drop.*)

LINDA. Tomorrow's bacon has made an appearance.

A POLICE CONSTABLE enters.

POLICE CONSTABLE. Good morning, ladies.

FIONA. Morning, officer.

POLICE CONSTABLE. What, may I ask, are you two girls doing out alone this late or early should I say?

FIONA. We were er . . . just admiring Hackney's architecture silhouetted against the dawn skyline.

LINDA (*mumbles*). Huh, ketch me admiring no phallic symbols I don't think.

POLICE CONSTABLE (*looking at watch*). What dawn?

FIONA. Moon. Against the pale glow of the moon.

LINDA. Winter solstice.

FIONA *stifles a laugh.*

POLICE CONSTABLE. Been to a party then?

FIONA. Yes.

POLICE CONSTABLE. Not thinking of driving I hope.

LINDA (*mimes turning a steering wheel*). No, just pretending.

POLICE CONSTABLE. Don't try and be funny with me, Miss.

FIONA. We left our car. We thought it best to walk.

POLICE CONSTABLE. Very advisable. Not on a yellow line I trust.

FIONA. No a private road.

POLICE CONSTABLE. Glad to hear it. Good morning.

POLICE CONSTABLE *goes out.*

LINDA. Morning all. Have a nice day.

FIONA. Shush.

LINDA (*warmly*). No officer, yes officer, we parked our non-existent car up a lamp post, officer.

FIONA. Tut, Winter Solstice.

LINDA. Dawn skyline.

FIONA. When we get round the corner we run right? Cos he'll be about to view your handiwork any minute now.

LINDA. S'okay. It's open to the public.

FIONA. You're so cool.

LINDA. He won't even notice it. Thick as shit. (*Then.*) For fuck's sake run.

Scene Twelve

Later the same day. BETTY's living-room. BETTY and IVY. JIM enters.

BETTY. Jim?

JIM (*irritated*). What is it, Betty? I'm late for work.

BETTY. Have you . . . I mean, would it . . . ?

JIM. Spit it out.

BETTY. I was wondering . . .

JIM. For Christ's sake, woman, I haven't got all day . . .

BETTY. . . . if I could lend ten quid off next week's housekeeping.

JIM. What? Now?

BETTY. Oh no next Christmas. What d'you think?

JIM. For what?

BETTY. Shopping.

JIM. Shopping? Betty, my love, it's Sunday. The poxy shops are shut.

BETTY. Not all of them.

JIM. You never go shopping on a Sunday.

BETTY. Well . . . I was thinking of popping out . . . for some fresh air.

JIM. Things are bad, Betty, but they ain't that bad. Fresh air don't cost a tenner.

BETTY. I meant . . . fresh air, not a lung-load of lorry fumes . . .

JIM. What? Where have you got to go . . .

BETTY. Er . . . Our Carol's . . .

JIM. They got an air filter in Islington then?

BETTY. Please Jim . . .

JIM. That don't cost ten quid.

BETTY. Five then, could I have five . . . ?

JIM. Blimey, Betty, since when did it cost a fiver to git to Carol's? And anyhow if they want you to babysit they can give you a lift there and back.

BETTY. Jim, I would like five quid.

JIM. I daresay we all would. (*He looks at his watch.*) But not until you tell me why and you'd better be quick about it.

BETTY. I'm your wife.

IVY. For God's sake, Betty, tell him, stand up fer yerself.

BETTY. Keep outta this, Mum.

JIM. Don't tell me let me guess. You both been invited to the Palace. (*Pause.*) Well, I gotta go.

BETTY *stands between him and the door.*

BETTY. I want to get a cheap-day return somewhere.

JIM. You'll be getting a one-way ticket to the funny farm if you don't make sense in ten seconds flat.

BETTY. I just thought I'd go for an outing.

JIM. Yeah, I grasped that much but WHERE?

BETTY (*pause. Mumbles*). Newbury.

JIM. Who bury? That rings a bell. Betty a joke's a joke. Now, what do you really want to do?

BETTY. Really, I thought I'd go . . .

JIM. Just knock these daft notions outta yer head once an' fer all. God Almighty, where did you git that idea?

BETTY. I got this letter inviting me.

JIM. Oh, how nice fer you. What did it say. Dear sister Betty, We hear you are a genuine East Ender what actually trod the same pavements as the Pankhursts . . .

BETTY. Jim!

JIM. Don't you Jim me. You'll be right here when I git back. D'you hear me, and we'll sort it out then. I can't waste no more time gabbing about it now.

BETTY. Please . . .

JIM. No way, Betty. No way. Gawd woman, I know you ain't bin hundred per cent lately but it's about time you tried to act normal.

He goes out.

BETTY (*to IVY*). Why did you have to blurt it out?

IVY. He wouldn't have given it to you anyway.

BETTY. No thanks to you. The one time it would have bin welcome and you didn't open your mouth and take sides.

IVY. Waste of time. Git more results reasoning with a brick wall, anyhow I got the money.

BETTY. I can't take it off you.

IVY. Yes you can. And you will, girl. (*She gives her two five-pound notes.*)

BETTY. Ta, Mum, I wish you'd come with me.

IVY. It's brass monkeys out there. It'd finish me off. Shame Enid can't git her act together.

BETTY. I s'pose I'd better git me stuff together.

IVY. Whatever you do, git a move on love.

BETTY (*from the kitchen where she is preparing a packed lunch*). Mum, did you ever get fed up?

IVY. Course I did! Why d'you think I had a different man every week.

BETTY (*sneers*). Humph.

IVY. You never forgave me for that one time, did you?

BETTY. I forgot that incident a long time ago. But you're right, Mum, I never forgave you. I'm sorry, honest. By the way, I've borrowed one of your thermal vests.

Pause.

IVY. I was on the game, Betty. It was the only way to get money, but I'm not making excuses, other women seemed to manage. That night, before you came home and he came round to court yer, I'd just shown a fella out and he got the wrong idea. Believe me, because this is the truth. I know I can't call it rape because I was in no position to, everyone would have laughed at me, but I did everything I could to stop him. Betty, it was totally against my will. He proved stronger than me.

BETTY. Why didn't you tell me at the time?

IVY. I tried to.

The doorbell rings.

BETTY (*crossing to the door*). Oh, Gawd what now?

IVY. Don't worry, it's probably the *Sunday Times* come to do an exclusive interview.

BETTY (*opening door*). Carol, what are you doing here?

CAROL *enters, looking as though she has been crying.*

CAROL. Oh, were you going out?

BETTY. Well . . . I . . .

IVY. Yes she is.

BETTY. Did you want something, I mean special?

CAROL. No . . . no . . . It doesn't matter.

IVY. Is Darrel with you?

CAROL. No. No.

BETTY. What's he doing?

CAROL. His nut. If you must know, we've run out of Alpen.

Well it was the third time this year but the way he went on . . . (*She is on the verge of tears.*) Oh . . . Mum . . .

BETTY (*takes CAROL's hand then starts to take her own coat off*). Come on, tell me what happened.

IVY. Git that coat back on, girl . . . You can both sort it out on the train. (*To CAROL:*) Your mother is going to do her bit fer peace. I suggest you go with her while that husband of yours does his pieces in bits, ha ha let him sweat.

CAROL. But what about Joe-Joe?

BETTY. About time Darrel learnt to look after his son for a whole day, don't you think?

CAROL (*pause*). Yes I suppose it bloody well is. All right then.

BETTY. Good. (*Slight pause.*) You know, I think the last thing we did together was buy the material for your wedding dress.

IVY. And it still will be if you two don't get a move on and stop jawing.

The doorbell rings.

CAROL. Oh, God help me, that's probably Darrel.

BETTY (*crossing to the door*). High time you got your own back then. (*She points to the kitchen.*) There's a tin of tomatoes in the cupboard. (*She opens the door. ENID enters with a suitcase.*) Enid, you changed your mind?

IVY. Gawd, Enid, that must be some packed lunch. What you got in there, half a horse's carcass?

ENID. Didn't you know, Ivy. I just stabbed the rag and bone man to death.

BETTY. Be serious, Enid.

ENID. Just landed the chip pan over bully boy Bob's bonce didn't I.

BETTY. Is he all right?

ENID. Talk sense. When has he ever bin all right?

CAROL. Is he badly hurt?

ENID. Made no difference. No sense. No feeling.

BETTY (*looking at suitcase*). Here, you're not planning to stay down there?

ENID. Do me a favour. I ain't going down there.

IVY. So, what you got in there, Bob or a dented chip pan?

CAROL. She's joking. You're coming with us, aren't you?

ENID. Am I hell!

BETTY. Where the hell are you going then?

ENID. Bognor.

BETTY. *Bognor*! Enid, it's the middle of bloody December.

ENID. I didn't have a stand-up fight with super gut so I could wallow about in mud all day.

IVY. You won't notice the difference on that beach.

BETTY (*to ENID*). That's just typical of you that is. We set this up to do something important fer a change but you, oh no not you. You take the opportunity to enjoy yourself.

CAROL. Don't be too hasty. Who ever enjoyed Bognor?

IVY (*gently*). Knock me down with a feather. Our Carol's made a joke. Quick, write it in your diary.

CAROL. Thank you, Nan.

ENID. Depends what you mean by important. (*To* BETTY:) So you go down there for a day. Right, fine. Come back. Nothing's changed. Big deal.

BETTY. So you go down to Bognor for a day. That's really earth-shattering, I must say.

ENID. Not fer a day. I'm going ter stay wiv me sister.

BETTY. Pardon?

ENID. I've left that stupid big wally.

BETTY. But Enid . . . Enid, what about the children?

ENID. The children? The children are practically fucking geriatric.

BETTY. You can't . . .

ENID. I have, Betty, I have. Bomb or no bomb I got round to thinking I ain't waiting around for it, biding me time stuffing a crew of big-bellied boozers.

IVY. Gawd Almighty, we got a true-life documentary on our hands. At this rate we're all going to feature on *Newsnight*.

BETTY. Carol, say something.

CAROL. Enid, I think you're very brave.

ENID. Ta.

BETTY. Say something positive. You've been watching too many films.

ENID. You won't talk me outta it, Betty.

BETTY. I'm really going ter miss yer.

ENID. You can come down and stay with me.

BETTY. It's not really sunk in.

ENID. I'm going to do something that will change me. You do what you want but I want something more.

BETTY. Huh, you don't want much.

ENID. Not really no. I just don't intend to hang around fer me arms and legs to be blown off before I gets round to putting me life in order.

CAROL. I think we should make a move . . .

IVY. Have you got the car, girl?

CAROL. Oh yes.

IVY. In that case I'll git me coat and come with you.

CAROL. Tell you what, Enid, if you come with us, I'll take you on to Bognor.

ENID. Are you sure? It'll make it a very long day.

CAROL. Oh bugger the Sunday dinner.

BETTY. And if we end up in Holloway, we can bugger the Christmas dinner an' all.

MASTERPIECES

Acknowledgement

I am indebted to Dusty Rhodes for seeing the film and letting me use her description of it, as published in the *Revolutionary and Radical Feminist Newsletter*, Autumn 1982, Common Ground Community Print Shop, Sheffield.

S.D.

Snuff

Snuff is a film which first appeared in the States in 1976, so called because the actresses were actually mutilated and murdered in front of the camera – 'snuffed out'. Many 'snuff' films have been made since then. Early in 1982 it was announced that the original *Snuff* film was being distributed in this country. Feminists protested immediately and the distributors withdrew the film but not before several hundred copies had been made. Women in Leeds' 'Women Against Violence Against Women' group found several shops advertising and hiring *Snuff*. We protested. Members of the Leeds licensing committee and other councillors were asked to see the film. Many did, most walked out unable to watch the mutilation and murder scene. They demanded that it should be destroyed. A group of women from WAVAW and local press and television also saw the film. We were numbed with shock. This murder was done for the pleasure of men. The Marquis de Sade, the 'honoured' pornographer, said, 'There's not a woman on earth who'd ever had cause to complain of my services if I'd been sure of being able to kill her afterwards.'

Dusty Rhodes (*December 1983*)

Masterpieces was first performed at the Royal Exchange Theatre, Manchester, on 31 May 1983, with the following cast:

ROWENA	Kathryn Pogson
YVONNE	} Patti Love
HILARY	
JENNIFER	
POLICEWOMAN	} Shirley Dixon
JUDGE	
IRENE WADE	
TREVOR, *Rowena's husband*	} Gerard Murphy
PSYCHIATRIST	
RON, *Yvonne's husband*	
MAN IN STREET	
MAN IN TUBE STATION	} Eamon Boland
PROSECUTOR	
CLIVE, *Jennifer's husband*	
PROLOGUE, *the Baron, the Peddler, the Consumer*	
POLICEMAN	} William Hoyland
TEACHER	
MAN IN TUBE STATION	
JUDGE	

Voice overs recorded by members of the Company

Directed by Jules Wright
Designed by Di Seymour
Lighting by Nigel Walker
Sound by Chris Coxhead

This production subsequently transferred to the Royal Court Theatre Upstairs on 7 October 1983, with the following change of cast:

TREVOR	} Bernard Strother
PSYCHIATRIST	

Directed by Jules Wright
Scenery by David Roger
Costumes by Di Seymour
Lighting by Nigel Walker
Sound by Patrick Bridgeman and Chris Coxhead

Masterpieces moved into the Royal Court's main auditorium on 5th January 1984.

Masterpieces is set in London. The events take place over twelve months in 1982 and 1983, and shift back and forth throughout the year.

Scene One

A restaurant. JENNIFER *and* RON, *and* TREVOR *and* ROWENA *are dancing.* YVONNE *sits at the table. Male monologue in three parts: all played by the actor who plays* CLIVE.

The sound of Concorde landing. The dancers freeze. Light on the BARON.

1. When I was at university, my one aim in life was to go into business and get rich quick. I was extremely ambitious and not about to wait around for middle-aged spread to set in before I made it. My enterprise, enthusiasm and hard work paid off. In the last few years the tax man has gleaned over two million pounds from me. I have always kept on the right side of the law and when I was first called a purveyor or filth, it upset my mother a lot, but ours is a perfectly normal profession run by ordinary nice people, not gangsters or kinky dwarfs in soiled raincoats. That is a ludicrous myth perpetuated by the media.

   We do sometimes lose stock in police raids, but we allow for the costs when building our stocks so, sadly, the consumer ends up paying more than he should.

   Profit margins are high. Our trade makes more money than the film and record business put together. It will be the growth industry of the eighties. Just as betting shops were in the sixties and casinos in the seventies. I sincerely believe, had it not been for the present repressive climate, I'd have received the Queen's Award for Industry long ago. My mother? Well, she soon stopped crying when I bought her a luxury house in the country.

The dance continues, then freezes. Light on the PEDDLER.

2. I suppose it was about ten, no twelve years ago when the market for naughty underwear and sex aids really opened up. Funnily enough I was working in a newsagents when this mate of mine told me there was a vacancy in one of what is now a large, established chain of shops and he could fix it for me. Well, I jumped at the chance and being the manager of a sex, I mean, private shop, I'm never stuck for something to say at parties even if it doesn't go down too well with the wife, know what I mean? The vast majority of our custom comprises normal healthy men. (*Slight pause.*) Oh, and women, that's why our shops have carpets on the floor, women like that, makes them feel at home. We have an in-joke about getting our underfelt. But seriously though, we've gone to great expense to get an easy atmosphere. It's just like wandering around a boutique. Of course we'll always have criticism from the frustrated politicians and their pathetic fanaticism for censorship. Hopefully, though, the majority of the population is liberated enough to wake up to the fact that we sell marital aids which enrich people's — men and women's — romantic lives, that we provide the practical side to sex therapy.

The PEDDLER *exits.* ROWENA *and* TREVOR *sit. Enter* CLIVE, *the* CONSUMER.

3. Oh, I suppose it depends what you mean by pornography. Yes I buy magazines, sometimes videos. It's not something clear cut or mechanical, sex I mean. Everyone has fantasies, don't they? And from time to time they need revising or stimulating otherwise like everything else it gets boring. It's simply a question of whatever turns you on. Let's face it, alcohol and cigarettes can kill people, looking at pictures never hurt anyone.

CLIVE *takes his place at the table.*
JENNIFER *and* RON *walk to the table and sit down.* RON *has been telling her a joke which has amused her. She is relieved, however, to be out of his grasp.*

TREVOR (*to* JENNIFER). I see he's kept you amused.

JENNIFER. Entranced.

RON (*to* TREVOR). We were chatting about holidays. Have you two made any plans this year?

TREVOR. We've sort of mutually agreed we can't afford it.

ROWENA. Might have a week in Cornwall.

RON. Package tour. Often works out just as cheaply if not cheaper.

CLIVE. That's what I keep telling Jennifer.

JENNIFER. Darling, I am not going on a package tour. As a breed, the British abroad are foul.

RON. At least you can usually guarantee a good dose of currant bun.

JENNIFER. They should all be shot.

RON. Pardon?

CLIVE. She is referring to her fellow-countrymen. We spent Christmas in Morocco last year. Never been the same since, have you darling?

RON. Apparently the food out there is horrible.

JENNIFER. The food is divine – so is the country. Only, for the rest of the crowd we went with, it might as well have been Margate. Do you remember all those hideous coach tours? – just like one of those office beano affairs.

ROWENA. Mother, don't be such a snob.

JENNIFER. God, you must be joking. Who can afford to spend a fortnight in Morocco at Christmas? This was the privileged élite.

CLIVE. At least you got your precious suntan. And enough juicy titbits to dine out on for the rest of the year.

JENNIFER. Yes, do you remember that day . . .

CLIVE. Not now, you've done it to death.

ROWENA. How come Mum always has the monopoly on funny stories?

CLIVE. Your mother has a warped imagination.

JENNIFER. He means because I'm a joke.

CLIVE (*through clenched teeth*). I did not mean that at all, darling.

RON. We heard a good joke in the pub, the other lunchtime. Do you remember, Trev?

TREVOR. I doubt it, I can never remember jokes.

ROWENA. Bad as me, darling.

RON. I wouldn't say that.

ROWENA. At telling jokes, Ron.

RON. Oh that's it, hang on. Two nuns walking through a forest, right? When a man jumps out on them and rapes them, one of them reckons, 'How are we going to explain to the Mother Superior that we've been raped twice?' The other one says, 'But, Sister, we've only been raped once.' 'I know,' says the first, 'but aren't we going back the same way?'

The men laugh, TREVOR *not as heartily as the other two.* ROWENA *rather hesitantly joins in.* YVONNE *doesn't even smile, while* JENNIFER *laughs uproariously and rather disconcertingly so.*

CLIVE. The only one I know is about the nun who was raped but she didn't mind because he was a saint. 'How do you know?' asked the other nuns. 'Because he had Saint Michael on his underpants.'

Same response only they don't find it as funny except JENNIFER *who laughs even louder.*

TREVOR. That's as old as the hills.

RON. What was the other one?

TREVOR. I don't know.

RON. Yes you do, I heard you tell it to Frank.

TREVOR. Oh.(*He is rather abashed.*) 'Help, I've been raped by an idiot.' 'How do you know?' 'Because I had to tell him what to do.'

There is the same pattern of response.
JENNIFER *laughs raucously.* YVONNE *remains silent but extremely uncomfortable, wishing she could just walk out.*

RON. What's your idea of an ideal date? She screws until four o'clock in the morning, then turns into a pizza.

Response is as for the first joke.

JENNIFER. I know a good one.

CLIVE. My dear, I don't think so.

RON. Come on, Clive.

CLIVE. You haven't heard my wife's jokes.

JENNIFER. Don't spoil it, there's a dear. Now there was this vicar and the headmistress asked him to give a talk to the fifth year.

CLIVE. Get on with it, darling.

JENNIFER. Do you mind?

CLIVE. Well you're hamming it up.

JENNIFER. How?

CLIVE. Fifth year, first year, second year, what does it matter? It's of no relevance.

TREVOR. Let her get on with it, Clive.

JENNIFER. Thank you, Trevor.

CLIVE. You've not heard the end yet.

JENNIFER. He won't live to hear the end if you don't stop interjecting.

CLIVE. You're dragging it out.

JENNIFER. Now you've got that out of your system may I proceed?

CLIVE. All right, if you think you must.

JENNIFER. Seconds away round two.

CLIVE (*to the others*). See what I mean?

JENNIFER. There was this vicar.

CLIVE. We know, we know. You've said that once.

JENNIFER. You've ruined the flow, so I'm going to have to start all over again.

RON. Let her get on with it.

JENNIFER. There was this vicar who was asked to give a talk about sex to the fifth year of a school in his parish. However, when he came to writing the appointment in his desk diary he didn't want to write sex as his wife might find it.

RON (*trying to be funny*). Find what?

JENNIFER (*grimaces*). His diary. So he wrote talk, at such and such a school, on sailing. The time came to give the talk and it was received very well. A couple of weeks later his wife met the headmistress in Sainsbury's and the headmistress said, 'Your husband gave a wonderful talk to our fifth year,' and the wife replied, 'I don't know how, he's only done it twice. The first time he was sick and the second time his hat came off.'

Although the men laugh they are less inclined to do so. YVONNE *smiles.*

ROWENA. Mother, trust you.

JENNIFER. Just wanted to prove I could hold my own.

CLIVE (*flatly*). Very adequately too, darling.

ROWENA. You're a bit quiet, Yvonne.

YVONNE. Well I . . .

TREVOR. Probably hasn't been allowed to get a word in edgeways all evening.

ROWENA. Don't look at me. I haven't been holding forth about woofers, tweeters, wattage and speakers all evening.

RON (*puts his hand over* YVONNE's). Still waters run deep.

JENNIFER. How sweet.

CLIVE. I'm seriously thinking of investing in a Bang & Olufsen.

ROWENA. Oh no, don't start Trevor off. He'll be green with envy.

JENNIFER (*to* CLIVE). What a shame you can't seriously think of an investment in tiling the bathroom.

YVONNE. How many men does it take to tile a bathroom? (*Pause.*) Three but you have to slice them thinly.

TREVOR. Couldn't you see your way clear to investing in one for me, Clive?

JENNIFER. I don't think tiles are the 'in' thing for stripped pine bathrooms.

ROWENA. I think he meant the hi-fi system. He's been on about getting a better one ever since I can remember — just a little boy's fantasy.

JENNIFER. I wonder what Freud would make of that.

ROWENA. Who cares?

CLIVE. Surely a social worker can't dismiss him out of hand?

ROWENA (*unsure*). Well . . . no . . .

CLIVE. He hit the spot in lots of ways.

YVONNE. Crap! Who's ever wanted a penis? What woman has ever wanted a penis?

JENNIFER *laughs genuinely*.

Have you ever wanted one, Row?

ROWENA. Er, yes, well, I wasn't defending him, very outdated ideas, ha. You were saying you weren't enjoying teaching much these days.

YVONNE. Actually Ron said that.

RON. Well, it's true, isn't it?

TREVOR. Row's pretty fed up with her job, aren't you?

ROWENA. Sort of. (*To* YVONNE:) D'you remember when we were at school, I said if it were the last choice on earth I wouldn't be a social worker and you said you'd rather clean toilets than teach?

YVONNE (*smiles*). Yes, high ideals of youth.

TREVOR. I suppose some goddess or other with her lack of

control over the inequality of the sexes drew you into
the nurturing professions, synonymous with the feminine role.

ROWENA. You can laugh.

JENNIFER. It must be very messy trying to shove the working
classes into inappropriate institutions when they clearly
don't want to go.

ROWENA. I can assure you I'm not like that, Mother.

JENNIFER. I'm sure you're not. I meant the concept as a whole.

CLIVE. You're as adept at analysing social work as you are at
telling jokes.

JENNIFER. Am I? How sad. I thought my jokes were really
rather funny. (*To* YVONNE:) Do you teach secondary age,
dear?

YVONNE. Yes.

RON. She hates it, don't you, love? It's the discipline especially.

YVONNE. I'd like to get out of teaching altogether.

ROWENA. What would you do?

YVONNE. I quite like the idea of proofreading. You know,
sitting in an attic all day correcting manuscripts.

TREVOR. Or womanscripts as the case may be.

RON. All those squiggly hooks and things would drive you round
the bend.

ROWENA. I don't think I'd like it much myself.

JENNIFER. Oh, it sounds quite appealing.

CLIVE. You would think that.

JENNIFER. Would I?

CLIVE. You're halfway there — round the bend I mean.

JENNIFER (*forced smile*). Oh, don't be mean, darling.

CLIVE (*forced smile*). Only joking, darling.

ROWENA. Is it all the preparatory work that's getting you down

YVONNE (*clearly doesn't want to talk about it*). Yes, yes,
everything.

RON. Come on, Yvonne. It's not that. You've always enjoyed teaching. It's the boys, isn't it?

YVONNE. Ron.

RON (*wants to explain his wife's unsociable behaviour*). I don't know if you're acquainted with adolescents today, but controlling them is damn near impossible.

ROWENA. I can imagine. I have nightmares about a couple of lads on my case load, but *en masse* I think I'd freak out.

TREVOR. Oh yeah? You've got a couple of headcases, but put you in front of a class of nubile sixteen-year-old boys and they'd have trouble controlling you.

JENNIFER. Ah ha, my daughter has another side to her.

ROWENA (*lightly*). Trev, please, not in front of the parents.

RON. It's all these girlie mags they bring in, playing on your nerves, aren't they, love?

ROWENA. Nothing's changed, they used to snigger at them in the cloakroom when we were at school.

JENNIFER. Same here, only in our day a nude ankle was enough to raise a snigger.

RON. I wondered what you were going to say then.

JENNIFER. Now, now, don't encourage me.

CLIVE (*to* JENNIFER). Darling, speak for yourself. I am not Victorian, I assure you, it takes more than an ankle . . .

JENNIFER. Thank you, Clive.

YVONNE. It's much more open and explicit now.

TREVOR. Is that necessarily a bad thing?

YVONNE. When a boy holds up a picture in front of the class and says, 'She's got more up top than you, miss', or 'Can you do this, miss?', yes it is.

TREVOR. I can see that it would provide a distraction from Gerard Manley Hopkins.

YVONNE. I teach history.

TREVOR. Or even King Lud and the Luddites.

ROWENA. What do you do?

YVONNE. What can I do? If I had my way I'd burn the lot of it.

TREVOR. Oh hang on, that's really rightwing.

YVONNE. Is it?

ROWENA. I've never thought about it much. I suppose if women want to do it and men want to look at it, where's the harm?

RON. I keep telling her most men look at it, and the more upset she gets the more the lads will play up.

ROWENA. Do they? (*Silence.*) Do you ever look at it, Trevor?

TREVOR. No, but I have seen it, some of the blokes at work leave it lying around.

ROWENA. You never told me.

TREVOR. I didn't tell you we had a digital thermometer or an electronic pencil sharpener either. So what?

ROWENA. And do you have any true-life confessions, Clive?

CLIVE. Is nothing sacred between stepfather and stepdaughter?

JENNIFER (*cheerfully*). Don't be modest, darling, you've got a video cassette library which could put the BFI out of business.

CLIVE. Oh films, I thought you meant filthy magazines.

JENNIFER. *Playboy* and *Mayfair* in the lav.

CLIVE. Oh, and you read the interviews in those, but I would never look at the really hard stuff. God, I couldn't bear the idea of children and animals used like that.

JENNIFER. I suppose it depends what you mean by pornography.

YVONNE. All of it, everything from adverts to . . .

RON. Love, it's totally innocuous.

TREVOR. I've got nothing against it. Just wish I had a low enough IQ to enjoy it.

ROWENA. Maybe it does have a positive side. To enable

inadequate men to act out their fantasies, save them from attacking anyone on the street.

YVONNE. Does social work for the child-batterer consist of showing them pictures of parents torturing their children, with the children appearing to enjoy it — as a preventative measure?

ROWENA (*unsure*). No.

TREVOR. Come on, there's absolutely nothing to connect it with violence.

YVONNE. It is violence, violence against women.

RON. All right, darling. Thank you.

YVONNE. I didn't mean to bore you.

JENNIFER. I'm glad you did. (*The* MEN *laugh.*) I mean, not bore us, not that you did but . . . What do the men on the staff think?

YVONNE. They don't give a damn. Even the local chip shop keeps a pile of magazines for the boys to browse through at lunchtimes.

CLIVE. Business is business.

YVONNE. It's a bloody conspiracy.

RON (*lightly*). Now love, don't act paranoid, especially in front of a social worker.

YVONNE. And who does the complaining about broken lights in corridors and lifts on estates? Is it a coincidence that they're all women or are they all paranoid?

TREVOR. What is it they say — 'Just because you think you're paranoid doesn't mean they're not all out to get you' or something?

ROWENA. It's very difficult for both sexes, boys have a lot of pressure on them to perform, you know.

YVONNE. Aren't we lucky to be living in a liberal society, next ll be poor little Hitler, wasn't he a victim of epilepsy?

ROWENA. You can't be so one-sided, Yvonne.

YVONNE. Crimes committed against women have never been credible, why change now?

RON. Amen. Yes, my love, we don't want to put Lord Longford out of a job, do we?

JENNIFER. Very stimulating thought. Oh, Clive, darling, you've gone very quiet.

CLIVE. I was contemplating getting my cheque book out. You know how that sends me into a frenzy of silence.

RON. Yes, time to make a move.

JENNIFER. Oh dear, I was just starting to enjoy myself. My main problem at the moment is . . .

CLIVE. Not now, darling. Your daughter specialises in problems all day long.

ROWENA. Unfortunately there is very little variation, unemployment or unemployment.

RON. Hey, that's what I meant to say to you, Row. There's a job going at my place. Just photocopying and stuff. If anyone you know can fill it — it's theirs.

ROWENA. Thanks, I'll bear it in mind.

RON. A nice girl though please, no troublemakers, punks or glue-sniffers.

ROWENA (slight edge). Even 'nice' people can't get work these days, Ron.

JENNIFER. It must be so boring for the poor devils.

CLIVE. You should know. The last time you worked, Noah was still painting the ark.

JENNIFER. With money life can be irksome, without it it must tediously boring.

CLIVE. Irksome?

JENNIFER. Well, apart from my horticultural cohorts, of course

CLIVE. Oh God . . . the damn women's flower arranging guild.

JENNIFER. We are far from damned, Clive darling, thank you.

TREVOR. What does it entail?

JENNIFER. Wondrous things, my boy. Not suitable for your delicate earholes.

RON. Does that apply to me as well?

CLIVE. Don't start her off.

JENNIFER. It's quite jolly really. We infiltrate exhibitions with our outrageous arrangements.

RON. A line in suggestive cacti?

JENNIFER. Oh no. Mine was a lovely dried number set in an oasis and for the base I used my diaphragm.

ROWENA. Mother, really.

JENNIFER. I have no use for it. It seemed a shame to think it was totally obsolete. And then Madeline grew mustard and cress in an empty pill packet.

CLIVE (flatly). Yes, very funny.

JENNIFER. Of course, not half as funny as your misogynist jokes.

CLIVE. Misogynist? Me?

JENNIFER. And then someone else grew these delightful little cultures — like ferns — on a sanitary towel.

The men look embarrassed. YVONNE laughs.

ROWENA. What on earth for? Why?

JENNIFER. Boredom. Everyone else is so stuffy. When we reached the change of life you know, menopause — we all decided we were perfectly entitled to act mad. We took a collective decision to be mad, as you might say.

CLIVE (mutters). I can't see how a decision actually came into it.

JENNIFER. On the contrary, it was a very intellectual discussion. We decided to get our revenge on society for writing us off. Mind you, we're running out of ideas.

ROWENA. If you're not careful you'll find yourself planting a daisy in the buttonhole of a man in a white coat.

JENNIFER. Ah, what does the future hold for your batty mother? What will I be doing in a year's time?

CLIVE. Don't tempt me.

JENNIFER. I often wonder, if I had a way of looking into the future, whether I'd bother.

YVONNE. I know I wouldn't dare.

TREVOR. See some terrible event and spend the time in between dreading it.

ROWENA. You're so pessimistic, Trevor, this time next year I reckon I'll have got promotion and you'll have your Bang & Olufsen.

CLIVE (*looks at his watch*). Unless we make a move, you won't be fit for work tomorrow, let alone next year.

CLIVE, JENNIFER, RON *and* TREVOR *go off.*

The sounds of a courtroom. ROWENA *moves to her court position.* YVONNE *watches her, then speaks directly to the audience.*

YVONNE. Rowena has this standing joke with me. Something along the lines of me being acutely aware of oppression from the day one of my brothers threw a copy of *Biggles Flies West* at me in my cot. Tch, that's a gross exaggeration. In fact, I can't remember seeing a book in our house. It was against considerable odds that I got to grammar school, let alone college. Not that it didn't cost a lot of teasing, both at home and down our street, and not that it taught me a lot either . . . a different way of thinking . . . a different set of values. (*Pause.*) But I was twenty-six before I learnt that the words 'I feel' and 'I think' were neither synonymous nor interchangeable . . . and there's no way I read that in any book.

The endless hours I've spent rejecting and rebelling against my mum and her catatonic, cast-iron clichéd philosophy of life, only to find a sort of grim truth in the wretched phrase — 'There's only one way to learn things — the hard way.'

Actually it was when I went away to college that I met

Ron at a party. He was working for his dad at the time in a mini-cab firm and there was something I really liked about him. Looking back, I think it was his MG sports car.

Exit YVONNE.

Scene Two

A crown court. ROWENA, JUDGE (*a woman*), POLICEMAN.

CLERK (*voice over*). All stand.

JUDGE. Rowena Stone, you are charged with the murder of Charles Williams. How do you plead — (*Silence.*) guilty or not guilty?

ROWENA. Neither.

JUDGE. Mrs Stone, as I'm sure you are well aware, this court does not have a procedure for neither. Are you guilty or not guilty?

Silence.

ROWENA. Not guilty.

JUDGE. Officer, would you be good enough to describe the events to the court in a little more detail?

POLICEMAN (*reading from a notebook*). On the seventeenth of this month I was proceeding in a westerly direction along Seven Sisters Road, when I noticed a commotion outside Finsbury Park Tube and the Inspector, I mean the ticket inspector . . .

JUDGE. Constable, just the events if you please, not a blow by blow account of your diary, otherwise you won't have anything new to say when you're cross-examined, will you now?

POLICEMAN. Madam.(*He attempts to précis his notes by reading faster.*) Anyway, when I got to the platform, I noticed a man, who was later identified as Mr Charles Williams, deceased, under the 10.15 p.m. from Walthamstow to Brixton tube train. An eyewitness who is prepared to testify to the fact said,

'She pushed him', whereupon I cautioned and questioned the accused who remained silent.

JUDGE. Did anything strike you as odd, constable?

POLICEMAN. Madam? (*He tries to think of something which might be construed as odd.*) Well, now you mention it, the tube driver kept jumping around shouting, 'Not another one, how many more bloody suicides am I going to get?' Obviously he wasn't fully aware of the situation and I think he was in a state of shock.

JUDGE. We are not assembled here to uncover the vagaries of your thought processes, constable.

POLICEMAN. We are trained in shock treatment, madam.

JUDGE. I meant anything peculiar in the manner of the accused?

POLICEMAN. Oh no, madam, she was as cool as a cucumber.

JUDGE (*to* ROWENA). Is this true?

ROWENA. No, I was in a state of shock.

JUDGE (*impatient*). Is the description accurate?

ROWENA. For the most part.

JUDGE. Specifically.

ROWENA. I believe it is impossible to proceed in a westerly direction along Seven Sisters Road, but the rest is true.

JUDGE. Mrs Stone, are you now changing your plea to guilty?

ROWENA. No.

JUDGE. I understand you have no defence lawyer.

ROWENA. Correct.

JUDGE. Mrs Stone, I propose to adjourn. To allow you time to reconsider your decision not to be represented and to give you time for legal aid to be arranged. Psychiatric reports will undoubtedly be called for.

ROWENA. Do you think I'm mad?

JUDGE. Fortunately, I do not have unlimited power. I am not in a position to label the sane insane or vice versa. I do feel obliged to say, however, how distressed I am to see you in front of me now, as I have always found your attitude to the law, in your professional capacity as a social worker, most sensitive and coherent.

ROWENA. Pity the same may not be said for the law's attitude to me. _— as a woman (?)_

JUDGE. Adjourned. _↳ for all women_

CLERK (*voice over*). All stand.

Scene Three

Playground sounds.

A classroom. YVONNE, *after school, sits there alone marking books. Voices off are those of a male teacher. Enter* IRENE WADE.

IRENE (*timid*). Mrs Hughes?

YVONNE (*looks up abruptly*). Mrs Wade.

TEACHER (*off*). Rogers, haven't you got a home to go to? Then I suggest you go. Now. Pronto.

IRENE. I hope you don't mind me coming to see you like this.

YVONNE. Is your husband with you?

IRENE. No, I came on my own. He doesn't know.

YVONNE (*relieved*). Oh, I see. (*Then:*) I really don't see how I can help you.

TEACHER (*off*). Gregory, get out of there and stay out.

IRENE. I've been very down lately, especially after I went to see Ian on Saturday.

YVONNE. Mrs Wade, you are talking to the wrong person. I was responsible for your son's conviction. If it hadn't been for me the whole matter would have been dropped.

IRENE. It's just . . . I don't know.

YVONNE (*abruptly*). You think he's been punished too severely?

IRENE. Well, I don't know.

YVONNE. Mrs Wade . . .

IRENE. Irene, please . . .

TEACHER (*off*). What are you lads doing skulking about the cloakroom area? I don't care, you shouldn't be here. Vanish.

YVONNE. Mrs . . . Irene . . . perhaps you should talk with the headmaster, you'd get a more sympathetic response.

IRENE. I know, he says the same as the lawyer. She'd only been raped but was unharmed.

YVONNE. I for one am not about to shout about how lucky she is, not today, or ever. If it hadn't been for me, no one would have bothered even to talk to her.

IRENE. Where is she?

YVONNE. She had to get a transfer. As though she hadn't been through enough and . . .

TEACHER (*off*). No, you can't go back and get it. It will have to wait until the morning.

YVONNE. And the worst of it is your son has been made a cult hero.

IRENE. If it had been my daughter I'd have wanted him hung from the nearest tree, but I don't . . .

TEACHER (*off*). Jamison, you disgusting brute, get out of here and report to the headmaster first thing in the morning. I can't find anything to laugh at. And that includes the rest of you as well.

YVONNE. Where were we?

IRENE. I wouldn't have your job for the world.

YVONNE. I'm sorry, some days I feel sort of schizophrenic, a cross between Joyce Grenfell and Attila the Hun.

IRENE. I understand. I won't take up any more of your time, Mrs Hughes.

YVONNE. No wait, Irene. I have no sympathy for your son. None. Not that I don't have any for you, but I do understand

if you feel it amounts to one and the same thing. (*Pause*.)
And my name's Yvonne.

TEACHER (*off*). This is the last time, clear off home!

IRENE. I . . . I just don't know what to say, or do, or anything.
I feel I could have stood by him over anything else . . . I'd
rather he'd done anything else.

YVONNE (*softer*). You feel he needs your support?

IRENE. He had all my support before. I don't know what I did
or didn't do wrong. I might make all the same mistakes again.
All those psychiatrists spent more time with me than they did
with him. Where did I go wrong?

YVONNE. You mustn't blame yourself.

TEACHER (*off*). I will not tell you again, Lawrence.

IRENE. Why not? Why on earth not? Everyone else is.

YVONNE. Nobody in their right mind — which doesn't
necessarily include the medical profession — is blaming you.
I'm certainly not. *always the woman's fault*
— in any circumstance

IRENE. Yes they are. They all are. A normal healthy boy rapes
a girl. Was I too prudish? Too open? Too domineering? Too
weak? Too much of a nag? Did I discourage him too violently
from playing with his genitals as a baby? Did I sit him too
viciously on the potty? Did I smother him? Did I neglect him?

YVONNE. For what it's worth, I know it's not your fault.

IRENE. When I used to read of those things in the paper, I used to
say castration was too good for them.

Long pause.

Can you tell me what I do with the love for my son?

YVONNE (*pause*). I'm sorry, I don't know.

IRENE. Perhaps you know what to do with this. (*She gives her
a carrier bag stuffed with magazines.*)

YVONNE (*pulls one out and looks at its cover*). But these go
back to seventy-eight.

IRENE. I always made it a rule that children should have privacy, but now he's away I thought, well, it would be wrong not to clean his room out — mind, they were well hidden. I suppose that was wrong as well.

YVONNE. You and your husband had no idea?

IRENE. I supposed all young boys looked at it. As for my husband, ha, it never bothered him.

YVONNE. You think your husband encouraged him?

IRENE. Didn't have to. He has a drawerful of his own. Only difference is, he doesn't have to hide it.

A MALE TEACHER enters, crosses to the window and bangs his fist on it.

TEACHER. Rogers, I told you to go home hours ago. Now get. (*To* YVONNE *and* IRENE:) Sorry.

Scene Four

HILARY's *flat. She is ironing.*
The day after the meal, ROWENA *has some evening visits, one of whom is* HILARY PETERS. ROWENA *is trying to be bright and breezy without appearing to be trying too hard.*

ROWENA. Hello, I'm from the Social Services, can I come in?

HILARY. If yer must.

ROWENA (*following* HILARY). My name's Rowena, can I call you Hilary?

HILARY. If that's what turns yer on. I s'pose you'll be wanting a cup of coffee.

ROWENA. No thanks, I've just had one.

HILARY. Not stopping long, then?

ROWENA. Are you busy?

HILARY. As a matter of fact I'm up to me eyes with the *Sun* bingo. I know the Social money ain't s'pose to go on luxu like the daily papers but then I'm a deviant, but of course you know that anyway.

ROWENA *tries to laugh casually.*

HILARY. Forgot me manners. Sit down. Won't you please?

ROWENA (*sits down*). Thanks. (*She tries to take in the surroundings subtly.*)

HILARY. Well, what d'yer want?

ROWENA. Nothing. Nothing special. I just called round to see if everything was all right.

HILARY. I might be thick but I know there's no such thing as door to door social work, not with this government anyway.

ROWENA. Okay, your previous social worker phoned me.

HILARY. Oh Gawd, the late Mrs Crawley.

ROWENA. She's not dead.

HILARY. More's the pity. No, I always used to call her the late Mrs Crawley on account of she was always late. Trouble with you lot, you read too deeply into things what aren't there.

ROWENA. Oh I see, and she asked me to pop in and see how you were getting along.

HILARY. And here I was thinking, one good thing about getting me transfer was getting you nosey bleeders off me back. (*Pause.*) No offence like.

ROWENA. It's just that I thought I'd introduce myself so that if you ever did need anything you'd know where to come.

HILARY. Ta.

ROWENA. You've got a little boy, is that right?

HILARY. What of it? You can't take him away you know, I look after him proper, he don't go without nothing.

ROWENA. I can assure you I have no intention of doing any such thing. What's his name?

HILARY. Heathcliffe.

ROWENA (*thinks this is a breakthrough*). Emily Brontë?

HILARY. Na, Kate Bush.

ROWENA. Who?

HILARY. The record, you know (*She sings.*) 'Heathcliffe it's me, it's Cathy —'

ROWENA. Oh. (*Then:*) My mum was reading *Ivanhoe* when she was pregnant with me. That's where I got my name.

HILARY. I don't blame you for changing it. Rowena's strange enough but Ivanhoe — God what a mouthful.

ROWENA. No, Rowena's a character in it.

HILARY (*flatly*). Oh, really.

ROWENA (*casually*). Do you still maintain contact with the father?

HILARY. S'no point.

ROWENA. Maintenance.

HILARY. You're joking. They'd only take it off me. The DHSS. Then after a couple of months he'd stop paying and I'd have to take him to court. No way.

ROWENA. Does he still see Heathcliffe?

HILARY. No.

ROWENA. Where is he?

HILARY. Dunno.

ROWENA. Heathcliffe?

HILARY (*sarcastic*). Oh dear me, now where did I leave him? Out playing on the window ledge? Or was it the M11? (*Then:* He's down his Nan's.

ROWENA. That's nice, does she live close by?

HILARY. As it happens.

ROWENA. Is there anything you're concerned about that I might be of any help with?

HILARY. Money.

ROWENA. Well, as you know we have no means of offering long-term financial support.

HILARY. You have no means of offering nothing. What d'you do, eh? All the people you see, the only thing what's wrong with their lives is money and all your fancy ideas and posh words can't cover up nothing. At the end of the bleedin' day the only advice you can give us is to march in and say (*She assumes a German accent.*) 'You vill learn to budget.'

Long pause.

Right, look sorry. I didn't mean to go on at yer — you ain't halfway as near as bad as the last one. Thatcher had nothing on her, I reckon her facepacks was made of chainmail.

ROWENA. We've had some complaints from the neighbours.

HILARY. I see, now you want to prove you can't be manipulated. Yeah, big word for me ain't it?

ROWENA. About men, drunk on the landing at all hours.

HILARY. Don't exaggerate.

ROWENA. It's not true then?

HILARY. I've got men friends, yeah. But then if I had female friends you'd reckon I was the other way and have my boy in care quick as a flash.

ROWENA. Hilary, I do not have the power to whip children into care unless there is proof that they're being maltreated.

HILARY. And then you whip 'em, in care, eh?

ROWENA. You know what I mean.

HILARY. I ain't never so much as laid one finger on him and I keep him looking real smart. Yeah, I know I look like something the Oxfam shop rejected but I always keep him smart. He has everything new . . . Nothing secondhand. Do you know how much a pair of kid's shoes cost?

ROWENA. And your boyfriends help you out? (*Pause.*) There must be better (*She corrects herself.*) easier ways of clothing Heathcliffe.

HILARY. Oh right. Hit me with 'em.

ROWENA. I know employment's hard to find.

HILARY. And I ain't exactly got golden bonuses either — no qualifications — on me own — a kid.

ROWENA. What did you do before he was born?

HILARY. I ain't never had a job then neither.

ROWENA. How old are you?

HILARY. Look at it on the bright side — I've only got another thirty-six years before I retire.

ROWENA. You've never worked?

HILARY. Not unless you count my CSE needlework project. You're s'posed to be a social worker. Where you bin?

ROWENA. Sorry.

HILARY. What for? Ain't your fault.

ROWENA. Do you enjoy, er, doing it?

HILARY. Do me a favour.

ROWENA. Why? Then, I mean, why do you do, er, it?

HILARY. They reckon we're all sitting on a gold mine, don't they?

ROWENA. That lucrative?

HILARY. Even I ain't heard of that one.

ROWENA. That much money in it?

HILARY. No, for me there ain't, no.

ROWENA. If you had a job would that be OK?

HILARY. What you going to do, give me yours?

ROWENA. I'm just thinking . . .

HILARY. Yeah, but who'd look after Heathcliffe? Me mum can't, not all day.

ROWENA. If we got him a place in a day nursery.

HILARY (weary). He's been on the waiting list since he was born.

ROWENA. If we could . . .

HILARY. And if a pig orbited the moon.

ROWENA. Is that what you want?

HILARY. What . . . a bacon satellite? Do you think I want to live like this? Course I want a job.

ROWENA. I can't promise but I'll do my best.

HILARY (*not nastily*). You sound like Mrs Crawley. She was a girl guide captain in her spare time. D'you really not want a coffee? S'no trouble.

ROWENA. Thanks. (*She looks at her watch.*) But I've got two other visits this evening.

HILARY. Blimey. You work unsociable hours.

ROWENA (*smiles*). Me?

HILARY. And I don't even get no sick pay neither. Honest, I want a job. I really do.

ROWENA. To want a job is hardly to be in the minority, to have one is.

HILARY. Do what?

ROWENA. Do you mind what work, er, which work. I mean the work you do — within reason?

HILARY. I'll take anything what'll give me enough money to live on — with proper wages packet and National Insurance.

ROWENA. I'll be in touch.

Scene Five

10 p.m. ROWENA is walking home after her last visit. A MAN walks behind her. (This is quite 'innocent'. There is no threat of attack.) ROWENA and the MAN freeze, then walk again.

ROWENA (*voice over*). Wish I wasn't wearing a skirt. I look quite respectable though. What am I doing out this late at night? Working. The only women who work at night are

stereotypes

prostitutes. Otherwise their husbands would meet them.
Don't walk fast, it will look funny. Don't slow up — inviting.
Don't look too nervous. Why the hell doesn't he cross over?

They pass each other. They look back.

ROWENA's *living-room.*

TREVOR (*grabs her*). Boo! Got yer.

ROWENA (*jumps out of shock*). Get away from me. What the
hell are you doing?

TREVOR. What's the matter? Jesus Christ.

ROWENA. Don't do that.

TREVOR. Do what?

ROWENA. Jump on me, you stupid sod.

TREVOR. Thanks a bunch, I was only taking the trouble to
welcome my wife home from a hard day at the office.

ROWENA. Well don't. *thinks he deserves praise*

TREVOR. Bloody hell. At least I don't loll in front of the telly
demanding my dinner.

ROWENA. Just go around scaring the bloody life out of me.

TREVOR. No need to bite my head off just because you're late.

ROWENA (*sits in a chair*). Everything took longer than I
expected.

TREVOR. Pity you don't get overtime, you'd be worth a fortune.

ROWENA. All right. I've earned an afternoon off in lieu. No,
spare me the toilet jokes.

TREVOR. I was going to say, you're looking rather flushed.

ROWENA (*groans*). Dreadful. How was your day?

TREVOR. Boring. Except Harriet's house burnt down, that's
why she was off.

ROWENA. Oh no, poor woman.

TREVOR. Yes, even I felt a bit sorry for her.

ROWENA. Was anyone hurt?

TREVOR. No, only the dog – burnt alive, but that appeared to be an ill wind anyway. Because, next door apparently had taken legal action against it because it had had a fight with their terrier and killed it. I ask you. How could you take a dog to court? What would it say when it got there? Alec reckons it would take a bow wow. Anyway that's hypothetical as it kicked the bucket Joan of Arc style.

ROWENA. Where is she now?

TREVOR. In the little doggie paradise. No, I s'pose after what it did the doggie hell.

ROWENA. No, fool, Harriet.

TREVOR. With relatives. (*Joking.*) You're home now, you're s'posed to switch the caring off.

ROWENA. You haven't got a job going have you?

TREVOR. You can't be that fed up.

ROWENA. Not for me, nana, that young woman I told you about who we thought was on the game, well she wants to get off.

TREVOR. Hey Row, you can't jump in all shining morality. If that's what she's chosen to do. — Choice to do + watch porn as well

ROWENA. <u>Choice</u>. That seems rather an inappropriate word.

TREVOR. Perhaps it's your particular values that are inappropriate.

ROWENA. Since when has wanting a job become a middle-class value?

TREVOR. When you choose to overlook the fact that by other definitions, she's a working girl.

ROWENA. She said she wanted a proper job. She doesn't like what she does.

TREVOR. Of course she said that to you. What do you think she was going to say — a screw a day keeps the tax man away.

ROWENA. I think she meant it.

TREVOR. Pull the other one. (*Then:*) You know they've been

wanting to tax it for years — just haven't found a way — short of inventing accountants to accumulate sperm returns.

ROWENA. Trevor.

TREVOR. Sperm is a perfectly respectable term.

ROWENA. Well that's it, then. Ron.

TREVOR. Interesting word association.

ROWENA. I'll give him a ring a bit later on.

TREVOR. I should have thought that dinner party was enough social intercourse to last a lifetime.

ROWENA. Stupid combination, Mum, them and Clive.

TREVOR. Your mother's one thing, but Yvonne, she's something else.

ROWENA. Poor Yvonne, we used to have such a laugh at school. I can't believe the change in her.

TREVOR. You say that every time we see them. If she laughed now the shock would kill her.

ROWENA. Mind you, it can't be easy being married to a man who pretends to be a reincarnation of Jack the Lad.

TREVOR. What do you mean by that?

ROWENA. Those banal jokes.

TREVOR. Honestly, sometimes you can be so snotty. Okay, so they weren't that funny, but couldn't you see he felt out of his depth, and with that bourgeois bitch who passes herself off as my mother-in-law it's hardly surprising.

ROWENA (hurt). Trev.

TREVOR (defensive). Well, she can't stand me.

ROWENA. That's purely projectionist. You can't stand her.

TREVOR. I know what projectionist means. She's cracked, round the bend, nutty, potty, and if she'd been one of your clients you'd have had her in the funny farm by now. But no, because of her breeding, nobody would dare slap a loony label on her. She's quite at liberty to pass as eccentric.

ROWENA. She's still my mum.

TREVOR. Yeah, well, sorry, it's just that, well, it was a perfectly enjoyable meal until Yvonne suddenly found her tongue, and then the atmosphere, well, we might as well have been in a fall-out shelter.

ROWENA. Maybe she had a point, she's unhappy.

TREVOR. There are ways and ways of making a point and a tirade from a friend's wife at a dinner party with one's in-laws present does not go down a bomb.

ROWENA. I thought you didn't care about your in-laws. Make up your mind. Besides which she's my friend, and your friend is her husband.

TREVOR. Don't let's bicker. I should count myself lucky I'm not your friend's husband. There for the grace of God etcetera.

ROWENA. She's very bright, you know.

TREVOR. I didn't say she wasn't. She made one or two intelligent remarks underneath the neurosis, but God, the way they were put across was so fanatical. Proofreader? How could she sit down and objectively proofread a Leslie Thomas novel? No wonder their sex life is a disaster.

ROWENA. Remember that stuff we were talking about?

TREVOR. What stuff?

ROWENA. Those magazines, could you bring some home?

TREVOR. What for?

ROWENA. Never looked at any before. Never know, it might improve my night life.

TREVOR. That and a Terylene duvet.

ROWENA. I thought my heavy breathing turned you on.

TREVOR. I've managed to distinguish the sighs of ecstasy from the intermittent asthma attacks. Spoilt it a bit.

ROWENA. What do you mean, their sex life is disastrous? How do you know?

TREVOR. What a scatty mind. That was about twelve sentences ago.

ROWENA. Well?

TREVOR. Ron told me one lunchtime in the pub.

ROWENA. Oh, do you often discuss your sex lives then? And what do you say about me, Don Juan? 'Trouble is, Ron old chap, nudge, nudge, snigger, snigger, I can't tell if she's actually orgasmed or if it's her allergy to the feather duvet.'

TREVOR. Of course not. It just spilled out one day. No wonder he's fed up.

ROWENA. Couldn't possibly be his fault though. Oh no.

TREVOR. For God's sake, Row, anyway I can't bring that stuff home.

ROWENA. Why?

TREVOR. Well, they'll think, I don't know what they'd think, but it would look funny.

ROWENA. Okay then.

TREVOR. It's just stupid. Tell you what, I'll buy you a copy of *Playgirl* instead.

ROWENA. Thanks, oh master.

TREVOR. Don't mention it, my darling.

ROWENA. Are you using the car tomorrow?

TREVOR (*teasing*). Might be.

ROWENA. Oh go on, let me. Can I, please? Clever Trevor.

TREVOR. Might let yer.

ROWENA. Go on. (*She kisses him.*)

TREVOR. For you, anything.

Scene Six

RON *and* YVONNE *at home.* YVONNE *is reading.*

RON. Right little ray of sunshine.

VONNE. So you have repeatedly told me.

ON. Life and soul of the party.

VONNE. Let's drop it, shall we?

ON. When it suits you, yeah, we drop it, but then you start opening your trap in public.

VONNE. I didn't bring it up, Ron, you did.

ON. If only by way of your bloody poface.

VONNE. I don't see what good it will do dragging it up again.

She continues to read.

ON. Oh don't you? No, but you don't see any point to communicating with your husband at all. Well that's the last we'll see of them in a long time. You know that silly cow Rowena can't stand you.

VONNE. Can't she?

ON. Why do you think you've not heard from her?

VONNE. Well, er, I'd not thought about it.

ON. Because, take it from me, she only sees you out of courtesy.

VONNE. She's not the sort.

ON. When was the last time she phoned? Eh?

VONNE. We've been friends for ages.

ON. You're an embarrassment, God, you're so involved with yourself, you can't see how stupid she thinks you are.

VONNE. She's the only friend I've got.

ON. Is that surprising? I mean, ask yourself. You want to listen to yourself, constant moan, moan, moan. Small wonder you have no friends. (*Knocks the book from her hands.*) You don't even try, do you? You can't even be bothered to talk to me. Do I really repulse you that much?

VONNE (*picks up the book again*). I'm not very happy.

ON. You're not happy? Christ, what d'you think I am? Over the moon, eh? Over the bloody moon. My God, my wife won't even speak to me, barely lets me come near her. Jesus Christ, Yvonne.

YVONNE. Please, Ron, not now.

RON (*mimicking her*). Not now, not now, darling. I've got a headache. A bad knee, athlete's foot, ringworm, tapeworm, aversion to sperm.

YVONNE. I can't take any more.

RON. You can't take any more? That's rich, you spoilt bitch. I wish they'd said something on the marriage contract. After five years your wife will be fucking frigid.

YVONNE. Ron, the neighbours.

RON. The neighbours, the poxy bloody neighbours. We have to listen to their squeaking bedsprings half the night. I'm sure they won't mind listening to the explanation of why they can't hear ours. I'm sure it'll be a relief to one and all. (*To the wall*:) Won't it?

YVONNE. Shut up.

RON. Typical. Anything you don't want to hear, like the truth, gets shut off. Shut out and shut up. Yvonne, you are married to me!

YVONNE. I'd noticed.

RON. Well, I can't say I had, not lately anyway.

YVONNE. What do you expect, eh? (*She screams.*) Shout at me all day, then expect me to make mad passionate love to you at bedtime?

RON. Don't give me that. I've tried every tack. Short of hanging myself, nothing but nothing I could do would please you.

The phone rings. Pause. Neither of them is about to answer it then RON *picks it up.*

RON (*sharply*). Hello. (*Then nicely*:) Oh hello, Rowena. (*To* YVONNE:) It's for you. (*He shoves the receiver towards her.*

YVONNE (*taking the receiver*). Hello Row. (*Pause.*) Oh, fine, fine. Yes, right. Here you are. (*She hands the phone back to* RON.) She wants to speak to you.

RON (*to phone*). Sorry, I automatically assumed . . . (*Pause.*) Yes, yes. It's still vacant. How old is she? Fine, yes, that'll be okay, as long as she's not a terrorist, ha ha. (*Pause.*) Oh thanks very much. Great. Give us a ring then. Bye.

YVONNE. What was that about?

RON. She wanted to speak to me not you.

YVONNE. About the job?

RON. Amongst other things. She didn't have much to say to you.

YVONNE. Not a lot.

RON. She obviously prefers to talk to me.

YVONNE. Only to ask you a favour. Still, perhaps I should go round and apologise.

RON. She reckons she'll invite us over to dinner, so I wouldn't bother. (*He sits next to* YVONNE *who tries not to tense.*) Don't worry, you can patch it up. Can we though?

YVONNE. Ron.

RON (*coaxing*). Come on, what's happened? Am I really that bad, eh? What's the matter? What's happened to us?

YVONNE. You think it's all my fault.

RON. I said 'we' didn't I? (*He strokes her hair.*) Let's forget it, mmm.

YVONNE. Umm.

RON. Coming to bed?

YVONNE. In a minute.

RON. Don't be long. (*He gets up and kisses the top of her head.*) You know I love you.

He goes out.

YVONNE (*hands over face, quietly*). I hate you.

Scene Seven.

HILARY. *Monologue.*

HILARY. When I was young, what am I saying? I mean when I was about thirteen I used to look at the boys in our class looking at us, and think how odd that they wanted to stick their cocks in us. Straight up, I did. Seemed such a peculiar thing. Anyhow, then I learnt it was natural and didn't think no more about it. Our school joined the grammar school that year and we was then comprehensive so all that meant was the grammar school lot done O levels and we, if we was really lucky, done CSEs. Also it meant like in the eyes of the boys that them lot were prudes and we was slags. I never figured out which ones were best to be in but I reckoned, looking back, we had the most laughs.

I told the social worker I ain't never had no qualifications but the truth of the matter is that's rubbish. I ain't entirely up shit creek 'cos I also got a CSE Grade 1 in Needlework — comes in handy sew to speak, ha ha. I weren't much interested in anything else. Nothing else on the timetable that is, but I tell you I could've got an A level, a Ph.D. even, in contraceptives. It weren't no fault of me own I fell for me kid.

Me and me mate Shirl had it sussed, we read everything we could lay our hands on. Having bin stuck with the label 'slag' it seemed stupid not to live up to it. But, as Shirl remarked at the time, if they only knew we aren't so much nympho-maniacs but contraceptomaniacs. I lost me virginity when I was nearly fifteen. I bunked off school. His parents were at work, not that it was a case of one thing led to another. No way. It was planned to the last letter — French letter. But them things are unreliable — the machine in the King's Head pub got 'British Made' on it — some cleverdick had written underneath, 'So was the *Titanic*'. So I made him get some of that Delfen foam stuff as well. I still think how brave he was going into the chemist to ask for it — but he must have thought it was worth it. What does I do though? Puts the applicator in the top of the bottle shaking on account of me nerves and the whole thing spurts all over the wall. Anyhow, we done it after we'd wiped it off. I don't know what I was expecting. (*She shrugs. Pause.*) He kept his socks on.

It was all getting a bit traumatised 'cos I don't know if you've ever had it off up the back of Ilford Pallie, but with foam, applicator and packet of three to contend with you sort of lose track of why you wanted to do it in the first place, know what I mean?

Anyhow, when me and Shirl was sixteen we decided enough was enough, and took ourselves off to the Family Planning. That was a real laugh only we was scared stiff at the time. We shuffled into the waiting room and grabbed a magazine and started to read it casual like. It was Shirl who had the nerve to look out, well, I don't know if it was nerve or whether there weren't much in the *Horse and Hound* what interested her. Anyhow we needn't have worried 'cos all you could see was pairs of hands clutching magazines, not a face in sight.

Then, oh my God, then we had this talk about all the different contraceptives. Me and Shirl reckoned we'd like to do that job, after all, that's what we spent all day talking about. Mind you, we started giggling like mad 'cos on this like card table with a green felt top was everything in the way of contraceptive wear you could imagine, looking really decrepit, 'cos they was only for show. The funniest thing was this pink plaster model of your insides like, you know, that picture in the Tampax instructions. Only having never seen a cross-section of me insides it was difficult to make out what was what — the fact that it was chipped to buggery didn't help matters none.

Anyway, they did our blood pressure but the weighing machine was broke, so they had to guess that, and then all these questions. I don't think they believed I was sixteen. Giggling in their faces couldn't have helped matters much. And then I had to have an internal. Can't tell you how much I'd been dreading it. There was some delay while I tried to figure out if I'd had sex in the last three days. 'Because of the sperm count my dear.' Then I said what did it matter 'cos we used a Johnnie anyway. They looked gobsmacked. I tell yer gobsmacked, like, 'Oh she might have an IQ after all.'

What they thought of me, I'm amazed they never sterilised me on the spot. I told 'em, I did, straight. I said, 'If I'd been doing it all this time with nothing I wouldn't be here. I'd be up the maternity ward, my dear.' I tell you I was so nervous when they told me to slip me lower garments off I took me socks off an' all. Then this plastic bag on a hand looms towards me treading on me clothes in the process, I might add. Shirl, lucky beggar, got out of it by telling them she was on, she wasn't but she's always one step ahead that girl.

Still it was easier, being on the Pill, like. Though didn't make much difference, more messy in another sort of way, if you know what I mean. I remember the name of it: Minilyn. I thought if I ever get a little house with roses round the door I'd call it Minilyn. Still at sixteen I was old enough to know m life had been mapped out. Not that I wasn't grateful to get th flat, I bloody was and it's really nice inside now.

So how did I get up the club? Well, Shirl cocked things up of her own accord, 'cos, like I told you, she never took no notice of what anyone else said. She figured out if you started to tak one packet straight after another you didn't have to worry about the week of the month when he didn't want it. So of course they found out and thought it was 'cos she was thick and took her off of it. So then she had one of those loop things, God, who would credit a little bit of wire with causing so much pain. There was times when she fainted, but one thin about Shirl, she weren't no coward. And as it turns out it wrecked her insides. She had it taken out last year and they reckoned she was probably infertile, tried to blame it on her getting VD or something — it weren't true. It had fucked her insides more than any Hampton Wick had done.

But they took me off it eventually 'cos of me blood pressure and I had to make an appointment for a cap fitting. Shirl made some stupid joke about inside leg measurements but I weren't having one of those coil things. Anyhow, I missed the appointment on account of me Nan's funeral. I remember thinking in the dust to dust bit, yeah and me from foam and rubber back to . . . yeah well — the bloke I was with didn't like going back to Johnnies much neither, that funny rubber smell really lingers on yer fingers. I discovered this stuff called 'C' Film. You have to insert it if you're a woman and he has to fit it on his whatsername like a handkerchief on a head but then I finds out that it's not effective until after an hour. S'ats okay fer a woman but have you ever known a bloke keep it up for an hour?

So what happens — round the back of the multi-storey car park one day and we'd only got one Durex — I taken to persuading him to wear two but I thought oh well, it's a chance in a million. And if I'm ever going to write me life story that's what I think I'll call it, *A Chance in a Million* but I wasn't done for. No. I know about douching. I read somewhere that there was something in Coca Cola what kills sperm. I don't know if it's true now. I suspect they took it out when they took whatever it was out that acts with Codeine. Any rate, we runs all the way to the off-licence. And this over-helpful shop assistant tries to persuade us that a can's cheaper than a bottle but we insisted on a bottle, then we had to buy a bottle opener, didn't we? He must have thought we were nuts — come to think of it, he was right.

Anyhow I douched meself with it — it seemed to have delayed reaction, it wasn't till I got home did I suddenly feel uncomfortable when I sort of erupted like in me best beige trousers. When I missed me first period I persuaded meself it was just worry but I sat up every night and prayed to God, said I'd do anything — even join the Salvation Army — threw meself down the stairs for good measure, but I don't reckon God took much to the idea of me with a tambourine. Me mum guessed, carted me off to the doctor's, saying, 'I didn't expect anything else of yer,' but the way she created it was kinda obvious she did. The doctor was a very nice, kind, moral man who thought abortion a sin. Bumbling sod. Still, I'm glad now 'cos I love my kid. That night me mum and dad had a set-to. He was carrying on at her: 'It's all your fault, you silly cow, you should have told her about precautions — you should have known that was the last thing she'd think about.' I laughed meself all through morning sickness on that one.

Scene Eight

ROWENA *is in her garden.*
    YVONNE *enters.*

YVONNE. Row.

ROWENA. Christ, Yvonne, hello.

YVONNE. Sorry am I disturbing you?

ROWENA. No, no, come through. Trevor never does anything in this garden except mow the lawn.

YVONNE. It's just that I saw the car outside — and then there was no answer at the door.

ROWENA. Oh hell, you can't hear anything over this. Shall we go indoors?

YVONNE. No, no, you carry on.

ROWENA. Do you want a cup of coffee?

YVONNE. No . . .

ROWENA. Or a drink . . . ?

YVONNE. No thanks . . .

ROWENA. Or something?

YVONNE. It's okay.

    Pause.

ROWENA. Nothing wrong?

YVONNE. No, no, I'm okay, fine. Fine.

ROWENA. Good. Good.

YVONNE. I only came round for a chat.

ROWENA. That's nice.

YVONNE. Well, no, to apologise really.

ROWENA. Don't be silly.

YVONNE. Last time we met I wasn't exactly on top of the world, if you remember.

ROWENA. Don't worry. We can't all be on top form all the time.

YVONNE. Only I seem to be perpetually wingeing.

ROWENA. You're no happier then?

YVONNE. You could say that.

ROWENA. How do you mean?

YVONNE (*lightly*). Oh, you know, waking up in the morning wishing you hadn't.

ROWENA. I'm sure it's not that bad.

YVONNE. I just wish moaning was a competitive sport. I'd be a world champ.

ROWENA. A holiday maybe?

YVONNE. I'm not a client you know.

ROWENA. I'm sorry, I didn't mean it to sound like that.

YVONNE. No. (*She smiles.*) I know.

ROWENA. Did Ron tell you he's fixed one of my clients up with a job?

YVONNE (*flatly*). Wonderful.

ROWENA. She's really thrilled about it.

YVONNE. How nice of him.

ROWENA. Considering she's totally unskilled, it was.

YVONNE (*flatly*). Is she attractive?

ROWENA (*shrugs*). Yes . . . yes I suppose so.

YVONNE. That's the only qualification she needs then.

ROWENA. Oh, come on. You and I didn't get our jobs because of what we looked like.

YVONNE. We have the dubious benefit of a white man's middle-class education coupled with the fact that my husband isn't our boss.

ROWENA. Jesus, you are bitter.

YVONNE. Yes.

ROWENA. What's the matter?

YVONNE. Nothing.

ROWENA. I think the sooner you get out of that school the better.

YVONNE. And I always thought the first principle of social wor was to get the clients to suss out the main problem for themselves.

ROWENA. I won't say another word.

Long pause.

YVONNE. I hate Ron.

ROWENA. Oh.

YVONNE. I hate everything about him.

ROWENA. Look, you have had a rough time lately, admittedly . . .

YVONNE. Especially sex.

ROWENA. But you can't take it all out on him. (*She pauses, awkward.*) Umm, yes well, we all go through times . . .

YVONNE. I don't hate the mechanics so much . . . I just hate Ron.

ROWENA. It's a phase.

YVONNE. Really.

ROWENA. Look, what do you want me to say? I thought it was school that was bothering you.

YVONNE. They're all mixed up together.

ROWENA. Oh Yvonne, I can't see how.

YVONNE. Men, it's all to do with the way men are taught to view women.

ROWENA. Now you've lost me.

YVONNE (*indicating her carrier bag*). Every week I seem to be confiscating this stuff at school, and as if that's not enough in itself, every week I get into trouble with the headmaster because the kids complain that it costs a lot of money.

ROWENA. Actually I wanted Trev to bring those magazines at the office home with him, but he wasn't too keen.

YVONNE. I'm not surprised.

ROWENA. Can I have a look at it?

YVONNE. Only if you think you must.

ROWENA *looks at the magazines in such a way that the audience is not exposed to their contents.*

Female monologues. (Voices over on tape)

. I suppose it would be stupid to say I did it because I wanted to be good at something and yes, okay, it gave me money and status — status, ha bloody ha. I wasn't dragged off to do it by the hair or anything but it was a different story when I wanted out. You don't get promoted in this lark. Your value is your body, when it starts to go, you get into the rough stuff and can be threatened within inches of your life — to do the nasties with animals and that. I tell you, the animals get treated like they was the royal corgies, you get treated like dirt.

. When I was a little girl, I was always being shown off to relatives, made to sit on uncle's knee. I learnt to flirt, was told that I was pretty and I liked the attention, I loved it. I still like my body being appreciated. When I was seven I was sexually interfered with by a male relative. I never told anyone. I'd learnt by then that I was dirty and it was my fault. I went into the business for money. I had no morals at that time, I was twenty and had a two-year-old daughter to support — sure the blokes assumed they could sleep with you whenever they wanted. I went to a meeting once where these women were talking about the links between violence and pornography. Huh, I told them it was a load of puritan bullshit. Makes me laugh now. It never occurred to me to take into consideration the abuse I'd suffered personally. All I ask is that my mother or daughter never find out.

You're supposed to do these pathetic antics, which would cause you permanent damage in real life, with ecstasy radiating off of your mug. Once in this game it's harder than you would imagine to get out. And if I go for a proper job, what would I say at the interview? 'Well, the last thing I did was a split beaver shot of me strapped naked to the front of an XJ6 I also 'starred' in a film specially made by a television company for the Falklands lads who watched the stuff to get their bloodlust up. What could I give them, poor as I am? If I were a wife or a mother I could give my man. But I have the commodity of my body, and so they took that.

ROWENA (*closes book*). I don't want to look any more.

YVONNE. I'm sorry, Row. I didn't mean . . .

Pause.

ROWENA. How they must hate us.

TREVOR *enters. Pause.* YVONNE *starts to clear magazines.*

No. Can you leave them?

YVONNE. I was going to burn them.

TREVOR. That's what the Nazis did with propaganda they didn't like.

YVONNE. I think I'd better go.

TREVOR. Goodbye.

YVONNE. See you Row.

She goes out.

ROWENA. Yes okay. (*To* TREVOR:) Did you have to be so rude?

TREVOR. Me? Bloody hell. You set me up didn't you?

ROWENA. I what?

TREVOR. Let's see Clever Trevor's face when he practically fall over the stuff. That'll be a laugh.

ROWENA. You must be joking. That's rubbish, talking of which just look at them.

TREVOR. What sort of a wanky idea is that?

ROWENA (*picks up a magazine*). Read that bit.

TREVOR. Yes, yes . . . atrocious, very badly written. (*Slight *pause*.) Rubbish.

ROWENA. Badly written? Trevor? These things go into millions of homes.

TREVOR. So does *Crossroads*, no need to get hysterical.

ROWENA. Next you'll be telling me to keep a stiff upper lip.

TREVOR (*calmly*). Rowena, love . . .

ROWENA. Don't you 'Rowena love' me.

TREVOR (*lightly*). I've started so I'll finish. I might be able to understand if I were a real pig but don't forget I was the one who introduced you to the *Female Eunuch* — the book as opposed to Yvonne.

ROWENA (*unbelieving*). Trevor!

TREVOR. Don't I do my share of the housework, the shopping, cooking . . . ?

ROWENA. And don't you always make a big show about it. Tell me what you've done; running to me for approval.

TREVOR. Don't twist things.

ROWENA. How many things do I do that go without recognition? Do I come running to you to say, 'Oh, Trevor look what I've done. The washing, the ironing, made the bed.'?

TREVOR. I've made the bed. It consists of straightening the duvet which takes approximately one second.

ROWENA. You know what I mean.

TREVOR. I've never raped anyone. I've never so much as attacked a single woman.

ROWENA. So that makes it okay.

TREVOR. In my book I should think so . . .

ROWENA. For other men to do it . . .

TREVOR. What can I do about that?

ROWENA. You could do something . . . I don't know, write, complain, about these . . . sex shops . . .

TREVOR. Sex shops? What do you know about them? They sell

sex aids for men and women.

ROWENA (*picking up a magazine*). According to this ad they sell whips, canes, dog collars, masks, hard-core porn, inflatable life-size dolls, torsos and electric vaginas for men to masturbate into. And it must be true because there it is — the mail order form.

TREVOR. All right, all right, don't lecture me for Chrissake.

ROWENA. I want you to understand.

TREVOR. To understand? To understand what? That you want total hostility between people in the street?

ROWENA. Trev . . .

TREVOR. Well, that's what you've got in your own back garden.

TREVOR *goes out. Lights fade.*

(*Interval.*)

Scene Nine

ROWENA *with a* PSYCHIATRIST.

PSYCHIATRIST. And you claim, Mrs Jefferson-Stone, that looking at pornography was the turning-point?

ROWENA. Yes.

PSYCHIATRIST. Enough of a turning-point to make you try to kill a man?

ROWENA. Yes.

PSYCHIATRIST. Would it also be true that you became obsessed with pornographic material?

ROWENA. I became obsessed with the way women are viewed by men.

PSYCHIATRIST. How did your feelings manifest themselves at the time?

ROWENA. I became extremely angry.

PSYCHIATRIST. Even though, subjectively, you had never been exposed to or threatened by sexual assault?

ROWENA. I felt sexually assaulted every time I went out —
adverts for everything from oranges to Opels, all sold with
women's breasts.

PSYCHIATRIST. You became prudish?

ROWENA. If that means I found it unacceptable, yes, I became
prudish. — *derogatory word*

PSYCHIATRIST. Can you specify — pinpoint — what exactly
you objected to?

ROWENA. The objectification of women.

PSYCHIATRIST. If you'll forgive me for saying so, you don't
strike me as the type of woman to be fanatical about this
sort of thing.

ROWENA. What sort of women would you expect to be angry at
the way women's bodies are cut up, mutilated and violated
for entertainment value?

PSYCHIATRIST. For a start you're wearing a skirt.

ROWENA. I am fully dressed, or had that escaped your notice?

PSYCHIATRIST. In the light of the conversation, indeed, it had
not.

ROWENA (*abruptly turns her chair away, then to herself*). I have
tried . . .

PSYCHIATRIST. To do what? Murder an innocent man.

ROWENA *roars with laughter.*

Mrs Stone, you are becoming evasive.

ROWENA. Why? Because I'm wearing a skirt?

PSYCHIATRIST. And incongruent.

ROWENA. I must try and answer the questions a little more
articulately then. In reply to the question of my dress
which seems to fascinate you.

PSYCHIATRIST. I didn't say that.

ROWENA. I could say, I can continuously compromise my
iconoclasm with conformist clothing camouflage when

complying with the correctness demanded of ceremonies such as these.

PSYCHIATRIST. That does not give much away except perhaps an obsession with the letter 'c'.

ROWENA *laughs.*

You lost all sense of reality at this time.

ROWENA. Quite the opposite. I gained all sense of reality.

PSYCHIATRIST. You also lost your sense of humour. That's true, is it not? — *like Yvonne.*

ROWENA. How can it be? You've made me laugh twice.

PSYCHIATRIST. As you are quite well aware, on neither occasion was I making a joke.

ROWENA. Then maybe you're in the wrong profession.

PSYCHIATRIST. What I meant was, I am given to understand, that during the last few months you wore jeans constantly.

ROWENA. If you believe that's a symptom of madness, I'd keep quiet if I were you.

PSYCHIATRIST. And in the last six months before you left your husband, your sexual life was unsatisfactory.

ROWENA. No. We didn't do it, which was very satisfactory as far as I'm concerned.

PSYCHIATRIST. And this contributed to your feelings of inadequacy.

ROWENA. I didn't feel inadequate.

PSYCHIATRIST. Do you masturbate?

ROWENA (*thinks — 'I don't believe this'*). Do you?

PSYCHIATRIST. I believe you've been seen by various colleagues of mine.

ROWENA. Indeed I've been subjected to a psychiatric battering.

PSYCHIATRIST (*trying to look at the reports in front of him with discretion*). Tell me about your relationship with your mother.

ROWENA. Go to hell.

PSYCHIATRIST. Would you concede that your opinionated and dogmatic nature shows an insecure assertiveness?

ROWENA. Tell me, would you concede, that you are a wanker?

PSYCHIATRIST. Mrs Stone, I am not of the opinion that you are insane and were it not for the seriousness of your crime be quite prepared to put it down to the premenstrual tension, PMT factor.

ROWENA. What, for 365 days of the year? Why that is magnanimous of you.

[handwritten annotation: — when all men blame women — moods on — so do women —]

Scene Ten

HILARY *and* RON *at work.* HILARY *is filing or trying to get on with some appropriate office work.* RON *is merely being 'friendly', i.e. he does not grope her, neither are his words loaded with lust.*

RON. How's it going, Hilary?

HILARY. Okay, thanks, Mr Hughes.

RON. Good. Enjoyed your first few weeks with us?

HILARY. Very much, thank you.

RON. I'm glad to see you like the job.

HILARY. Ta.

RON. Good, good.

Pause.

HILARY. Nothing wrong is there? I mean, I'm sorry about those invoices but it was the photocopier really.

RON. No, no, it could happen to anyone. I thought we could go for a drink at lunchtime.

HILARY. It's okay, thanks, I don't drink lunchtimes, it makes me nod off in the afternoon, know what I mean?

RON. A coke then?

HILARY. I never drink coke, ta.

RON. How about after work then?

HILARY. I've got to collect me little boy.

RON. I thought your mother did that.

HILARY. From the nursery but I have to go straight to her place of work.

RON. Well, tomorrow lunchtime it is then.

HILARY. It's really very kind but I have to do me shopping lunchtimes.

RON. Kind, nothing, I always take new members of staff to lunch. It's a tradition.

HILARY. Oh.

RON (*jokey*). No need to sound so enthusiastic.

HILARY. I'm sorry, Mr Hughes.

RON. Ron.

HILARY. Ron.

RON. Are you finding it too long a day?

HILARY. Oh no, it's great really. No, it's just right.

RON. How far do you go?

HILARY. Pardon?

RON. How far do you have to travel?

HILARY. Oh, it's easy on the tube.

RON. Where do you live again?

HILARY. Er, like I say, it's only twenty minutes on the tube.

RON. I remember now. Finsbury Park. How silly of me. I go that way most evenings. I can drop you off.

HILARY. It's very nice of you but . . .

RON. No buts . . . It's no trouble.

Scene Eleven

JENNIFER *and* CLIVE'*s living-room.* CLIVE *is about to watch a video. He puts it in the recorder but doesn't get a chance to switch it on. Enter* JENNIFER.

JENNIFER. Did you buy it?

CLIVE. No, my darling, I hired it.

JENNIFER. Oh no, Clive, how many times do I have to tell you? It's a racket. Hiring of videos is just a front for those places to get your address. Now we'll get the damn thing pinched again.

CLIVE. I don't see why that should bother you.

JENNIFER. And what has my husband got to entertain himself with? (*She picks up the cassette case.*) *Violate the Bitch.* Don't you have something a little more romantic, say in French with subtitles, *Violez la biche*, so much prettier don't you think?

CLIVE. Who rattled your cage?

JENNIFER. Rattled. Me?

CLIVE. Go to bed.

JENNIFER. What makes you think I want to go to sleep?

CLIVE. When it comes to a toss up between sleep or my company with regard to entertainment potential, sleep usually wins. (*Pause.*) What's the matter?

JENNIFER. I'm bored. It's hell.

CLIVE. True.

JENNIFER. I think I was biologically determined to be bored. My first rattle probably bored me.

CLIVE. People who are bored are usually extremely boring. Why don't you sit down and watch this with me? It might rejuvenate your interest in other toys.

JENNIFER. The only movement to come out of the dying embers, darling, is the bloody death rattle.

CLIVE (*weary*). Oh, go to hell.

JENNIFER. What do you mean, go? Heavens, don't try to tell me that there's a worse existence than this. Perhaps I'd better ring the Samaritans.

CLIVE. Ring the blasted Pope for all I care, but stop opening and shutting your poisonous mouth before the verbal battering does permanent damage to my ears.

JENNIFER. Fine. When you stop martyring yourself and stop wimping about like a henpecked eunuch and stop watching this filth.

CLIVE. I have had enough.

JENNIFER. I would have thought so, yes, but in the light of your unsociable viewing hours, the odds are stacked against you. If you're henpecked, what does that make me — cocksucked?

CLIVE. Hardly.

JENNIFER (picks up the video). What do you have to buy all this trash for?

CLIVE. You're so narrow-minded.

JENNIFER. I bloody well am not.

CLIVE. If I'd imagined for one minute how you'd have turned out, I'd never have married you.

JENNIFER. And if I'd known you'd knock off three secretaries concurrently, maybe I'd have thought twice about marrying you.

CLIVE. At least they didn't nag.

JENNIFER. Nag? You know why the dog is considered man's best friend? Because you can hit, shout at and abuse dogs and they still come back for affection.

CLIVE. Whereas women sulk.

JENNIFER. Or worse still, kick back and commit crimes of disobedience. A nag by any other name.

CLIVE. Then I suggest you stop making yourself hoarse.

JENNIFER. Ha, ha, ha.

CLIVE. You, do you know something? You're mad, mad as

a hatter, you should have been certified years ago.

JENNIFER. Thanks a bunch. And if they'd used you as a yardstick to measure sanity by I would have been. If you're the walking, breathing model of normality, it's a compliment to be mad.

CLIVE. Jesus, I feel sorry for your first husband. It must have been the biggest relief of his life when he dropped dead.

JENNIFER. Shut up.

CLIVE. And your freaky children, God, not that I don't feel sorry for them. Having you as a mother must surely qualify them for some state benefit.

JENNIFER (sarcastic). Oh, but of course having you as a stepfather made up for all that.

CLIVE. At least I get on far better than you ever did with your foul daughter and son-in-law.

JENNIFER. It's not her. It's him. Creep.

CLIVE. You were pleased as punch when she married him.

JENNIFER. I must have been in a trance, persuading myself that a man whose only asset was a double-barrelled name would make my daughter happy. It's a scientifically known fact that to have a brain and a double-barrelled name is a genetic impossibility.

CLIVE. At least they've dropped the other name and the hyphen.

JENNIFER. I haven't heard from her since then.

CLIVE (sarcastic). Oh dear, that's come as a big shock.

JENNIFER. I wonder if anything's wrong.

CLIVE. What could possibly be wrong? The discovery that beanshoot and lentil quiche gives you cancer? She can't stuff another green pepper because it's ideologically unsound to penetrate vegetables.

JENNIFER. Frankly, you couldn't stick your prick into a green pepper properly.

CLIVE. My dear, a green pepper certainly has more feeling than you do.

JENNIFER. Oh Clive, I hope we're not getting into one of our na, na, na, na, silly arguments.

CLIVE. You started it.

JENNIFER. We are.

The doorbell rings.

CLIVE. Jesus, who the hell can that be at this hour?

JENNIFER. Probably one of the video burglars. You answer it in a manly voice.

CLIVE *opens the door.*

CLIVE. Rowena.

ROWENA. Clive.

CLIVE. Good grief, we were just talking about you, weren't we, darling?

JENNIFER. Rowena, are you all right? What on earth are you doing here? Is Trevor with you?

ROWENA. I'm on my own, Mother. Nothing's wrong. Just hadn't seen you for a long time. Sorry I didn't get round to ringing back when you called. How are you both?

CLIVE (*puts his arm round* JENNIFER). We're fine, absolutely. At one. Aren't we darling?

JENNIFER (*smiling*). Ace.

ROWENA. Mum, I er, I wanted to talk to you.

JENNIFER. Oh dear, I rather think you pre-empted this conversation by giving me a copy of *My Mother Myself* last Christmas.

CLIVE. I think I'd better be making tracks. It's nice to see you Rowena. Maybe you and Trevor could come down for a weekend some time.

ROWENA. Thank you, Clive.

CLIVE. Good night all. (*He kisses* JENNIFER.)

JENNIFER. Good night, darling.

CLIVE *goes off.*

ROWENA. I feel rather silly coming this late at night.

JENNIFER. Nonsense, dear. Clive always reckons I'm less able to relax than a sex maniac dosed with Spanish Fly. Sorry, I forgot you get paid not to mock the afflicted.

ROWENA. Mother, do you have to act batty all the time?

JENNIFER. Do you want me to act bitter?

ROWENA. It was a stupid idea me coming to see you.

JENNIFER (sits down). Rowena, I am far too inhibited to proceed into an embarrassing mother–daughter baring of soul, but I am only half as obnoxious as I appear. What brings you here?

ROWENA. Nothing, I only wanted a chat. Have you seen anything of Mark?

JENNIFER. Unfortunately, Clive had rather an aversion to him. Ever since he wore that earring to mum's funeral. Mark, I mean, not Clive. God, Clive thinks it's cissy to carry a handkerchief. Hence he always appears more sniffy than cissy.

ROWENA. I thought Clive liked Mark.

JENNIFER. Did you? I should never have married a younger man.

ROWENA. At least I didn't make that mistake.

JENNIFER. No, you married that big dick Trevor.

ROWENA. Mother.

JENNIFER. Sorry, little prick.

They both laugh.

ROWENA. Are you and Clive happy?

Silence.

JENNIFER. No.

ROWENA. Oh? You always seem so happy to me.

JENNIFER. Why do you ask then?

Brief pause.

Since the time I married him, Clive has had numerous affairs and what did I do? I read all the right books, I became a perfect cook in the kitchen, perfect hostess in the dining-room and perfect mistress in the bedroom. When that failed, I became mistress in the bedroom, bathroom, living-room, kitchen and lavatory.

ROWENA. Why are you telling me all this?

JENNIFER. Because you bloody well asked and because it was part of a big fat lie which accumulated in the notion that a facelift at forty would make me happy. When it didn't I stopped bending over backwards, literally, for him, and instead unleashed the acrimonious recriminations which I'd kept bottled up for years.

ROWENA. I'm sorry, I never knew.

JENNIFER. I don't want your pity. I've given as good as I've got, well, nearly. If I kill him I'll rot in prison as an evil scheming bitch. If he kills me he'll get a suspended sentence because I was neurotic and nagged. We are always responsible for their crimes but we carry the can for our own.

ROWENA. Does he still have affairs?

JENNIFER. He tries but he can't fulfil the false image in his head of how a woman should behave.

ROWENA. Because women's sexual identity has been manufactured.

JENNIFER. Perhaps you should write an article in *Community Care*.

ROWENA. Do you remember that night we went out to dinner?

JENNIFER. How could I forget?

ROWENA. Did you think Yvonne made sense?

JENNIFER. Oh yes.

ROWENA. Why didn't you back her up?

JENNIFER. I wasn't aware it was a debate. Next time I'll round up a chief whip. Look, darling, it's no good putting your head in the sand and crying about it.

ROWENA. Why not?

JENNIFER. For one thing you get grit in your eyelids. (*Pause*.) Sorry. (*She sighs*.) It's late. I'd better switch the electric blanket on in the spare bed. I take it you're staying, course you are. I've forgotten whether you're a breakfast person or not.

ROWENA. I don't think you ever knew.

JENNIFER. Huh, many's the time I can remember mediating between you and Mark over who had the most Rice Crispies. It was practically bloody lunchtime before you two actually got round to eating them after listening to them going snap crackle and pop for hours. Anyway, you'll have to make do with toast.

Pause.

I never really liked being a mother much. I'd always looked forward to the time when we could be friends. (*Slight pause*.) God knows, the company round here is awful. (*Picks up the video*.)

ROWENA (*takes the video from* JENNIFER). Is that what you do? Watch these things with him?

JENNIFER. I used to but not any more. If they did to dogs what they do to women on the screen, there'd be a public uproar.

ROWENA. But he still buys them.

JENNIFER. I did once dump the lot in a bucket of water, but not unpredictably he took violent exception to the event.

ROWENA. Not surprising.

JENNIFER. Do you know how much they cost?

ROWENA. Tough.

Scene Twelve

TREVOR *is putting the finishing touches to the table.* YVONNE *and* RON *are coming to dinner. The sound of a door slamming.*

TREVOR. Not a moment too soon, love, look. (*He gestures towards the table.*) All my own work. They'll be here any minute. Oh no, what's up? This evening visiting is getting a real bind. Don't tell me, Hilary's murdered Heathcliffe and hidden him in a cupboard.

ROWENA. She's left the job.

TREVOR. I'll restrain myself from saying I told you so.

ROWENA. Fucking hell.

TREVOR. Suppose it was quite ungrateful of her.

ROWENA. There's a limit to gratitude.

TREVOR. I know sometimes it's really tedious when people don't behave according to plan.

ROWENA. Ron has been offering her lifts home and automatically assumed he could sleep with her.

TREVOR. She shouldn't have accepted the lifts then, she's not as innocent as that.

ROWENA (*sarcastic*). It's that simple, that clear cut, isn't it?

TREVOR. It's not as if she's averse to sleeping with men for gain.

ROWENA. Oh fuck off.

TREVOR. Look, you know things aren't good mutually — and I used the word advisedly — between him and Yvonne, so he has a bit on the side.

ROWENA (*louder*). A bit on the side?! So it could be anyone — he has a universal right . . .

TREVOR. She only had to say no — like you do, often enough. If matricide means beating the mattress to death we can both plead not guilty with a free conscience.

ROWENA. Don't you understand at all why I'm so angry?

TREVOR. Why take it out on me? I haven't done anything.

ROWENA. Except condone the idea that half the human race are mere objects with suitable orifices.

TREVOR. Don't be totally ridiculous.

The doorbell rings.

ROWENA. Don't answer it.

TREVOR. For God's sake, stop acting like a petulant child. She's your friend, make a bloody effort. (*He opens the door. Very politely.*) Hello Ron, Yvonne, how nice to see you . . . come in . . . Row's just got in from work . . . I don't know if you want to change, darling.

ROWENA. What into — a mute frog?

RON. Oh there's no need, you look perfectly lovely, Row.

TREVOR. Row? Drink everyone? (*He pours them all a glass of wine.*) There you go . . . umm, well . . . Row?

ROWENA. Just adjusting the *bonhommie* to automatic pilot. How are you Yvonne?

TREVOR (*to* RON). Can't seem to get her out of jeans these days.

YVONNE. The same. I've written to publishing firms about another job.

ROWENA. Good.

TREVOR. Shall we take a pew before the avocados shrivel before our eyes? Yvonne? Ron? (*He gestures towards the table. They sit.*)

ROWENA. Time for the last supper.

ROWENA *sits.*

RON. This all looks very good. There was really no need you know. That girl was a good worker but I suppose you know she up and left.

ROWENA. Yes.

RON. It was the hours.

ROWENA. I heard.

RON. It was nice to have her about the place — bright spark.

ROWENA. I'm sure.

RON. I'd be willing to give her another chance.

ROWENA. How chivalrous of you.

RON. Don't worry, it won't prejudice me against anyone else you might put my way.

ROWENA (*deliberately drops a knife on her plate, pause*). You've got a nerve.

RON. A charm, a certain brash charm.

YVONNE. Charm? Charm, my arm.

RON. No need for pleasantries, love.

ROWENA (*to* RON). How dare you rape that woman.

RON. That's no woman, that's my wife.

ROWENA. Hilary, one of my clients.

RON. Don't be so possessive. I was one of her clients, and do you mind, there was no force involved.

ROWENA. No fucking choice involved.

TREVOR. Rowena, you're giving fucking a bad name.

RON. Look, I did her a favour, I gave her a job don't forget.

ROWENA. I'm not about to, nor is she.

RON. At least she's now got some work experience.

ROWENA. I don't believe this.

RON. And of course I'd be prepared to give her a reference.

ROWENA. Oh, I'm sure, I'm sure.

RON. So, right? There's no need to take on, okay.

ROWENA. You bastard.

TREVOR (*still trying to save the situation*). Now you're taking the name of the illegitimate in vain.

The following lines, up to RON's *and* TREVOR's *exit, are all delivered at top speed and volume.*

ROWENA. Get stuffed.

TREVOR. Just shut it, will you?

YVONNE. Why should she?

RON. You stay out of this.

ROWENA. Why should she?

TREVOR. Just leave it.

YVONNE. Oh, you'd like that wouldn't you?

RON. Who told you to open your trap?

TREVOR. For Chrissakes, drop it.

YVONNE (to RON). Who gave you the right to breathe?

RON. Shut it before I shut it for you.

ROWENA. Get out of my sight. Get out of my house.

TREVOR. Leaving aside the theory, all property is theft. It's our house.

YVONNE. Clever Trevor.

ROWENA. Shut up Trevor.

TREVOR (to YVONNE). You make me sick.

YVONNE. The feeling's mutual.

RON. Just bloody well piss off.

ROWENA. No, you piss off yourself.

TREVOR. Shut up.

YVONNE. No, you shut up.

TREVOR. You stupid bitch.

RON (to ROWENA and YVONNE). You make me ill — the pair of you.

YVONNE (screams). Then get out.

RON. Don't worry. I won't spend another moment with you — you fucking hysterical hag.

YVONNE. The truth, the elusive truth, slipped inadvertently from the pig's mouth.

RON. I'm off. (*He goes out.*) Witch.

TREVOR. Ron wait for me. (*He goes out.*)

   Long pause.

ROWENA. Ah, well, Trevor never makes enough for four.

YVONNE. I'm not very hungry.

ROWENA. What are you going to do?

YVONNE. Leave him.

Scene Thirteen

A cold but sunny spring day. ROWENA, YVONNE *and* JENNIFER *are having a picnic. The atmosphere between them is warm and relaxed. The pace is slow.*

JENNIFER. I don't think I've been on a picnic since you were little.

ROWENA. I must confess it wasn't a habit I thought I'd be keeping up.

YVONNE. It's nice though . . . reminds me of when I was a kid . . . rolling down grass slopes in the park . . .

ROWENA. Trying to fend off the wasps from the jam sandwiches . . .

YVONNE. Playing run outs . . .

ROWENA. Playing on the swings in the park till after dark.

JENNIFER. When the only thing you had to worry about was forgetting your dinner money for school.

YVONNE. I didn't even have to worry about that. I used to get free school dinners.

ROWENA. And I had packed lunches and (*To* JENNIFER:) you used to throw anything in them that just happened to be in the fridge at the time . . .

YVONNE. Which, as far as I remember, was usually beetroot . . .

ROWENA. That's right, we used to share my packed lunches, and your dinner tickets and have two dinners together a week . . .

YVONNE. And sell off the extra one and spend the money in the tuck shop on Fridays.

JENNIFER. I see . . . It's all coming out now . . . Did you ever sell off the packed lunches?

ROWENA. You must be joking. We'd have had to pay someone to eat beetroot sandwiches.

All laugh. Then silence.

JENNIFER. I always used to loathe the spring . . .

YVONNE. Seems one of the most unlikely things to loathe.

JENNIFER. All that stuff about everything new . . . growing . . . new start and all that only served to make me want to squash it all.

ROWENA. You've never allowed yourself to be optimistic . . .

JENNIFER. I think it was more the awful feeling of being left behind. (*Pause.*) Still, at last I'm starting to blossom. I've become more adventurous in my old age.

YVONNE. You've got the Family Planning Association to sponsor a flower arranging exhibition?

JENNIFER. No, that was a load of rubbish . . . I'm going on holiday to Greece. How's that for starters?

ROWENA. Nice. Are you going on your own?

JENNIFER. Originally yes, but I wondered if you two wanted to come with me . . .

YVONNE. That sounds like a great idea . . .

ROWENA. Hang on, we can't even afford . . .

JENNIFER. On me I meant. It's the least I can do to make up for the beetroot sandwiches.

ROWENA. When?

JENNIFER. Easter?

ROWENA (*to* YVONNE). What do you think?

YVONNE. I'd love it.

JENNIFER. Right, that's settled then.

Silence.

ROWENA. Well, I suppose we better start making a move . . . get all this packed up.

YVONNE. I sort of wish we didn't have to go back . . .

JENNIFER. If we stay here much longer we won't have to, we'll die from exposure . . .

YVONNE. Shame the sun had to go in.

JENNIFER. The sun never goes in. It just gets obscured by clouds.

ROWENA. Very poetic, Mother.

JENNIFER. See, how's that for optimism?

Scene Fourteen

Tube station. It is 10.30 p.m. A man enters. There is the sound of a train pulling in. He sits on a bench, half-asleep, free to doze. ROWENA rushes on to the platform. As the train pulls out another man enters smoking a cigarette. There is the sound off of a tube approaching on another platform. The man looks at his watch. Pause. He casually saunters up the platform towards ROWENA who doesn't look at him. Long pause. He then says something to her which we don't hear. She turns away and weighs up the options of whether to run back up an empty, dark passageway or stay where she is. She moves away from him deciding that the next train will arrive any minute and she'll be safe. He approaches her again very fast. Very close to her face. She shoves him violently. He falls on the track. There is the sound of a train. Simultaneous blackout. Lights flash on ROWENA looking back at the track. Blackout. The train screeches to a halt.

Scene Fifteen

Music: the tune from Scene Eight. A POLICEWOMAN *stands in the shadow behind* ROWENA. *There is the sound of a knock at the door and then front door opening. All dialogue to the end of the scene is pre-recorded.*

ROWENA. Hello Hilary I . . .

HILARY. Go to hell.

ROWENA (*firmly*). Hang on. (*Then:*) The nursery rang to say that Heathcliffe hasn't been for the last couple of days. Is he all right?

HILARY. He's okay so you can stop concerning yourself.

ROWENA. Then why hasn't he . . . ?

HILARY (*very aggressive*). Cos I ain't bin well.

ROWENA (*relieved*). Oh, I see. (*Then:*) Have you been off work?

HILARY. You're quick.

ROWENA. Don't worry, I'm sure Ron will understand.

HILARY. I'm sure he does.

ROWENA. Luckily he and his wife are coming round to dinner this evening. I'll explain . . .

HILARY. Save yerself the trouble. I've told him to stuff his job.

ROWENA (*pause*). Well . . . sure . . . if that's your choice.

HILARY (*shouts*). Just what's it to you anyway? Nothing. All you bloody care about is Heathcliffe. You don't give a bleedin' monkeys about me.

ROWENA. Look, can I come in . . . ?

HILARY. No, you can fuck off.

ROWENA. Hilary . . .

HILARY. I wish to God I'd never set eyes on you — you and your bleedin' friends.

ROWENA. He did give you a job.

HILARY. Yeah, oh yeah, and I'll give you three guesses what he expected in return an' all.

ROWENA. What?

HILARY. What d'you think? Use yer imagination.

ROWENA. The bastard! Hilary I'm sorry . . .

HILARY. And that's about all you can afford to be an' all. 'Sorry'. 'Cos you ain't ever going to know what it's like to be thrown on the shit heap. You got enough qualifications, security and money to have some sodding choice. Well mine is the D bloody HSS crap. Or on me back. What a bloody joke and I thought working was s'posed to give you some self-respect. Ha bloody ha.

ROWENA (*angry rather than lost for words*). God, I don't know what to say.

HILARY. Why bother to say anything? You just have your nice dinner party, smooth everything over and live happily ever after.

The sound of the front door slamming.

Women must make the choice

Scene Sixteen

Courtroom. JUDGE, COUNSEL FOR THE PROSECUTION.

JUDGE. Mrs Stone. Mrs Stone. (ROWENA *faces the* JUDGE.) We have heard the evidence, including extensive psychiatric reports which suggest you are removed, vague, uninvolved, and failed to maintain normal, acceptable patterns of communication. Prudish to the point of being sexually repressed — frigid. Is there anything you would like to say?

ROWENA. Yes. (*She reads from a piece of paper.*) Douglas Coles pleaded guilty to the manslaughter of his wife and got two years' probation because it was proved she was neurotic and nagged. Gordon Asher strangled his wife and got a six-month suspended sentence. (*In future productions more up-to-date examples can be substituted for these.*)

JUDGE. Please don't waste this court's valuable time with

irrelevant material. You have chosen to present your own defence. I suggest you do so by re-examining in your own words the events leading up to the crime.

ROWENA (*pause*). He spoke to me.

PROSECUTION. I am speaking to you. Do you mean to say that if I were standing in a tube station I might meet my end?

ROWENA *does not respond.*

What did he say to you?

ROWENA. I don't remember.

PROSECUTION. You don't remember? (*He speaks louder.*) Do you remember the crime? The consequences? The punishment for a few words exchanged?

Silence.

JUDGE. Please try to elaborate a little, Mrs Stone.

ROWENA. I'd been to see a film, a pornographic film. I was extremely angry.

JUDGE. You are not at liberty to avenge the pornography industry in this country. We have censorship laws for that.

ROWENA. The laws are a load of cock.

PROSECUTION. Mrs Stone, I really must . . .

JUDGE. Indeed, the laws will need looking into if they provoke this callous sort of attack from so-called sane women. What was this film?

ROWENA. A snuff movie.

PROSECUTION (*in response to* JUDGE's *puzzled look*). M'lud, a film or films made in the United States where, according to reliable reports, the participant is actually killed in front of the camera.

JUDGE. What, in real life?

PROSECUTION. Yes, m'lud.

JUDGE. So, on seeing this film you thought you'd go out and kill a man?

ROWENA. No, it was a coincidence. I didn't want to speak to that man. He insisted, when he got too close for comfort I became angry and shoved him.

PROSECUTION. Unfortunately, on to the line, at the time when the train was coming. Why didn't you shove him back on to the platform?

ROWENA. I . . .

PROSECUTION. Because this was an act committed in cold blood, regardless of the accused's inexplicable preamble . . . Watching a film cannot be construed as anything but an objective experience. The man was a complete stranger and there is no foreseeable way that it could be described as a crime of passion. He leaves a wife who would not be a widow today if it had not been for the calculated acts of this woman.

ROWENA. What was he doing harassing me then?

PROSECUTION. Harassing you? You can't even remember what he said. 'Have you got a light?', or 'Can you tell me the time?' Are you seriously suggesting that innocent remarks should be deemed incitement to murder?

JUDGE. Mrs Stone we have heard the evidence. One thing is indisputable. A man has lost his life as the direct consequence of the action taken against him by you. A man whom you have admitted you never met before. I would suggest to you that the evidence you have put forward is nothing more than an irrelevant fabrication to further some fanatical belief that the laws concerning pornography in this country are inadequate. But that is of no concern here.

He looks at her. She looks directly back at him.

Do you understand, Mrs Stone, that it is now up to this court to determine whether you are guilty or not guilty?

Silence.

CLERK (*voice over*). All stand.

ROWENA *and the* POLICEWOMAN *move forward into an 'empty' room. The* POLICEWOMAN *sits on a bench.*

Scene Seventeen

ROWENA *and* POLICEWOMAN. ROWENA *is absorbed in her own thoughts. There is silence.*

POLICEWOMAN. Is there anything I can get for you . . . ?

ROWENA. What? Oh. No . . . Thanks.

POLICEWOMAN. Cigarette. (*She offers her one.*) What was it like?

ROWENA. Sorry?

POLICEWOMAN. The film you saw.

ROWENA. Oh, that.

POLICEWOMAN. What was it like? Er, don't . . . If you don't want to.

Pause.

ROWENA (*very quietly*). Well, the first part was badly made and like a lot of films it contained a good deal of violence and shooting. I think it was loosely based on the Charles Manson story. Then it changes, it becomes real. It's a film studio during a break in the filming. The director is near a bed talking to a young woman. He gets turned on and wants to have sex with her. They lie on the bed and he kisses her. She then realises that they are being filmed. She doesn't like it and protests. There is a knife lying on the bed near her shoulder. He pins her down as she attempts to get up. He picks up the knife and moves it round her neck and throat. There is utter terror on her face as she realises that he is not acting. She tries to get up but cannot. The film shows shots of his face which registers power and pleasure. He starts to cut into her shoulder, and the pain in her face . . . It's real . . . Blood seeps through her blouse. Her arm is held down and he cuts off her fingers. It is terrible. I have watched a woman being cut up and she is alive. He then picks up an electric saw. And I think no . . . no he can't use it. But he does. Her hand is sawn off . . . left twitching by her side. Then he plunges the saw into her stomach, and the pain and terror on her face. More shots of his face of power and pleasure. He puts his hands inside her and pulls out some of her insides. Finally, he reaches in again and pulls out her guts and holds them above his head. He is triumphant.

Long pause.

That's it. The end. And I kept forcing myself, to pretend that it was only a movie.

POLICEWOMAN. No. It happens. I've seen photos, hundreds of photos of little girls, young women, middle-aged women, old women . . . with torn genitals, ripped vaginas, mutilated beyond recognition. I try to not think about it.

ROWENA. I'm going to have a long time to think about it.

POLICEWOMAN. We do our best to convict them.

ROWENA. Yes. (ROWENA *moves away*.) I don't want anything to do with men who have knives or whips or men who look at photos of women tied and bound, or men who say relax and enjoy it. Or men who tell misogynist jokes.

Blackout.

one leads to another
all degrade women.

NEAPTIDE

This play is dedicated to all the friends, both mothers and teachers who have shared their experiences with me, and whose help and encouragement have been invaluable.

Acknowledgement
My grateful thanks to Dr Phyllis Chesler for permission to quote from her interpretation of the Demeter myth and her book *Women and Madness* (Avon Books, 1972).

S.D.

Neaptide was first performed at the Cottesloe, National Theatre, London, on 26 June 1986, with the following cast:

CLAIRE, 27	Jessica Turner
POPPY, 7, *her daughter*	Lucy Speed
VAL, 29, *Claire's sister*	Catherine Nielson
JOYCE, 57, *mother of Claire and Val*	Mary Macleod
JEAN, 30, *Claire's flatmate*	Sheila Kelly
SID, 58, *father of Claire and Val*	Anthony Douse
LAWRENCE, 31, *Claire's ex-husband*	Michael Bray
COLIN, 30, *Val's husband*	Peter Attard
WALTER	Marc Bellamy
SID JUNIOR } 4, *Val's twin sons*	Richard Lawrence
JUSTIN, 5	John Sinclair
SPENCER, 6 } *Jean's sons*	Ruben Patino
BEATRICE GRIMBLE, 51, *headmistress*	Janet Whiteside
LINDA FELLOWS, 33, *games mistress*	Theresa Watson
ANNETTE POLLARD, 54, *domestic science teacher*	Jeanne Watts
MARION LANDSDOWNE, 32, *needlework teacher*	Anna Keaveney
CYRIL BARRETT, 64, *physics teacher*	Anthony Douse
ROGER CUNNINGHAM, 29, *English teacher*	Roderick Smith
DIANE	Miranda Foster
TERRI } 17, *sixth form pupils*	Jacquetta May
YOUNG DOCTOR, *male*	Peter Attard
OLDER DOCTOR, *male*	Anthony Douse
NURSE, *female*	Jacquetta May
CLERK OF THE COURT, *female*	Miranda Foster
BARRISTER, *male*	Peter Attard
FLORRIE, *voice only*	Jeanne Watts

Directed by John Burgess
Designed by Alison Chitty

The play is set in an outer London suburb. The events take place in March 1983.

PART ONE

Scene One

A hospital. TWO DOCTORS, *both men, one some years older than the other, stand by* VAL's *bed. A female* NURSE *hovers in the background. They are all oblivious to* VAL's *first speech.*

VAL. The performers in this pit are as old as the witchcraft trials. Centre stage. The powerful male Doctor-Inquisitor. In the wings, a subservient female Handmaiden-Nurse. Stranded on a mud flat, myself, a Witch-Patient.

The DOCTORS *appear to be in the midst of a deep conversation when* JOYCE *enters.*

OLDER DOCTOR (*with genuine concern*). I'm afraid you can't see your daughter at the moment, she needs plenty of rest. Perhaps you would care to wait outside? (*With a gesture he indicates to the* NURSE *to show* JOYCE *out of the room. Exit* JOYCE *with* NURSE. *Then to the* YOUNGER DOCTOR:) I wasn't on duty last night. Strictly speaking, March will see to this one.

YOUNGER DOCTOR (*smiles*). Hare March?

OLDER DOCTOR. Don't tell me, on top of everything else our quack colleague is German.

YOUNGER DOCTOR. I meant as in 'Mad as . . .'

OLDER DOCTOR. Oh, I'm with you now. Hum yes. (*Shaking his head over* VAL.) Probably have her flung out inside a week.

YOUNGER DOCTOR. With disarming success, no doubt.

OLDER DOCTOR. And who'll have to mop up the long-term backlash. Hum? Caught up in the unfortunate irony of psychiatric policy – concentration of short-term solutions. Our analyst friend is careful not to contravene that.

YOUNGER DOCTOR (*drily*). What's the difference between a

cow chewing the cud and a therapist chewing gum? The cow has an intelligent look on its face.

OLDER DOCTOR (*wryly*). I'll leave it to you then. (*He exits.*)

YOUNGER DOCTOR (*calls off*). Staff.

The NURSE *enters.*

NURSE. Yes, doctor.

YOUNGER DOCTOR. Did you manage to dredge the social worker's report up?

NURSE (*offers him the medical notes which include a photocopy of the social worker's report*). Yes, I'm afraid there's not much to go on though.

YOUNGER DOCTOR (*taking the file*). Is there ever? (*He sighs. Flicking through them.*) Huh, that's a fat lot of good. (*He hands the notes back to her.*) Still make it available to Dr March, we mustn't allow accusations of unco-operation to fly around the ward. Children?

NURSE. Doctor?

YOUNGER DOCTOR. Has she got any offspring?

NURSE. Yes, two.

YOUNGER DOCTOR. And do we know, pray, who is looking after them?

NURSE. The maternal grandmother is to collect them from the nursery and look after them until their father gets in from work. In fact she's outside now.

YOUNGER DOCTOR. Who? Who is?

NURSE. Mrs Jones's mother. Shall I tell her she can come in?

YOUNGER DOCTOR. Oh yes, yes.

They both exit.

NURSE (*as she goes through the door*). You can come in now, Mrs Roberts.

Enter JOYCE. *She crosses to the bed, pulls up a chair and sits down very unconfidently.*

JOYCE. Hello love, how are you feeling? (*Pause.*) Don't worry about the boys, they're fine. We took them to playschool this morning. They were ever so good, no tears or nothing and I'll collect them for as long – (*She stops herself.*) – for as long as they want to go. (*Pause.*) Colin's rearranging his timetable at work so not to worry. He sends all his love. (*Pause.*) He's beside himself, I mean he's very concerned. Well, we all are, we all are. For you. That you get well, back to your old self. (*Finally.*) Have you got a message for him? (*Silence.*) Val?

VAL (*quietly*). Here I sit, mad as a hatter with nothing to do but either become madder and madder or else recover enough of my sanity to be allowed back to the world that drove me mad.

JOYCE (*shocked*). I don't think I can remember all that. What on earth possessed you to come out with a mouthful like that?

VAL. I didn't say it.

JOYCE (*gently, slightly patronisingly*). Oh, Val, who did then? The washstand?

VAL. Some woman years ago. I don't think there are any original states of mind left to reclaim.

JOYCE (*sighs*). Val, love, this won't do. Now, I've brought you a clean nightie and two flannels.

Scene Two

Afternoon. Sunday. Two days previously. CLAIRE's *living-room.* CLAIRE *is sitting in an armchair.* POPPY *is sitting on her lap. She has been reading* Mrs Plug the Plumber *to* CLAIRE. *There is a Mother's Day card, which* POPPY *has made, on the mantelpiece.*

POPPY (*reading*). Ah well, all in a day's work, said Mrs Plug. I'm going to go home and have a slap-up supper, this job is driving me round the bend. (*She slaps the book shut.*)

CLAIRE (*laughs*). Poppy, it does not end like that.

POPPY. I know. I thought it was boring for you.

CLAIRE. Now, have you got your Nan's present ready?

POPPY. Yes, I've hid it behind the chair.

CLAIRE. Good.

POPPY. It's your turn.

CLAIRE. What is?

POPPY. It's your turn to read me a story, you promised.

CLAIRE. It's just that they'll be here soon.

POPPY. You promised.

CLAIRE. Okay, okay, which one . . .

POPPY. Pepsi-phone.

CLAIRE. Persephone.

CLAIRE *picks up a book.*

In the beginning, if there ever was such a time, Demeter, the goddess of life, gave birth to four daughters, whom she named Persephone, Psyche, Athena and Artemis. The world's first children were unremarkably happy. To amuse their mother – with whom they were all passionately in love – they invented language, music, laughter – and many more useful and boisterous activities.

One morning Persephone menstruated. That afternoon, Demeter's daughters gathered flowers to celebrate the loveliness of the event. A chariot thundered, then clattered into their midst. It was Hades, the middle-aged god of death, come to take Persephone, come to carry her off to be his queen, to sit beside him in the realm of non-being below the earth, come to commit the first act of violence earth's children had ever known.

Pause.

. . . and thus they each discovered that in shame and sorrow childhood ends, and that nothing remains the same.

Persephone's sisters came home without her. Demeter raged and wept. She bound up her hair and turned wanderer, but could not find her eldest daughter anywhere on earth.

POPPY. No, because she wasn't on the world, she was underneath it.

CLAIRE. Finally the sun spoke and told Demeter what had happened, that her daughter was married and a queen. He counselled her:

'Why mourn the natural fate of daughters – to leave their mother's home, to lose their virginity, marry, and to give birth to children?'

POPPY. Silly sun.

CLAIRE. Demeter was grieved beyond and before reasoning.

POPPY. She was vivid.

CLAIRE. What?

POPPY. Raging mad.

CLAIRE. Oh, livid.

POPPY. Yes, hopping livid.

CLAIRE. Remembering an oracle's prophecy of a splitting, a scattering and an exile, she said to the sun:

'Yea, if that be the natural fate of daughters, let all mankind perish. Let there be no crops, no grain, no corn, if this maiden is not returned to me.'

And she stopped the world.

POPPY. Brillo, that's my favourite bit.

CLAIRE. And because Demeter was a powerful goddess, her wishes were commands and Persephone returned, but she still had to visit her husband once a year and during that time no crops would grow. However, neither husband nor child nor stranger would ever claim her as his own. Persephone belonged to her mother. That was Demeter's gift to herself.

Silence.

POPPY. Did she really stop the world?

CLAIRE. Why do you think nothing can grow in winter and all the leaves fall off the trees?

POPPY. Do you really believe that? Really and truly?

CLAIRE. Well, I certainly like it better than *Cinderella* or *Sleeping Beauty*.

POPPY. Don't stop there, what happened to all the others?

JOYCE (*off*). Hello? Anyone at home?

CLAIRE. In here, Mum. (*To* POPPY:) When they've gone it's bath and bed, okay.

POPPY. Aw Mum.

Enter JOYCE *and* VAL.

JOYCE. You should really keep the door locked. I could've been anyone. Hello love. (*She kisses* CLAIRE.) Hello Poppy.

POPPY *hugs* JOYCE, *then goes and gets* JOYCE's *present which is a daffodil in a brightly painted pot.*

CLAIRE. I'm glad you could make it, Val.

VAL *smiles. They sit down.*

JOYCE. We let your father and Colin go for a drink, so it's just us together. (*To* CLAIRE:) Thought you'd appreciate that. Now don't go putting the kettle on. We've had so many cups of tea it's a wonder I've not turned into a watering can.

POPPY (*presenting* JOYCE *with her present*). Happy Mother's Day, Nan.

JOYCE (*very pleased*). Oh Poppy, thank you. It's lovely. Did you grow it yourself?

POPPY (*considering this*). Well, I put it in a cupboard under the stairs for ages but it grew by itself really. I painted the pot though.

JOYCE. And very nicely too. Who are these?

POPPY (*pointing at the pictures*). This one is you, Nan. This one is Val and this is Sybil and –

JOYCE (*correcting*). Aunty Val and Aunty Sybil.

CLAIRE. Yes and this one is Claire.

JOYCE (*correcting*). Mummy.

POPPY (*affirming*). Yes, that's right, my Mum.

JOYCE. Honestly, Claire, if children grow up using their parents' names it's no wonder they end up rioting.

CLAIRE (*handing JOYCE a wrapped gift*). Happy Mother's Day.

JOYCE. Oh thank you. (*Pleasantly.*) Gawd, I'm a bit frightened to open it. I'm never sure what I'll get from you. What with tea towels about sinking into his sink.

CLAIRE. That was years ago.

JOYCE. It was still too late then. I've spent the best part of my life with my arms in Fairy Liquid. Anyway, I just hope it's something I can show your father.

CLAIRE. If you usually show him the cardigans people give you from Marks and Spencer before you change them for thermal underwear, yes, you can.

JOYCE. All right, don't take . . .

POPPY. Oh, open it, Nan, open it.

JOYCE (*opening it and finding it is a cardigan from Marks and Spencer*). Oh it's very nice, thank you, Claire. And I got a card from Sybil yesterday.

VAL. Oh Sybil, Sybil, Sybil. What a name to call a child, don't dribble Sybil.

JOYCE. There's no need to be like that, Val. She was named after my mother and you know full well I didn't want any of you named after her. God knows your christening was a trauma and a half, Val, but when it came to Sybil's I just didn't have the strength to take another scene behind the font. Anyway, I don't know if they have such a thing as Mother's Day out there, but my card had the Statue of Liberty on it, so I don't know whether that was by design or coincidence, but it only says she'll ring tonight. I only hope she gets the time lapse right. I have no desire to be wished 'Happy Mother's Day' at three o'clock tomorrow morning, thank you very much.

CLAIRE. I'm sure she won't. Do give her my love.

JOYCE. Yes, of course. You know it's on an island, don't you? Did you know that?

CLAIRE. Manhattan?

JOYCE. I know that's an island don't I? No, the Statue of Liberty is stuck out in the water on something no bigger than your garden and, you know, here was I thinking it was like Eros slap bang in the middle of things. I said to Sid, I did, just as well I've never been on Mastermind not knowing something like that. He laughed, that's why I married him, he's a good laugh, your father.

CLAIRE. You should see the Statue of Liberty for yourself. Sybil's always saying she'd like you to go over and visit.

JOYCE. What with? That's what I'd like to know.

CLAIRE. You can get quite a cheap fare and there's Dad's redundancy money.

JOYCE. We can't go throwing that about traipsing round the world. Have you lost your senses? And what's your father s'posed to do – go down the dole and say, 'Be good lads and just pop the next few Giros in the post to New York'? That would make them roll in the aisles, I'm sure.

CLAIRE. Sorry, it was only . . .

JOYCE. An idea. Yes, well, the very idea. I'm not so sure as I want to go over there in the first place and I can't for the life of me fathom why Sybil flounced off there. I still wake up of a night in a cold sweat praying she's not been mugged.

CLAIRE. Oh, Mum.

JOYCE. I do, you know, I do, and fancy, I ask you, of all the places to live in New York she ends up in somewhere called SoHo. Other people over there at least have those normal numbered addresses like 42nd Street.

CLAIRE. She's a journalist, nothing else.

JOYCE. I know it's only a name and what's in a name but you don't have to face the neighbours: 'And where's your daughter living these days, Mrs Roberts?' 'Well, actually, in New York's SoHo.' Well, the way they look you'd think I'd just said she'd dropped dead.

CLAIRE. So how are you?

JOYCE. And where's that err . . . Joan?

CLAIRE. Jean. She went to her mother's for the weekend.

JOYCE. Did she take the boys with her?

CLAIRE. No, actually they're staying with Riq until tonight.

JOYCE. Oh, is he still hanging around?

CLAIRE. She and Riq have been lovers for five years.

JOYCE. It's about time they jolly well got married then.

CLAIRE. That's their business, Mum.

JOYCE. And, it's a good deal better than some other people's arrangements.

CLAIRE (gently). Now, Mum.

JOYCE (sighs). Still it's your life, each to their own, live and let live, that's what I always say.

VAL (deliberate sarcasm). Ha. Ha.

CLAIRE. Val?

VAL (snaps). Fine, fine, I'm fine.

JOYCE. Course you are, course she is, just not been herself, right now . . . lately. (*To* CLAIRE:) Now don't you start probing and upsetting everyone. I notice nobody bothers to ask how I am. I suppose I'm not worth bothering with.

CLAIRE (*curtly*). I just did, only you ignored it.

JOYCE. Sometimes, frankly, it's just as well not to ask. Life's not a bowl of anything much. Especially with neighbours banging away into the night – they've even got an hydraulic cat-flap, God alone knows why, on the twelfth floor. Still, moaning about it doesn't get you anywhere. Laugh and the world laughs with you, weep and you weep alone, that's my motto.

VAL (*quietly*). One by one we all file on down the narrow aisles of pain alone.

JOYCE. Pardon? Val?

VAL. Thought I'd finish where you started.

JOYCE (*choosing not to take this up*). What a life, I ask you. I tell you I need one of those *Help* programmes all to myself. I thank God I'm not a Catholic, that's all I can say, not that he's not the best pope so far, this one.

VAL (*flatly*). Hurray, hurray, it's Mother's Day.

JOYCE. What's got into you these days, Val? You used to be so sensitive.

CLAIRE. Mum!

JOYCE (*to* CLAIRE). Which is more than I can say for you, I'm afraid, young lady.

CLAIRE. Woman.

JOYCE. Oh Claire, where is all this nitpicking getting you? (*Firmly.*) I'll tell you one thing for nothing: when you were born they didn't say to me, 'Mrs Roberts, you've got a lovely little baby woman.'

CLAIRE. I'm sure they didn't say 'You've got a lovely little baby lady' either.

JOYCE. Whereas Val could have been a poet, couldn't you, dear?

I'll never forget when I met one of her lecturers, he said you've got a potential . . .

VAL (*flatly*). The distortion of abortion is a Catholic contortion from which I can only conceive that the Papist is a rapist.

JOYCE. Well, you haven't been feeling very well lately, have you? No, no, we won't go into that now. Every day in every way getting better all the time. You look much better than when I last saw you. Doesn't she?

CLAIRE. Did you ever enrol for those cookery classes, Mum?

JOYCE. What went wrong? Oh, what went wrong? I didn't mind that you were all girls, oh no I didn't. I just wished that you'd all turn out like those Brontë sisters. (*VAL and CLAIRE exchange exasperated looks.*) Yes, well, that was a load of pie-in-the-sky nonsense. For a start their father was a priest. I don't suppose for one minute that many great lady – (*She looks at CLAIRE.*) – women novelists had dockers, unemployed ones at that, for fathers. (*To CLAIRE:*) There, that's what you should be going on about in your sociological stuff.

CLAIRE (*controlled*). That's what I do go on about, Mum, only my analysis isn't quite so succinct.

JOYCE. And that's another thing. I bet Charlotte Brontë didn't talk to her mother like that.

CLAIRE. If I remember rightly her mother died when she was seven.

JOYCE. And that's where I'll be, in the grave, thanks to you. Things you've put me through.

CLAIRE (*through clenched teeth*). Mother, please.

JOYCE. It wasn't for the want of trying, my girl, didn't I always encourage you to play with the vicar's daughter?

VAL *laughs out loud*, CLAIRE *suppresses a smile*.

Now what are you laughing at? They were a very nice family. Mark and Harriet – wonderful people, and I hoped by you mixing with their daughter Mary some of the respectability might rub off.

CLAIRE. Mum? Mary had three abortions by the time she was eighteen.

JOYCE. Well, with a name like that she was hardly blessed. Still, it's quite something to have your father called by God like he was.

VAL. Probably all he heard was a dog with a sore mouth, going 'Mark, Mark'.

JOYCE. Val! Please not in front of the child.

POPPY. Did you know, Nan, 'god' spells dog backwards.

JOYCE. Poppy!

CLAIRE. Poppy, I think you've overstepped the mark.

POPPY. But it's true.

JOYCE. Is this what it comes down to, one of my daughters calls the Pope a sod, the other says he's a rapist, and my granddaughter goes one further and calls God a dog. Heaven help us, on Mothering Sunday as well.

Silence.

POPPY. I didn't call God a dog.

CLAIRE. Mum, we've done all right. Everything considered. And we owe that to you. (*To* POPPY:) No, I know you didn't, love.

JOYCE (*to* CLAIRE). I've taken enough blame for everything. Don't start on me.

CLAIRE. Look Val and I went to university, neither you nor Dad went there. And we weren't pushed into it like loads of others. Mum, you were always saying don't get married like you did at nineteen and regret it.

JOYCE. Regret it? Regret it? What have I got to regret? I might have said don't get married at *sixteen*, but I didn't say don't get married at all or fornicate or emigrate or crack up or go the other way or whatever. My God, I wanted three daughters like the Brontës and I ended up with a family fit for a Channel Four documentary. Regrets, me? It's you lot that should have regrets.

CLAIRE. I give up.

JOYCE. Now you know how I feel – I gave up a long time ago.

CLAIRE. Why do you have to criticise me all the time?

JOYCE. Me? Criticise? Just what do I criticise you about?

Enter JEAN *behind* JOYCE.

CLAIRE. Hi, Jean.

JOYCE. Personal cleanliness is the last thing I'd criticise you for – you can tell that by your fingernails – spotless. (*She sees* JEAN.) Oh, hello Joan – did you have a nice time?

JEAN (*flatly*). I went to my mother's.

JOYCE. Not a good recipe for success, if my mother was alive today she'd wish herself dead again. Poor woman, God rest her soul.

JEAN *sees the way the conversation is going and exits.*

Not that there's not plenty I could be having a go at you for.

CLAIRE. Perhaps not now, eh, Mum?

JOYCE. I wonder whether my feelings ever get taken into consideration.

CLAIRE. Mum!

JOYCE. Don't worry, I know – L-I-T-T-L-E E-A-R-S.

Pause.

POPPY. Little ears, what does that mean?

JOYCE. Nothing, love, it's slang for Nanny's got a big mouth.

POPPY. Mum? There's only three. Demeter had four.

CLAIRE. You're the fourth.

POPPY (*pointing at* JOYCE). So you're Demeter.

JOYCE. Don't point dear, it's rude.

POPPY (*nodding towards* VAL). You're Psyche and Aunty Sybil can be Athena.

VAL. Do you learn this at school?

POPPY. No, Claire – (*She looks at* JOYCE.) – Mummy tells me.

JOYCE. Course, Val did her degree in the classics, didn't you love.

VAL. I never finished it.

JOYCE. No, but only because nature had something better designed for you, didn't it? Not that your father and I weren't upset at the time because we were, we were, but Colin is a very decent man and he's done the best thing by you, he has. You have a marvellous husband and a lovely family, sometimes I think you don't realise how lucky you are, I don't.

CLAIRE. Did you ever enrol for those brass rubbing classes, Mum?

JOYCE. Oh, that's just typical of you, stick your head in the sand, hear no evil, see no evil, but (*She stops herself.*) I tell you this much: a social worker had never so much as put a finger on the doorbell until . . .

CLAIRE (*harshly*). Mum, leave it out, please.

JOYCE. It's all very well you saying, 'Mum, please', but that won't solve anything.

CLAIRE. And nor will your carrying on about it.

JOYCE. Honestly. Have you no shame?

CLAIRE (*slowly*). Will you stop picking on me.

JOYCE. Me? Me? Picking on you? Huh, I like that. It's usually only drunk and insane mothers who are considered unfit for parental control.

CLAIRE. Shut up.

VAL. Stop it. Stop it. Stop it.

JOYCE. There, look now, what you've done now. Look.

CLAIRE. I haven't upset anyone. If anyone's upset anyone . . .

JOYCE. What about me and my ties with her?

CLAIRE (*shouts*). Drop it please.

Enter SID.

SID. Drop what? I came straight in, the door was open.

JOYCE (*startled*). Oh Sidney, love, it's you. Where's Colin?

SID. Trying to park the car. This must be getting into a trendy area, can always tell when the Citroëns are double-parked. Hello there, Val, Claire. And how's Poppy?

POPPY. Hello Grandad – you can be – (*To* CLAIRE:) Who can he be? I know, Zeus.

SID. That's my cleverest granddaughter. (*To* CLAIRE:) And if I'm Zeus, who are you?

POPPY. Pepsi-phone.

SID. Now me, I'm somewhat Carling-Black-Label-prone myself.

POPPY. Where have you been?

SID. Tell who this one's taking after. (*He looks at* JOYCE.)

JOYCE. He's been to the pub, as if we need ask, when he knows full well that we haven't got the money for him to go swilling beer down his neck with.

SID. You know what her latest economy is now? Eh? Keeps the curtains drawn so the sunlight doesn't fade the carpet.

JOYCE. Someone's got to budget.

SID. Nothing will budge it either, the pattern will be stuck on it a long time after we're gone. Hey, Poppy, do you want to sit on my knee?

POPPY. No thank you.

SID (*to* CLAIRE). If that kid grows up with any weird ideas, I'll kill you.

CLAIRE. Oh really? Not before I kill you, I suppose.

JOYCE. What are you going to do, stab him to death with your 'Women Against Violence' badge?

VAL (*to* SID). Leave her alone.

SID (*to* CLAIRE). D'you hear me?

CLAIRE. Father, your theories of biologically-inherited traits are about as informed as your vocabulary.

SID. Don't sauce me, girl, you're not too big to feel the back of my hand.

CLAIRE. You what?

Enter COLIN.

JOYCE. Ah ha, hello Colin, how lovely to see you. We were just going to make a nice cup of tea – would you like one?

COLIN. No thanks, if it's all the same. It's just that I've left the boys with the neighbours. How are you feeling, Val?

VAL. Fine.

COLIN. Oh well, no worse, that's better. Are you ready?

SID. I know what I meant to say – you didn't show up for that game of arrows last Tuesday.

COLIN. Sorry about that, but I like to spend time with my family.

JOYCE (*to the* WOMEN). What a lovely man. (*To* SID:) He's got better things to do with his money than booze it away, not like some I could mention.

SID. You want to know something, my wife's so mean, when she tried to get the last bit out of the toothpaste tube she broke her foot.

COLIN *feels he has to smile.*

JOYCE. What are you coming as, Les Dawson?

SID. Wish I was.

JOYCE. You know very well that's not true. I cut them in half and use a rolling pin. (*To the* WOMEN:) He loves me really.

SID. I'll tell you another thing.

VAL. Shut up.

COLIN. I think we'd better be making tracks. The boys will probably be demolishing next-door's patio by now.

JOYCE (*to* VAL). Don't worry about your father, he's just trying to do his impression of a river – small at the head and big at the mouth.

COLIN (*to* SID). Can I give you a lift?

SID. Very kind of you, boy. (*To* JOYCE:) Come on then, let's be having yer.

CLAIRE. Bye, Dad.

POPPY. Bye, Grandad.

SID. See you soon, Poppy, Claire.

COLIN. Shall we make a move?

CLAIRE. Take care, Val.

VAL *nods. Exit* VAL, COLIN *and* SID.

JOYCE. We must have a family get-together more often. It's been lovely to see you. Thanks very much for my presents.

POPPY. S'okay. Bye, Nan.

JOYCE *kisses* POPPY *and then* CLAIRE.

CLAIRE. Bye, Mum. And stop worrying.

JOYCE. What else am I supposed to do? What else can I do? Sometimes you forget –

SID (*overlapping, off*). Come on, stop jawing, girl.

JOYCE. Any rate, enough said. Bye. (*Exit* JOYCE.)

POPPY *and* CLAIRE *sit down*.

CLAIRE. Phew.

POPPY. I don't know which one is more crackers, Nan or Aunty Val.

CLAIRE. Val's not crackers, love. She's depressed.

POPPY. What's that?

CLAIRE. It's . . . it's . . . I think it's like when you feel angry but can't show it, so you feel sort of sad.

   Enter JEAN.

JEAN. Coast clear?

CLAIRE. Just about. Where's Riq?

JEAN. He's putting the boys to bed.

CLAIRE. Come on Poppy, I'll run the bath for you.

POPPY. I'll do it.

CLAIRE. Okay. I'll come up for a chat when you're in bed.

POPPY. I'll shout when I'm ready. (*Exit* POPPY.)

CLAIRE. Was your weekend really awful?

JEAN. Worse. How was yours?

CLAIRE. Very quiet, apart from this evening; Mum's beside herself.

   Enter LAWRENCE.

JEAN. We should have locked the back door.

LAWRENCE. I want a word with my wife. Alone.

JEAN. Your wife doesn't live here.

LAWRENCE. Claire. Clever clogs.

CLAIRE. Lawrence, how many more times. This sort of confrontation is s'posed to be done through our solicitors.

LAWRENCE. I want a word with my ex-wife in private.

CLAIRE. Say what you want to say and go.

LAWRENCE. I want to see my daughter then.

CLAIRE. Don't be so irresponsible.

LAWRENCE. It was my turn to have her this weekend.

CLAIRE (*quietly angry*). No, Lawrence, it was your turn last weekend, but you rang up and cancelled it because your wife –

LAWRENCE (*overlapping*). She does have a name you know.

CLAIRE. Abigail had to go and look after her dad.

LAWRENCE. So I should have seen Poppy this weekend.

CLAIRE (*as if to a child*). No, Lawrence, last weekend and next weekend. (*Then.*) For Christ's sake, it's Mother's Day. Even in your perversity, do you not think it's somehow fitting for my daughter to be with me today?

LAWRENCE. You're going to have plenty of time to be sorry enough . . .

JEAN (*coldly*). I thought I told you to leave.

LAWRENCE (*to CLAIRE*). We've got everything sewn up.

CLAIRE. You think?

LAWRENCE. The sordid details are going to make you look unfit to have a goldfish bowl in your care.

CLAIRE. I should have taken an injunction out.

LAWRENCE. Not worth it now.

They both look at him.

Don't worry, I'm going.

Exit LAWRENCE.

JEAN. How many more times?

CLAIRE. At least it will be out of his hands soon. Whatever happens he won't be able to just drop in.

JEAN. I can't believe the way he carries on.

Pause.

CLAIRE (*changing the subject*). Do you think you and Riq will ever live together?

JEAN. You sound as bad as my mother.

CLAIRE. Sound as bad as mine come to that.

JEAN. I've got everything I want from a relationship. So has he, except he has to do his own washing.

CLAIRE. Let's get everything ready for tomorrow.

JEAN. Sunday evening, ugg, work tomorrow, it's so depressing.

CLAIRE. My job's the one thing I've got going for me.

JEAN. And you're good at it. How's po-faced Marion these days?

CLAIRE. She found some obscene graffiti last week. Probably kept her going all weekend.

JEAN. Any excuse for her to go tittle-tattling to the Head. Funny how some people never grow out of attention-seeking.

CLAIRE (*mock dramatic*). And worse, she thought the culprit was one of the lower sixth in my group.

JEAN (*smiles*). Sounds nasty.

CLAIRE. It'll blow over.

JEAN (*getting up*). Come on, I'll set the table, anything to make breakfast more bearable.

Scene Three

The next morning. Breakfast bedlam. JUSTIN, SPENCER and POPPY sit at the table. CLAIRE is trying to clear away as they go along. JEAN *is trying to cut* JUSTIN's *hair.* JUSTIN *and* SPENCER *are fighting over the cut-out model on the back of the Rice Krispies packet.*

SPENCER (*grabbing the packet; to* JUSTIN *so* JEAN *can't hear*). It's mine.

JUSTIN (*screams*). Arhh, he's not getting it, is he Mum? Mum, is he? It's mine. It's mine. I want it. Mum? Mum? Tell him.

JEAN (*twisting* JUSTIN's *head back in position*). Hold still, Justin.

SPENCER. It's my turn, you promised me. Mum, not him, didn't you, you did, you did, in Sainsbury's.

JUSTIN. You liar. She never. It's my turn, put it back, it's mine.

SPENCER (*jeering*). Ha ha hee hee. I've got it now so it belongs to me nar nar.

JUSTIN. It's not, you can't have it. It's still full up. Put it back.

SPENCER. Finders keepers, losers weepers.

JUSTIN. Give it me. Now.

SPENCER. No.

JUSTIN *makes a lunge for the packet. The scissors miss his ear by a fraction.* JEAN *grabs the packet and puts it back on the table.*

JEAN. Just piss off. (*She puts the scissors down and sits to eat her own cereal.*)

JUSTIN (*to* SPENCER). She told you to piss off. Piss off. (*He puts his tongue out.*) She told you to piss off.

POPPY (*telling* CLAIRE). Jean said 'Piss off'.

CLAIRE. Morning isn't the best time for any of us.

SPENCER *has picked up the scissors and is cutting out the back of the packet with little regard for the contents.*

JUSTIN. Mum! Mum! He's doing it, look, look, tell him off.

JEAN (*rounds on* SPENCER *and grabs the scissors*). Behave or I'll cut your head off.

JUSTIN. She's going to do a Henry the Eighth on you.

JEAN. Justin, shut up.

CLAIRE *and* JEAN *sit down to their respective bowls of cereal.*
SPENCER *and* JUSTIN *continue to prod and pinch each other until*
SPENCER *bangs his spoon into* JUSTIN's *bowl of Rice Krispies.*
JEAN, *in response, flicks a spoonful of her cereal into* SPENCER's
face.

JUSTIN (*laughs*). You got paid back.

SPENCER. What did you do that for, Mum? Mum? What did you do that for?

CLAIRE. Jean?

JEAN (*foul mood*). I haven't got three degrees and spent seven years training to be an educational psychologist not to know how to treat my kids.

SPENCER (*wingeing*). You said you would cut my head off.

JEAN. Spencer, talk properly.

SPENCER. And you said 'piss off'.

JEAN. If I hear one more word out of you, you'll be reading about how you drowned in a bowl of Rice Krispies in next week's *Beezer*.

JUSTIN. He couldn't read about it if he was dead.

JEAN. What have I told you about trying to be too clever, Justin? (JUSTIN *opens his mouth to reply*.) I don't care. Shut it. We're late as it is. (*To* CLAIRE:) I'll give you and Poppy a lift if you like.

CLAIRE. Thanks, we'll both get told off if we're not there before the bell.

POPPY. Oh, they don't mind. They know you're a teacher.

CLAIRE. Well, my headmistress knows I'm a mother, but it doesn't seem to work that way around.

JEAN (*to* CLAIRE). What about having time off?

CLAIRE. I've got it all worked out.

JEAN. That's good, well, you know.

CLAIRE. Not that Lawrence wouldn't rearrange the school timetable if he could to make it as awkward as possible all round. Bastard.

POPPY. My dad isn't a bastard. I'll tell him you said that.

CLAIRE. You can Poppy. Sadly, he's heard me call him worse things than that.

JUSTIN. What's a bastard?

CLAIRE. Sorry, Justin, I used the wrong word. I was angry but that word was inappropriate – wrong.

JUSTIN. Yes, but what's . . .

POPPY. When Jean's angry with Riq she calls him a wanker.

CLAIRE (*firmly*). Thank you, Poppy.

JUSTIN. What's a wanker? (*Pause.*) What's a wanker?

CLAIRE (*looks at* JEAN, *who has bowed out of the conversation in favour of charging over the mess on the floor with a carpet sweeper*). It's . . . er . . . someone who err . . . wastes a lot of time on themselves.

JUSTIN (*to* SPENCER). Wanker. Wanker.

SPENCER. Takes one to know one, you are, yourself, you are . . .

JEAN. Right out to the car both of you. (*Brandishing scissors.*) Or I'll make both your nostrils into one.

JUSTIN. Wank off. Wank off.

JEAN. Just one big hole.

The BOYS *run to the door.*

SPENCER. Wouldn't be as big as your mouth.

The BOYS *exit fast.*

JEAN (*shouts after them*). And don't tempt me by playing under the wheels. Stand by the door. (*To* CLAIRE:) I'll just get my things together and I'll be with you. I don't know which goddess is responsible for Mondays, but I could strangle her.

CLAIRE (*helps* POPPY *on with her coat*). Ready, love?

POPPY. She forgot the scissors.

CLAIRE (*smiles*). I think she was only joking.

Scene Four

Staff room. Before school. MARION *and* ANNETTE *are marking exercise books.* CYRIL *is reading the sports pages in* The Times. LINDA *is sorting out arm bands.* ROGER *appears to be trying to mate two paper clips. There is a knock at the door.*

CYRIL (*without looking up*). Go away and come back after the nuclear war or Easter, whichever happens to be the latter.

ANNETTE. Honestly, Cyril, it's lucky they can't hear you.

CYRIL (*mumbles*). Blasted kids.

Another knock.

ROGER. Well, whose turn is it?

ALL OTHERS. Yours.

ROGER. Okay, okay. (*He goes to the door and opens it to* DIANE *and* TERRI.) Yes girls, what can I do for you?

DIANE. We'd like the key to the stationery cupboard in the commerce room.

ROGER. What? (*He looks at his watch.*) Is this shift work? We haven't had assembly yet.

DIANE. Miss Grimble wants some stuff run off and we didn't finish it on Friday.

ROGER. And where's Miss Whatsit Evans who's supposed to be in charge of that room?

TERRI. She's off sick again.

ROGER. Well, I don't know . . .

TERRI. Ahh, go on, Sir.

ROGER. Don't go away. (*He goes to the board, which has various keys on it, and selects one.*)

ANNETTE (*curtly*). Really, I think you should go with them, Mr Cunningham. Keys are not to be taken from this room without being accompanied by the teacher.

ROGER (*defensively*). But Miss Do–da Evans is off sick.

ANNETTE. Precisely.

DIANE. We'll bring them straight back, Miss.

ROGER (*giving DIANE the key*). Here you are, but if we read that the Russian warheads were made from two dozen gross of Her Majesty's drawing pins, we'll know who the culprits were, ha ha!

TERRI (*forcing a laugh*). Thank you, Sir.

MARION (*calls*). Please shut the door.

No response.

CYRIL. They're all born in a barn.

ANNETTE. Someone should make sure the key is retrieved. Those two aren't renowned for their reliability. (*She sighs.*) I don't see why it should always be me. (*She exits.*)

ROGER. Suit yourself, Annette. At the beginning of the day some of us enjoy our little peace.

CYRIL (*mutters*). Piss off.

MARION (*shocked*). Pardon, Cyril?

CYRIL (*smiles innocently*). Piece of sanity.

MARION (*nodding towards the open door*). Some chance with the whole school gawping in.

ROGER (*hotly*). All right, all right, I'm shutting the door. (*He goes over to the door, slams it in* MISS GRIMBLE's *face. She promptly opens it, pushing him out of the way.*) Sorry Miss Grimble, didn't see you there.

Enter BEA GRIMBLE.

BEA (*briskly*). Obviously. (*To the others.*) Morning all.

EVERYONE (*various versions of*). Good morning Miss Grimble.

BEA. Is Mrs Anderson here yet?

MARION. Not so far, Miss Grimble.

BEA. Bother.

LINDA (*helpfully*). It's very unusual. She must have got held up – the buses on Mondays are . . .

BEA. No matter, I'll try and catch her later on. (*She turns to go, then, as an afterthought:*) No more disgusting business in the toilets to report then, Miss Landsdowne?

MARION. Not as far as I am aware, Miss Grimble.

ROGER. Aye, aye, what's this then?

BEA (*coldly*). Since when have the girls' lavatories been your concern, Mr Cunningham?

ROGER (*weakly*). I beg your pardon.

Exit BEA GRIMBLE.

CYRIL. She was looking for Claire on Friday evening as well. Wonder what that's about.

ROGER. I'm more interested in Marion's revelations. (*To* MARION:) Come on, don't keep us guessing.

MARION. I'd have thought Miss Grimble made it quite plain that it was nothing for you to worry about.

ROGER. I'm sure you'll tell me at your own convenience. (*He laughs at his own joke, probably because nobody else does.*)

CYRIL. It's bad enough starting a new week without you cracking on like a crazed cockatoo, Cunningham. Give it a rest.

ROGER. Cyril, you are dry to the point of being wooden.

CYRIL. The rot has set in. What d'you expect? This place is a blight on my life.

MARION. Boys, boys.

Enter CLAIRE.

ROGER (*ever jocular*). Why, if it isn't Ms Anderson at last.

CLAIRE (*fake smile*). Master Cunningham, fancy seeing you here on time.

ROGER. And a bit ruffled you are too. Where have you been hiding him, down the leg of your dungarees?

In fact ROGER has never seen CLAIRE wearing dungarees, but this fits his image of her.

CLAIRE (*ignoring ROGER*). Morning, Linda, Marion, Cyril.

They respond appropriately.

ROGER. Our beloved Virgin Queen was looking for you.

CLAIRE. Typical, the very morning I'm late. What did she want?

ROGER. Didn't say, but it's my bet I'm conversing with the next deputy headmistress.

CLAIRE. Don't talk rubbish.

Enter ANNETTE.

Morning, Annette.

ANNETTE. Good morning, Mrs Anderson.

ROGER (*to CLAIRE*). Anyway, she dropped a bombshell about some goings-on in the girls' toilets and Marion was too abashed to enlighten me. I was wondering if you could put me in the picture.

CLAIRE. I have no idea what you're talking about. Marion?

MARION. I found some graffiti last week.

CLAIRE. Oh, that.

ROGER. Something juicy, I hope it was about me.

MARION. Hardly.

ROGER. Come on, then, you've got us all on the edge of our seats.

MARION (*embarrassed but trying to be nonchalant*). It was a phone number amongst other things . . . for a gay switchboard.

ANNETTE. That euphemism is quite disgusting. It's quite wrecked the poetry syllabus. Instead of being an expression of joy, it's an excuse for muffled titters. Who do you think wrote it

MARION. More than likely one of the sixth form. There's some queer fish in your group, Claire.

CLAIRE. I wouldn't say that.

ROGER. Queer being the operative word. I was only thinking when Diane Collier came to the door that she was a bit butch.

ANNETTE. It doesn't bear thinking about.

CLAIRE (*to* ROGER). Just because she can see through you. In fact she's probably more intelligent than you.

CYRIL (*to* ROGER). That's not saying much.

MARION (*to* ANNETTE). I've always found her strange. Do yo remember that campaign she started in the third year for girls to do metalwork? Luckily it was knocked on the head.

ANNETTE. Humm. She was so good at home economics, but had the audacity to tell me it was boring. At least, I think that's what she meant by announcing it was creatively deflating.

CLAIRE. This is supposed to be the age of equality.

MARION. Whatever it's supposed to be, it's certainly not the age of perversity. Not in this school anyway. We must be on guard for hanky-panky or horseplay.

CLAIRE *picks up a copy of the* Daily Mirror, *which is on the table, and hides behind it.*

ANNETTE. You know, I saw a marvellous version of *Macbeth* a couple of years ago, with Peter O'Toole.

ROGER. Did you pay for him to accompany you?

ANNETTE (*coldly*). He was in it.

MARION. How wonderful.

ANNETTE. Roger, I'm sorry to say this but you make me ill.

MARION (*to* ANNETTE). Go on, dear.

ANNETTE. Mind, not that the blood wasn't ridiculously overdone.

ROGER. I bet you'd have preferred it medium-rare.

ANNETTE (*regardless*). But it brought a whole new perspective to the characters of the three witches, you know, a hint of, er, female intimacy . . . between them . . . which gave a real tinge of reality to their evilness.

CLAIRE's *newspaper twitches.*

CYRIL (*with laboured consideration*). You know when I was at college –

ROGER. Shakespeare was still doing the rewrites.

CYRIL. Cunningham you are more stupid than most of the fourth form.

MARION. Just take no notice, Cyril.

CYRIL. We had an extraordinary woman in our year, trained to be a PE teacher – always wore men's clothes, rumour had it that she wore a truss on the hockey field.

On the words 'PE teacher' LINDA *grabs a newspaper and hides behind it.*

ROGER. You ever heard of pre-penile dementia, Cyril?

CYRIL. It's true.

ANNETTE. In any event, Marion's right, we better keep our eyes well-peeled.

The bell goes.

ROGER (*eagerly*). Unto the breach, dear friends, or fill the gap with our non-sexist teaching.

The others start to make a move. CLAIRE puts the newspaper down.

CLAIRE (*smiles*). I wish someone or something would fill that gap in your face.

ROGER. Ah ha, the pink maiden surfaces from under *The Mirror* – well read?

CLAIRE (*stonily*). What a big wit you are.

Scene Five

The same day. The staff room after school. Everyone except ROGER is collecting books etc. to go home.

ANNETTE. Miss Grimble's having a word with them now, before they go home.

MARION. Were they kissing on the lips?

ANNETTE. Yes.

ROGER. I presume you mean . . .

MARION. Mr Cunningham, you are obscene.

ANNETTE. I can quite believe it of the other one, but not Terri, mean, she's quite attractive.

CYRIL. I don't believe it of Diane. Like I said, this woman at college wore men's clothes and when she played hockey . . .

ROGER. Just because one doesn't wear a codpiece does not necessarily mean avowed heterosexuality.

MARION. There just isn't anything natural about women kissing each other.

CLAIRE (*blurts out in spite of herself*). Oh yes, there is. (*Silence.*) I mean, er, there can be, for comfort, you know, at a funeral or such like.

ROGER. If I dropped dead, would you kiss Marion?

CLAIRE. If you dropped dead, I'd kiss everything in this school, including the dog shit in the playground.

ROGER. You'd do that for me. I'm so honoured.

ANNETTE. Spare us, Mrs Anderson, don't encourage him.

MARION. Ignore him. You know social intercourse only excites him.

LINDA. Anyway, I don't know what you're on about. I practically had to prize Terri off one of the boys from Drylands Park on the playing field this afternoon.

CYRIL. Could have been after his box.

LINDA. The cricket season hasn't started yet.

ROGER. How's that then, you've awakened our games mistress. Interesting to see who comes out to defend what. Next into bat, Mrs Anderson.

CLAIRE. I'm not defending anything. (*She starts to collect her stuff together.*)

LINDA. And I'm off home. Bye all.

Chorus of goodbyes. Exit LINDA.

ANNETTE. It's the parents I feel sorry for.

ROGER. Can't be very fruitful knowing there are bent genes in the family tree.

CYRIL. Luckily they can't reproduce themselves.

MARION. Public tolerance wouldn't trust them with the next generation.

ROGER. Some of them do have children, though.

ANNETTE. Don't be ridiculous, how can they?

CYRIL. You'd be surprised, Annette, there are ways to get round anything these days.

ROGER. Even nature.

MARION. Not many ways round the unhappiness it must cause.

ROGER. I wouldn't worry, Marion, it only affects women who can't get men.

CLAIRE, *bag packed, coat over her arm, is about to slink out.*

ANNETTE. Oh, Claire.

CLAIRE (*startled*). Yes? What?

ANNETTE. I'd almost forgotten. She wants to see you as well, before you go.

CLAIRE. Me? What for?

ANNETTE. I don't know. She didn't say.

ROGER. Oh dear me, what are you teaching them, Mrs Anderson?

ANNETTE. Roger, I hate to say this, but could you please shut your mouth?

ROGER. She'll probably want to see me next, with some winge about there not being enough *Romeo and Juliet* on the syllabus.

MARION. Rest assured, no one in their right mind would want to see you.

ROGER. Just let her try. I'll give her a run for her money.

MARION. And if we're lucky, she'll give you your money and tell you to run. Can I give you a lift, Annette?

ANNETTE. Very kind of you, dear, goodnight everyone.

CYRIL. Come on, Cunningham, buy me a drink down the pub.

ROGER. What? And miss the revelations of Mrs Anderson's hush-hush rendezvous with our revered leader?

CLAIRE. I do not intend to be any longer than I have to. I'm going straight home after the confrontation.

ROGER. Oh go on, tell us, I'll wait.

CLAIRE. You'll be waiting a long time then, won't you? You know your problem, you're all id.

Exit CLAIRE.

ROGER. What's id?

CYRIL. Short for idiot.

Scene Six

The Headmistress's office. DIANE *and* TERRI *stand in front of the desk.* BEA GRIMBLE *sits behind it, fiddling with her fountain pen.*

BEA. This, as it appears to me, is a very serious matter. Would you care to offer any acceptable explanation?

TERRI (*spilling words in panic*). Yes, yes, it wasn't what you think at all. I was, er, like, just daydreaming about my boyfriend, with my eyes shut, you know how you do. Sorry, how one do . . . does?

BEA. No. Do enlighten me.

TERRI. A real good-looking, I mean, clever, intelligent, nice, very decent boy and Diane didn't see me and bumped into me by a mistake and we lost our balance, very silly, really.

BEA. Really. Is that a fact? Because it seems to me that maybe I should introduce school medicals, as everyone lolls round this place with their eyes shut. And tell me, Terri, do you often spend your days in the cloakroom, eyes closed, daydreaming about boys?

TERRI. Oh yes. I mean no. Although I've had hundreds of boyfriends but I'm going steady now with a boy, but I don't let it interfere with my school work.

BEA. I'm very pleased to hear it. What have you to say for yourself, Diane?

DIANE. Not a lot.

TERRI (*quickly*). It's true.

BEA. What is?

TERRI. What I've just said. She means she's got nothing to add.

BEA. Do you speak for Diane as well?

TERRI. No, no. I hardly know her.

BEA. I thought you were good friends?

TERRI. Oh no, that was the third year, second year, well not even in the first year. We were friends at primary school but we lost touch.

BEA. Until today.

TERRI. Yes, no, no, it was an accident, Miss Grimble, you know how clumsy adolescents are.

BEA. Indeed. (*Pause.*) Now, I must get this business straight. I'm sorry but I have to ask you, Terri: did you kiss Diane and umm, have you had an intimate relationship with her or anyone else for that matter?

TERRI (*almost shouts*). Men. (*Then.*) Men, er, boys and then not *intimate* intimate, but you know . . .

BEA. Thank you. That will do. And Diane, will you deign to tell us the truth about yourself?

DIANE. I am a lesbian.

BEA (*quickly*). Terri, you may go.

TERRI *bolts for the door and exits, shutting it behind her.*

I beg your pardon.

DIANE (*slowly*). I said . . .

BEA. Thank you, that will do. What do you mean by walking in here and . . .

DIANE. But Miss Grimble, I know that hypocrisy is a value you don't encourage. Surely you didn't expect me to lie?

BEA. Just what would you have me encourage?

DIANE. I've never felt you would protect, let alone perpetuate prejudice.

BEA. As far as awareness goes I'm taken to be a leading light in this authority, but I don't need to remind you that we are very much stuck in a backwater – though whether this would be tolerated anywhere is doubtful. (*Firmly.*) Now, as long as you keep your private life to yourself, and the subject is never, I repeat, never mentioned in this establishment again – you can go.

DIANE. It's what I am, it's not a hobby that I can keep shut up in an attic, even if I wanted to.

BEA (*controlled*). You will keep quiet. Do you hear me?

DIANE. If I don't say it, who will? We are nowhere in history books, sex education leaves us out, the media makes us into gross caricatures, when society does recognise us, it's only to oppress and . . .

BEA (*the voice of generous authority*). Diane, while it is between you and me, I am prepared to let the matter rest, but once a name is put on it publicly, it will involve condemnation from staff, parents and pupils alike. And once the education authority gets wind, it could affect the whole community.

DIANE (*defiantly*). That's not my problem.

Pause.

BEA. In that case you'll have to be transferred.

DIANE. I won't.

BEA. I'm sure you need no reminding that I am the headmistress of this school, not the inspectorate of people's preference of partner. You will do as I say or leave.

DIANE. But I'm in the middle of my mocks.

BEA. You should have thought of that before you tried to make a travesty of me. Get out of my sight.

DIANE. But . . .

BEA. NOW!

DIANE *exits to find* TERRI *outside*.

TERRI. What happened?

DIANE (*snaps*). Well, I didn't win no luxury cruise to Lesbos.

TERRI. I don't suppose you did, fancy coming out with it like that. What happened to what we agreed to say?

DIANE. I didn't agree to say anything.

TERRI. You said to me to say what I felt best saying.

DIANE. You felt best coming out with all that?!

TERRI. The point is, I got away with it, didn't I? Couldn't you see that old Bea was prepared to accept anything but the truth? Rudest word she's ever heard is pantie-girdle.

DIANE. And that makes you feel better, getting away with what? A load of silly lies.

TERRI (*angry*). Well, I hope you're able to come up with a stronger word than silly because when the others find out, our lives will be hell.

DIANE. That remains to be seen.

TERRI. So all you've proved is that you've got more courage than me. (*She half turns.*)

DIANE. Look, I didn't mean . . .

TERRI. No, and you didn't have to either. (*She exits.*)

DIANE. Terri? (*She goes after her and bumps into* CLAIRE.)

CLAIRE. Hello, Diane, what's happened?

DIANE (*nods towards* BEA's *office*). She reckons I've got to leave.

CLAIRE (*shocked*). Leave?

DIANE. Can you try and explain to her?

CLAIRE. I'm not sure . . .

DIANE (*flatly*). No, I didn't think you would be.

Exit DIANE. CLAIRE *knocks on the door.*

BEA. Come.

CLAIRE *enters the office.* BEA *has tried to regain her air of authoritative calm.*

CLAIRE (*tense*). You wanted to see me, Miss Grimble.

BEA. Ah, Mrs Anderson, do take a pew. I expect you have an inkling as to why I asked you here.

CLAIRE. Well, I . . .

BEA. I did try and get hold of you this morning, but you were rather elusive.

CLAIRE. I'm sorry I was late.

BEA. No matter. I have spoken to Mr Graham at EO6.

CLAIRE. But I was only a few minutes late. I was here by the bell.

BEA. No, no, that is of no consequence. Mr Graham was most understanding, although it's slightly unusual. As from this week I'd like to appoint you as acting deputy head.

CLAIRE. Do what? I mean, pardon?

BEA. With an honorarium to your salary of course.

CLAIRE. I'm sorry. I mean, what a surprise.

BEA. I know you're young, but your qualifications are first class, literally, and you're a very popular member of this establishment with staff and pupils alike.

CLAIRE. Thanks. Err . . . thank you. Thank you very much indeed. It's a great honour.

BEA. If you'll forgive me for saying so, you look quite perplexed. What did you think I was going to say?

CLAIRE. I thought it was about Diane Collier.

BEA. Oh, that wretched child. It's too despicable for words. I've been on to St Saviour's only they won't take her. They say they've got enough sexual perverts without starting a new trend with the girls.

CLAIRE. But . . . (*Carefully.*) I mean . . . with all due respect, isn't that a bit drastic?

BEA. Drastic, no, I don't think so. Heavens, you're not condoning the girl? (*Then.*) Are you?

CLAIRE. Heavens, no, (*Beat.*) no, (*Beat.*) no. It's just that she's very clever.

BEA. Too damn bad. She's got to go.

CLAIRE. But forcing her to go isn't very good publicity.

BEA. It doesn't bode too well, I agree. Now, as acting deputy head, have you got any better suggestions?

CLAIRE. It did occur to me that maybe, if she agreed to see an Ed. Psych.

BEA. Excellent, excellent. I'll call Mr Forthingay.

CLAIRE. No. I mean, I know he's very good.

BEA (*nods*). Knows his stuff.

CLAIRE. But I'm thinking of one who specialises in this sort of thing.

BEA. What's his name?

CLAIRE. Jean, Jean Boyd. She's a woman.

BEA (*disappointed*). Oh.

CLAIRE (*hopefully*). She's got a PhD.

BEA. Very well, I'll leave it in your capable hands and I'll announce your appointment in assembly tomorrow.

CLAIRE. Thank you, Miss Grimble.

CLAIRE *leaves the office, shutting the door behind her, and bumps into* ROGER.

ROGER. So what did she want?

CLAIRE. You'll know soon enough.

ROGER. Go on, you can tell me.

CLAIRE. Go away. (*She starts to walk,* ROGER *trying to keep up with her.*)

ROGER. Luckily, I have more appeal for my students.

CLAIRE. Because your discipline is atrocious.

ROGER. I encourage them subtly, of course, to feel good about themselves.

CLAIRE. Huh, subtlety is an adjective that has escaped your description for the best part of your life.

ROGER. Like today I complimented them by telling them that one of the rewards of teaching A level English was that it attracted mostly girls. Unfortunately in my position it's like looking at a box of chocolates when you're on a diet.

CLAIRE. I hope they reported you.

ROGER. They loved it. Giggles and blushes all round. Had them eating out of my hand. Except that Diane Whatsit girl. D'you want a lift home?

CLAIRE. No, just get out of my way.

Scene Seven

Monday evening. POPPY *and* JEAN *are in the living-room. Enter* CLAIRE.

POPPY. When she comes in I'm going to give her the biggest hug and kiss. Mum. (*She rushes to meet her.* CLAIRE *picks her up and kisses her.*)

CLAIRE. How was school?

POPPY. Horrible. I got told off again for talking and our teacher told us a story about Jesus being nailed to a cross and I said if that was on a film on telly my mum wouldn't let me watch it. But d'you know what? She wanted us to draw a picture of it.

CLAIRE. Oh. What did she say?

POPPY. She said, next time I wanted to butt in, I was to put my hand up.

CLAIRE (*nods*). Uh huh.

POPPY. So I did.

CLAIRE. Oh?

POPPY. I had to. You know what she said next? That Jesus forgave the robbers and muggers that were hanging round him and they went to heaven.

CLAIRE (*shrugs*). That's how the story goes.

POPPY. I said, if someone mugged my Nan I wouldn't forgive them and my Nan would be really mad if they ended up in heaven with her. She would, wouldn't she?

CLAIRE. What did Miss Stokes say to that?

POPPY. Get on and draw your picture. And guess what? Tony Sudenham did one of Jesus and used real blood.

CLAIRE (*shocked*). Whose?

POPPY. He cut his knee at playtime and there was enough for the hands. Show off. Huh, he cried when he fell over, though. The boys mostly did muggers with tattoos but our table didn't. What did you do today?

CLAIRE. Well, I got made acting deputy head.

JEAN *looks up from the book she's reading.*

JEAN. That's fantastic, well done.

POPPY. Brillo, Mum. Now you can boss everyone about.

CLAIRE. Not quite.

POPPY (*jumps up*). I forgot, I forgot. I made a present for you. Wait there. (*She exits.*)

CLAIRE. Thanks for collecting her for me.

JEAN. It's no trouble especially as your meeting with Miss Grimble proved fruitful. That's great news, Claire, couldn't be better.

CLAIRE. Unfortunately, one small cloud on the horizon. Diane came out today . . .

JEAN. Can't you tactfully shut the closet door before she gets flushed away altogether.

CLAIRE. In style, in the headmistress's office, whilst the headmistress was still in there.

JEAN. What is it they say, better latent than never?

CLAIRE. Really, Jean, that's a Roger Cunningham remark!

JEAN. Sorry. Mind, it's a great idea for updating a Bessie Bunter story.

CLAIRE. Beatrix the matrix wants her transferred to St Saviour's.

JEAN. St Saviour's??!

CLAIRE. Only they won't take her.

JEAN. If she's in the sixth form she could leave.

CLAIRE. But she stands to get at least two A levels.

JEAN. Oh, how we cling to academia.

CLAIRE. I suggested that we get an Ed. Psych. in.

JEAN. Are you mad? They're all a bunch of wankers.

CLAIRE. Not just any Ed. Psych.

JEAN. Oh, I'm with you. It's okay by me.

CLAIRE. You know, just nod and mutter a few clichés.

JEAN (*agreeing*). Yes, some large fib about if a fuss is made of this at this stage it could be habit-forming.

CLAIRE. That's it, that sort of thing.

JEAN. Talking of which, I hope you didn't betray yourself.

CLAIRE (*flatly*). Throughout the day I invalidated myself three times. If that's what you mean.

JEAN. And a cock crowed thrice?

CLAIRE. Roger Cunningham visibly preened himself but his feathers will soon ruffle when he hears of my promotion.

Re-enter POPPY with a large piece of paper, rolled up, in one hand, and a book in the other.

POPPY. Here it is. (*Unrolling the paper.*) It's a picture of a woman holding the world still.

CLAIRE. Poppy, it's lovely. Thank you. We'll put it on the wall.

POPPY. Mum, would it be okay if Sharon comes round tonight?

CLAIRE. Yes, I should think so.

Doorbell.

POPPY. That'll be her. (*She rushes to the door.*)

CLAIRE (*laughs*). Just as well I said yes.

POPPY (*off*). Hello Nan, hello Sharon. Mum's in there.

JOYCE. Thank you, Poppy.

JEAN and CLAIRE exchange glances. JEAN gets up as JOYCE enters.

There you are. (*She sees JEAN.*) Oh hello . . .

JEAN (*nods*). Joyce.

JOYCE. That's funny, that's my name too.

JEAN. I know, hello Joyce, my name's Jean.

JOYCE. Oh yes, sorry Jean. You know a friend of Poppy's walked up the street with me.

CLAIRE. Oh, that's Sharon.

OYCE. She looked at me like I was off the telly and said, 'Hey, are you Poppy's Nan?' Like I was wonderful or something.

CLAIRE (*teasing*). You're complaining about that?

OYCE. I just wonder what the child has told her, any rate, that's not the point.

CLAIRE. Do you want a cuppa tea?

OYCE. I didn't come all the way over here to have a cup of tea, did I? That's what you think of me, shut the old girl up with a cup of tea.

CLAIRE. Sorry.

OYCE. I know. I know. But I've been stewing on it all day. Colin had a quiet word with me yesterday and he's so worried about Val. He asked me if I'd pop round this evening because he has to work late but we're not to let on to Val.

LAIRE. We?

OYCE. You get on with her so much better than me. It's just a feeling; I don't know – you know what they're like these medical people – love drama – take you away in the middle of the night, so if you weren't disorientated in the first place, you soon will be, waking up in an ambulance at two in the morning.

LAIRE. They won't be able to take Val to hospital if she doesn't want to go.

OYCE. She just seems to have let go of herself. Please, Claire?

AN. Don't worry, I'll see that Sharon gets home all right.

LAIRE. Okay, Mum, I'll come with you. I'll get my coat and tell Poppy where I'm going.

OYCE. Thanks. (*Exit* CLAIRE. *Silence.*) Claire told me you're one of these psychological people. What do you think about our Val?

AN I don't really know her, but from what I can see, I think she's just unhappy.

JOYCE. Humph. Well, happiness doesn't grow on trees.

JEAN. Nor does powerlessness.

Enter CLAIRE with her coat on.

CLAIRE. Come on, I'm ready.

Scene Eight

VAL's *living-room.* VAL, COLIN, SID JNR *and* WALTER.

COLIN. Right, shall I put these two to bed before I pop out?

VAL (*shakes her head*). No.

COLIN. Don't worry, I'll only be twenty minutes at most. I'm sorry, I've got to get this paperwork back to Tim, it won't wait until the morning. You wouldn't believe how hectic things are at the office. All of a sudden Easter holidays have become very popular.

VAL (*flatly, quietly*). You don't have to spy on me.

COLIN. Val, please . . . love, don't give in to those ideas. (*VAL turns away.*) Believe me, I only want what's best, really. Anything, Val . . . I'd do anything to get you back to your old self. (*VAL nods.*) I'm just at a loss as to what to do. Are you sure you'll be all right . . . you only have to say.

VAL (*nods*). You go.

COLIN. Like I say, I won't be long. Okay, I'm going. (*He puts on a jacket.*) Now Walter, Sid, behave yourselves until Daddy gets back. (*He kisses VAL and exits.*)

COLIN *has left his briefcase behind.*

SID. I'm a condor.

WALTER. I'm a condor.

Both play aeroplanes, making appropriate noises, running round the settee on which VAL sits.

WALTER. Mummy, play. Control over. Come in. Over, over.

SID. Control Tower come in. Mummy! Come in! Mummy!

VAL lies on the settee.

WALTER (*shakes her gently*). Mum, you are the control tower.

SID. She's not.

WALTER. Mummy no good.

SID. Come on. Nice Mum.

WALTER. Sleep. No good.

SID. Mummy runway.

WALTER. Yeah, Mummy play.

They both run round the settee. Then one at a time crawl over VAL, stand on the arm of the settee and jump off. They are about to do it for a second time when VAL grabs WALTER, not viciously, and sits him on the floor. In the tussle a glass of orange juice gets knocked over. WALTER isn't hurt but shocked, wailing.

Ahh, Mummy, ahhhhhhhh, it hurts, it hurts.

SID. Orange gone. Broken. Mummy. (*He starts wailing.*)

Both continue to cry. VAL, helpless, sits, vaguely stroking their hair. SID looks at the glass.

Orange gone.

WALTER. Get nother one.

SID. Play boats, play boats.

WALTER. Yeah.

They both exit to the kitchen. The sound of a scraping chair as they drag it across to the sink and then the sound of a tap running. COLIN re-enters.

COLIN. Forgot the sodding papers, didn't I? (*He picks up his briefcase but is torn by the sight of VAL.*). Val, love, please just talk to me. I don't know what to do, can't you see how much I love you?

VAL. I don't want to take responsibility for this relationship any longer.

COLIN (*gently*). Val, I don't know what you mean. I don't come from a home, a place where relationships were discussed. If anything was wrong something got broken after a lot of shouting, I understand that. How do you expect me to cope with this? No one ever taught me what to do or how to behave, let alone how to respond, it's not the sort of thing that ever gets mentioned in schools. What's the use of knowing that Barnes Wallis invented the bouncing bomb or what SALT stands for, or remembering the French for grapefruit when you've never ever been to France. And nothing, if I could remember it all, nothing would be of help, I learnt nothing that I could apply to my life. (*Pause.*) I love you because you're strong. I never wanted a woman at home who was little more than a servant because that's all my dad knew of marriage. I don't want a wife, not in that sense, but I want you, Val, you, you and the boys – you're all I've got. I'm so proud of you. I want to make this work. Just tell me what to do and I will try. Honest to God, Val, I need you. Can't you . . .

He turns.

Oh hell . . .

He gets up. Exit COLIN.

After a long pause, VAL *gets up. She goes over to the window and smashes her fists and arms through it. The sound of breaking glass prompts* COLIN *to re-enter.*

Christ Almighty. Val. Oh God. (*He crosses to her. Then, gently:*) Now, let's have a look, come on, put your hand over, we've got to stop the blood. Oh why love? (*Looking round frantically for a bandage.*) Where's the plasters? Oh Val, have we got any bandages? (*Opening and shutting drawers.*) I knew we should have bought that first-aid kit when we saw it in Argos. (*He takes off his jacket and shirt and proceeds to wrap the shirt around* VAL's *arm.*)

There, sorry, sorry, come on, we'll have to get it seen to . . . Where are . . . Sid? Walter? (*He exits to the kitchen.*) Get off the table. What did you tell them to do, flood the place? (*He re-enters with* SID *and* WALTER.) Come on, you two get in the car. (*He steers* VAL *with his arm.*) Come on, love. Why? Oh why?

SID. Where are we going? Where are we going?

WALTER. Mummy Mummy.

Enter CLAIRE *and* JOYCE *through the front door which* COLIN *has left open.*

CLAIRE. Sorry, we did knock . . . oh what's happened?

COLIN. At last. Thank God. Why didn't you come earlier?

JOYCE. Val, what have you done? What's she done to her arm, what the hell's happened? Colin, what . . .

COLIN (*nods to the window*). She cut herself. Please could you two stay here and look after the boys.

JOYCE. I'll come with you.

COLIN. Please.

CLAIRE. We'll stay here, Mum. Colin, at least put your jacket on. Now, let's have a look.

COLIN (*feeling his bare chest*). Oh God. (*Putting on his jacket.*) Don't touch that, she's losing blood.

CLAIRE (*swiftly takes the sleeve off the shirt, redoes the bandage so it's tighter*). It's not that bad, it will need stitches though, Val.

COLIN. Please I must get her to hospital.

JOYCE. You're not going to let her stay in hospital, are you? Colin, answer me, are you?

COLIN. I'm not going to have her bleed to death on the carpet.

JOYCE. I'm coming with you.

CLAIRE. No, Mum.

COLIN. No. Stay here. (*He propels VAL through the door. They exit.*)

JOYCE (*shouts after him*). Don't you dare let them do anything but sew the arm up.

SID. Mummy gone. (*He starts to cry.*)

WALTER. Daddy gone. (*He starts to cry.*)

CLAIRE. Only for a little while. They'll be back soon. Come on, come here for a cuddle.

CLAIRE *cuddles* WALTER; JOYCE *cuddles* SID.

JOYCE (*feeling SID's feet*). Their shoes and socks are wringing wet. Poor loves. (*She gets up, finds a towel and dries their feet. She puts clean socks on them then stuffs the shoes with newspaper.*)

CLAIRE. They're almost asleep.

JOYCE. Did she try and slash her wrists?

CLAIRE. No, it was further up the arm. Physically it wasn't bad.

JOYCE. But why?

CLAIRE. Mum. (*Nodding towards the boys.*) We must try and keep calm. I'll take these two up and read them a story.

JOYCE. You're right. I feel so useless.

CLAIRE. You can't do anything until Colin gets back.

JOYCE. You see to them and I'll try and do something to the window.

CLAIRE *exits with* SID *and* WALTER.

While JOYCE *boards the window up, she talks to* CLAIRE *although* CLAIRE *can't hear her.*

I was in Woolworth's the other day. You wouldn't remember when nothing in there was over sixpence. It seemed like magic when I was a child. Until I was caught stealing a bar of chocolate and tasted nothing but humiliation. Mind, it's all changed now, but what hasn't? I don't think they can have any store-rooms in

Woolies, you know, because it seems that all the stock is on the shelves. Rows and rows of the same thing but some of them are still good value. Any rate, I was just comparing the price of the wrap and seal bags when but a few feet away this man went off his nut. I was going to say 'off his trolley' but you might have got confused with shopping trolley and thought I was going to have a dig at the way men don't seem to be in control of the things, let alone what they buy. Do you know that most wives have to write the shopping list in order in accordance to how you go around the shop otherwise you can find a pile-up round the poultry. All it takes is for one of them to be a vegetarian and it needs the assistant manager and a pair of wire cutters to de-mesh them. Anyhow, that's beside the point – this chap didn't even have a basket. He was just stood there standing and he blew a gasket. Flipped. Shouting and screaming words what nobody could make out but sounded like something like 'Alley Waly Gumbroil' and he started smashing his fist over and over the massive piles of soaps so there were bars of Lux, Fairy Toilet, Shield, Imperial Leather – you name it, flying all over the shop. Literally. It was quite a few moments before he was apprehended and, as he launched attack after attack into what was left of the display, so even the plastic price labels attached to the chrome racks started pinging from place to place. I caught myself thinking: let them punch soap all over the show, as long as they don't hit their wives.

Not that any of you have ever been hit by a man, to my knowledge anyway. Colin is such a lamb, isn't he? And it wasn't so long ago that our Val thought God's grand plan meant a Shreiber fitted kitchen. As for Lawrence, he was nothing like he is now. D'you remember he used to wear so many badges that when I saw him without them his shirt had so many perforations I nearly dunked him in a cup of boiling water. Yes, like a teabag it was. Oh, and in the winter he wore those silly loud jumpers with reindeer prancing all over them. Talk about migraine, I tell you, Claire, you was lucky to get away without a brain tumour. Not that I was a hundred per cent, to say the least, behind you leaving him like that, it must have been a real blow to his do-da. But well, before that, mind, he used to make quite an effort to get on with me. Clever that, because I know you're not supposed to have favourites and I treat them all the same – you were always special to me. So he knew what he was doing when you first started going out together. My instinct is to say courting but you all cringe and say, 'Aw Mum, no one says courting these days'. Well, my vocabulary has had a lot of new words prised into it over the years, and you have to be careful because there's a lot of difference between 'going out' and 'coming out'. I tell you sometimes, I get so tongue-tied I don't know whether – but what's that to do with anything. Nothing. Where was I? Oh yes, so he had me sussed out, as they say. Invited me to his bachelor pad for Sunday tea. He apologised for the state of it. Apparently there'd been a party the night before. It was a bit messy and he must have noticed that I was almost wearing myself out sitting still while the hoover lay dormant. So by way of distraction, he told me that someone had arrived with a bottle of sherry which had been made in South Africa and as a matter of principle he'd poured it down the sink. Myself, I couldn't help thinking it was a pity Vim wasn't made in South Africa. His family was worth a bob or two, I can tell you. Well, you could tell for yourself they went to the theatre practically every other week and that, but him, he had no time for it, turned his back and shunned the lot of them, and he was always raving on to me about authentic working-class culture – whatever that is when it's at home. I'd supposed he meant the group of fire-eaters on stilts who blocked the pavement, outside the Town Hall, when Nalgo were on strike.

We are talking about a man who used to call coppers pigs, the Beak – right-wing scum, and the law – by that I mean the legal system the whole shebang – 'a heap of shite'. But being who he is he can use it any way he wants because that's what it's there for and I should know, amount of times he told me.

Not that this turncoat soft-peddling didn't eat at him, because it did. He took his contrary ideas and guilt and inflicted them on a therapist. Didn't last long though. He told me, while I was still speaking to him that is, why he'd jacked it in. 'Huh', I said to him, I said, 'Lawrence, it's a fine to-do, in this day and age when the ultimate in humiliation for a grown man like yourself is when your therapist yawns at you'.

Enter CLAIRE, not having heard a word coherently.

CLAIRE (*impatiently*). Mum, can you keep the noise down. They're asleep.

JOYCE. I'll never understand what came over you. He wasn't such a bad bloke. He might have had some weird ideas but then, let's face it, he wasn't the only one.

CLAIRE (*angrily*). For Christ's sake don't start all that up now!

Scene Nine

Friday morning. Staff room. Breaktime. ROGER eating a packet of crisps. Enter CLAIRE.

ROGER. Good morning, deputy éclaire, our matriarch's mentor and minion.

CLAIRE. Mr Cunningham, as acting deputy head, I must remind you of your place which, were it not for the advantages awarded to the unfairer sex, would be down a lavatory pan.

ROGER. What a superb metaphor. Ms Anderson, one may venture even for you Milton has not lost his uses.

CLAIRE. Indeed he hasn't, I sincerely hope you take after him. (*She drops the book,* The Complete Works of Milton, *which ROGER has open on a table.*) Go blind and wank yourself into oblivion.

ROGER. Fortunately, my paradise isn't lost to a loud-mouthed . . .

CLAIRE. Language, sir, language, we simply cannot tolerate your hot hyperboles in this school.

ROGER *is stopped from shouting any further adjectives by* MARION *entering, followed by* ANNETTE.

CLAIRE (*about to walk past them, to* ROGER). Have a nice day.

MARION. Claire, Claire, have you seen this? (*Brandishing a copy of the school magazine.*)

Enter LINDA.

CLAIRE (*to* MARION). No. (*To* LINDA:) Hello, Linda, how's things?

LINDA (*looking at* MARION). Fine.

CLAIRE *shows no interest in the magazine and* ROGER *takes it from* MARION.

MARION. Liberal teaching methods are to blame. They can't say I didn't warn them.

LINDA. Don't go overboard, Marion, it's simply the agitation of one girl.

MARION. Girl? If you can call her a girl. I'm not aware of any pronouns for neuters. Actually, I supposed you'd be the best person to ask about that, Roger.

ROGER (*looks up, offended*). Just what do you mean by that?

MARION. Is there another pronoun other than he or she?

ROGER. 'It' – no man's land.

MARION. Quite.

ROGER. Anyway, if you'll excuse me. I can't stand here all day discussing the ins and outs of hermaphrodites.

MARION. No, you can't, Miss Grimble's coming.

ROGER. Don't get excited, Marion, she always makes that noise – it's chronic bronchitis. (MARION *looks confused.* LINDA *and* CLAIRE *act as though no one is in the room. A little louder; he continues for the sake of talking.*) What do you call a shiny receptacle from which ale is poured from a great height? – Beer Tricks Thimble.

Enter BEA GRIMBLE *with* CYRIL *in tow. She gives* ROGER *a withering look.*

CYRIL (*as they enter is muttering to* BEA, *who is totally oblivious of him*). And rumour has it, when on the rugger field.

BEA. Please take a seat, I want a word with you all. Don't worry, Miss Pollard is with the sixth form. This is a very serious matter. Ah, Mrs Anderson, would you sit here next to me. (MARION *is forced to change places with* CLAIRE.) Thank you, I'm sorry I've not had time to discuss this with you personally, Claire, but in view of the urgency of the matter, I'm sure you'll understand. Now, have you all seen a copy of the school end-of-term magazine?

MARION. I have, Miss Grimble.

BEA. In view of the fact that I've forgotten my reading glasses amidst the fracas, would you care to read for us?

MARION (*quickly*). No, I would not. (*A look from* BEA.) I couldn't, I couldn't possibly. I mean its sentiment is completely beyond my comprehension.

BEA. Quite likely. Very well. (*She looks at* CLAIRE.)

CLAIRE (*reluctantly*). I'll read it.

BEA. Thank you. (*She hands them all a copy.*) Back page.

CLAIRE. From here?

BEA. Yes. (*She sighs.*) It's not really the sports fixtures that concern us today. (*She nods to* CLAIRE.) Thank you.

CLAIRE (*reads*). Women should never again have to apologise for loving each other. How natural is it to spend your life in service to a man? When I deny through silence I am only reinforcing my isolation. I am a lesbian and I am not alone.

Silence, during which CLAIRE *does not look up.*

BEA (*almost sadly*). I don't think it's too hard to nail down the author of that. There is, however, another piece in the third person. Perhaps we should hear that?

She nods to CLAIRE *but* CLAIRE *passes the magazine to* MARION *who is left with little choice other than to read it.*

MARION (*reads*). It is about time the education system recognised the hypocrisy it transmits while trying to be liberal in its purporting to care for the individual. Its liberalism is total reactionary rubbish and sexist crap. We are not allowed freedom of choice over our sexuality, which if it is different to that as suggested by the hierarchy of this establishment, is evil. We have a right to our identity and we are not going to be silenced by a smack in the gob from this fascist, poxy school.

ROGER (*stifles a laugh*). That's told us.

BEA. You'll be laughing on the other side of your face if I find the culprits, who obviously can't string a sentence together to be in your English A level group. (*Silence.*) Yes, it renders me speechless, what do you make of it, Mrs Anderson?

CLAIRE. I agree, the syntax is foul.

BEA. Is that all you have to say?

CLAIRE. No. (*Slight pause.*) I mean . . . it's dreadful, disgraceful, disgusting.

MARION. I don't understand how it got there.

BEA. Someone or something obviously typed it on to the last stencil and put it back in the pile awaiting duplicating and collating. Although how they obtained the key will, I suppose, remain a mystery.

MARION. Ah, Miss Evans has been off and . . .

BEA. Miss Evans's attendance or lack of it in this school is not the topic under discussion, that is a matter for this evening's Board of Governors meeting. But this (*Jabbing at the article with her finger.*) business must on no account be allowed to get that far. Which is why we are thrashing it out now. Perhaps Mr Cunningham is the best person to enlighten us as to the precise, punctuation aside, meaning of the wording.

ROGER (*studying the wording*). Educational, i.e. learning.

BEA. Don't try and be funny, Mr Cunningham. This is not a merry jape. I am quite aware of the connotations of 'educational', 'hypocrisy', 'sexuality' and 'rubbish'. Neither do I need David Owen to point out the connection between 'liberalism', 'reactionary' and 'fascism'. I am stumbling over poxy.

ROGER. Ah, it's . . . the clap.

BEA. And what's that when it's at home, a new wave dance step?

ROGER. Venereal disease.

BEA. God help us all. Is that rife, as well? It would seem that this institution is nothing but a hotbed of perverted promiscuity.

CYRIL (*thoughtfully, matter of factly*). Rest assured, Beatrice, it is impossible for women to transmit syphilis to one another. The germ can only breed in the heat created by the friction of the erect penis in the vagina.

BEA (*looks as though she might be sick*). Spare us, please.

MARION (*shocked*). Cyril, I thought your degree was in physics.

CYRIL. I am qualified to teach biology, only I always considered it more of a woman's subject.

BEA (*recovered*). Indeed. Thank you, Mr Barrett.

CYRIL. My blood pressure runs amok at the thought of teaching fifth form girls the ups and downs of menstrual cycles.

BEA (*firmly, singsong*). Thank you.

ROGER. On your bike, Cyril.

BEA (*raising her voice*). Mr Cunningham.

ROGER. Poxy, Miss Grimble, is used as an expletive, a swear word. Obviously, the authors or authoresses do not hold the school in very high regard.

BEA. Obviously. (*Slight pause.*) Mrs Anderson came up with an excellent formula for negotiation but it has gone too far for us to put it into operation.

CYRIL. They must be helped in some way, surely.

MARION. I don't know about that – it must be stamped out, this sort of thing breeds like wildfire.

BEA. What do you suggest?

MARION. For what?

BEA. For those who fly in the face of the fabric of society.

CLAIRE. I know it goes against . . .

MARION. It goes against everything decent people hold dear.

CLAIRE. Such as?

CYRIL. God and the family. To name but everything in two.

BEA. Not that the nuclear physics goes against God and the family, I don't suppose, Mr Barrett?

ROGER. Never mind the Holy Trinity. Marion's right, if this thing doesn't get hushed up there's no telling what will happen. It's a real threat to the other girls.

LINDA (*everyone including herself is shocked at this outburst*). You think so? You really think so? You think the possibility so attractive to girls in this school, let alone society, that they will relinquish the security of friends and family? Are you really suggesting that the possibility is so viable that they, with nothing less than gay abandon, will shrug off all social pressures and become outcasts? (*Stunned silence, then half-mumbled.*) Although if they all did they wouldn't be outcasts . . .

MARION. Which is why it mustn't be allowed to get to that.

CYRIL. Oh God, we'll have the papers round here, none of us can handle that.

ROGER. Why should we? This would never happen in a mixed school. I've always said it was unhealthy.

BEA. There is nothing unhealthy about girls failing, Mr Cunningham.

ROGER. That's as may be, but you felt the need to appoint male staff.

BEA. On the contrary, it wasn't me, it was the poxy Equal Opportunities Commission.

ROGER. Oh.

BEA. None of this is solving our dilemma. I want you all to send every girl in the school who could possibly be a (*Slight pause.*) whatever, if you follow my drift, to me.

CLAIRE. With all due respect, Miss Grimble, that could implicate all the girls in the school.

BEA. I hardly think so.

LINDA. It might be just the one girl. We don't actually know that there's more.

BEA. We cannot afford to take that chance my dear. There is definitely more than one style of writing and too many leaks can sink the ship.

MARION. We don't know who'll get hold of this. (*Brandishing the magazine.*) Anyone could read it.

BEA. Precisely. That's why those responsible must somehow be rounded up and be seen to be punished.

MARION. I suppose if they mean what they say they'll become visible to us. I mean hold a meeting. Shouldn't be hard to find them.

BEA. Good. Good. Thank you, Miss Landsdowne. With a bit of luck we'll be shot of this matter before the end of term. From now until then I'd be very grateful if we could have all hands on deck. Anything suspicious, send them to me. (*She gets up.*) Is that clear?

Various responses of 'Yes' with varying degrees of enthusiasm. BEA GRIMBLE crosses to the door and opens it.

ROGER (*mutters*). What a gay day.

BEA (*turns*). Mr Cunningham, you are provoking me beyond the pale. (*Parting shot.*) Humm, poxy? Old-fashioned words for me are just as sufficient. Nincompoop seems to fit the bill adequately in your case.

She exits.

CYRIL (*gets up and stumbles after* BEA, *mumbling*). Miss Grimble, if I could have a word with you about the blocked Bunsens.

CLAIRE (*more to herself than anyone in particular*). I just don't believe this.

MARION. Miss Grimble's right, though, this matter's got out of hand.

ROGER. Or in hand, depending on how you see it.

MARION. It's a good job Annette isn't here, as she'd be sorry to have to say how you make her feel.

ROGER. Huh, well, what a good thing we haven't got an Easter pantomime. The poor creature playing Mary Magdalene would well and truly be in the spotlight.

MARION. Don't be stupid. Anyway she was always washing our Lord's feet.

ROGER (*mimicking* BEA GRIMBLE). Oh, Miss Landsdowne, don't tell me foot fetishes are rife as well? I'm so pleased to see you're not taking this lying down. Come along now, ladies, time to get your fingers out. (*He laughs and exits.*)

MARION. Shame he couldn't marry Miss Evans and catch whatever it is she's got.

LINDA. The shame of it is that it couldn't be terminal.

MARION. Really now, Linda, that's nasty. I wouldn't wish that on anyone. (*She looks at her watch.*) I could put the couple of minutes before the bell to worse use than a quick cruise round the sixth hangouts. (*She exits.*)

CLAIRE (*still holding the magazine*). What am I going to do?

LINDA. Don't look at me.

CLAIRE. Not unless there was a hundred per cent rebellion and every girl in the school said she was gay.

LINDA. Could you have agreed to that when you were their age?

CLAIRE. No. The only common denominator is silence.

LINDA. I don't know how you can say that with this screaming up at you. (*She takes the magazine from* CLAIRE *and drops it on the table.*)

(*Interval.*)

Scene Ten

Hospital day room. VAL *sits in a chair doing the crossword. Enter* CLAIRE.

CLAIRE. Hi.

VAL. Not particularly.

CLAIRE. Sorry.

VAL. Take no notice. If madder only had one 'd' it would be an anagram of dream.

CLAIRE. Armed with unfulfilled ones.

VAL. Something like that. (*She puts the paper down.*) What about you?

CLAIRE. Oh, all right. (*Pause.*) Well, I might have been if one of the girls hadn't come out at school; that could have been copeable-with only, to that headcase of a man I had the misjudgement to marry, getting married means that nothing stands in his way of getting Poppy, even though he never bothered to see her for three years, even though he's unreliable about access now, that matters nothing except of course that I will be forced through a farce which masquerades as justice. It wouldn't be so bad if an article hadn't appeared in the school magazine, which apart from repercussions to my job (*She stops herself.*) Sorry, Gawd, listen to me. Maybe you and I should swop places.

VAL. Maybe we're in the same boat.

CLAIRE. Here I am trying to prove what a normal mother I am.

VAL (*raising her voice*). Where are the 'normals'?

CLAIRE. Shush, keep your voice down.

VAL. Where are they, this invisible minority who can put their hands together and thank God every morning that they were born one of the great, white, washed normals?

CLAIRE. They sit in judgement, perched on benches, tightly permed, decaying wigs balanced on their heads. Looking like ten-stone owls.

VAL. If it wasn't so serious it would be ludicrous.

CLAIRE. We seem to be caught in a horrendous fairy-tale.

VAL. Huh, that's true, the doctors in here are clones of the Brothers Grimm. Mum tells me you and her had words.

CLAIRE. Words, huh. Screams more like. We had a furious row. What did she go and bother you with that for?

VAL. Because she's afraid for you.

CLAIRE. Well, she should try and do something about it instead of finding fault all the time.

VAL. You know, you were always her favourite.

CLAIRE. Rubbish. I'm the scapegoat. She just launched into why didn't I stay with Lawrence and God knows what.

VAL. Well, I've asked her to bring some make-up in for me.

CLAIRE. Oh?

VAL (*with irony*). Seems that you get on better in here if you spend an hour in front of the mirror each morning. And Mum was over the moon about me starting to take an interest in myself again.

Scene Eleven

School corridor. Lunchtime. CLAIRE approaches a classroom door which has a notice saying 'Meeting – girls only' on it. A lot of voices can be heard above the noise of a record which is playing in the background. The impression should be of about twelve girls in the room.

CLAIRE (*opens the door*). Shut that thing off. (*The record player is turned off.*) What is the meaning of this? Now, get out of here and play tennis or something. Go on, file out of the other door quietly. Now. Not you, Diane, would you please come here?

Pause. DIANE comes out of the room. CLAIRE shuts the door behind her, takes the notice off the door, folds it and hands it to DIANE.

DIANE. Miss?

CLAIRE. Have you gone stark staring crackers?

DIANE. No.

CLAIRE (*now calm*). Let's talk sensibly about this.

DIANE. All right, you first.

CLAIRE (*firmly*). What is all this about?

DIANE. Haven't you read the school magazine?

MARION, a pile of exercise books under her arm, crosses from left to right and comes within earshot of DIANE's next speech.

CLAIRE (*noticing MARION and talking more softly*). Try to be . . .

DIANE (*angry*). No. I'm not going to try to be anything, least of all forcing myself to act normal. I hate the word, normal is a lie. You're always on about change, well I don't know about you, but I intend to change things.

Exit MARION.

CLAIRE. Standing in the dole queue won't change much. The only way to change the system is from within.

DIANE (*flatly*). Cop out.

CLAIRE. You think so?

DIANE. Every day making another compromise until you become so demoralised you hate yourself. (*Long pause.*) What about all those thousands of women who were burnt as witches? It was you who told us that it was because they were independent and men were frightened of them. (*Silence.* CLAIRE *still doesn't respond*). What are you thinking?

CLAIRE. Something stupid, like how nice to be seventeen when the only dirty word is 'compromise'.

DIANE. You're only a generation away.

CLAIRE. A generation? Bloody cheek.

DIANE. You going to grass on us all then?

CLAIRE. I'm going to have to think about it.

DIANE. Thank you. (*Exit.*)

Enter MARION. *She crosses to* CLAIRE.

MARION (*conspiratorially*). I've notified Miss Grimble, she wants to see you in her office after school.

CLAIRE (*extremely angry, coldly*). Thank you, Marion. Do you not think I am capable of my own dirty work?

Scene Twelve

BEA's *office. Enter* CLAIRE.

BEA. Good work. I hear you caught the lot of them at lunchtime, in the act, I mean red-handed. I mean, you know, at this meeting, whatever. (*Pause. She starts again.*) Have you made a list of names?

CLAIRE. No.

BEA. Right, let's do that now. (*She pulls up a chair by the corner of the desk so they are sitting almost next to each other. She indicates* CLAIRE *to sit, which she does. Silence.*)

CLAIRE (*slowly*). Miss Grimble.

BEA. Beatrice, my dear, in the confines of this room.

CLAIRE. Miss. Beatrice, Beatrice.

BEA. Yes?

CLAIRE. Do you think this is all really necessary?

BEA. Oh? Don't tell me all this will disappear by itself. That the Easter vac and a gorged dose of chocolate egg will put the equilibrium back in their defective hormones.

CLAIRE. It's just that we are committed to an anti-sexist policy in this school and . . .

BEA. We are, we are and I am the living proof of that, am I not? They wanted a man for this job. Oh yes, they did, you know. Ludicrous, isn't it? However, that is an aside and nothing whatsoever to do with these rampant flauntings.

CLAIRE. But Miss Grim . . . Beatrice.

BEA. Call me Bea . . . all my friends do.

CLAIRE. I don't . . . it's a question . . . I feel we . . . that I, that is . . .

BEA (*kindly but with laboured patience*). Claire, it's Friday evening and I'm sure we both have better things to do. Now let's make a list of the names and get it over with. (*She picks up a pen.*) First off, Diane Collier, we all know that.

CLAIRE (*snaps*). No.

BEA. Come on now, she told me herself.

Long pause.

CLAIRE. You're going to have to put my name at the top of that.

Silence.

BEA (*stunned*). You mean? I hope you don't mean what I think you mean. Do you? I mean, what do you mean?

CLAIRE. Just that.

BEA (*shakes her head*). No.

CLAIRE (*nods her head*). Yes.

BEA. Hell fire, it's an endemic. (*Then.*) No, no, you can't be, you're married and . . .

CLAIRE. Divorced. Don't you mean epidemic?

BEA. And you've got a little girl. What nonsense. I know what I mean, it's your vocabulary that's flagging.

CLAIRE. I left my husband to live with a woman. Anyway, it's not a disease of any description.

BEA. Yes, yes, plenty of women do that, doesn't mean a thing. Cheaper way to live. I'm all for frugal living.

CLAIRE. Because I wanted a relationship as well as . . .

BEA. Claire, let's just pretend you didn't say that.

CLAIRE. I don't feel any of us should have to pretend anything.

BEA (*sharply*). Are you still living with her?

CLAIRE. No, she . . .

BEA. And do you have a . . .

CLAIRE. No.

BEA (*relieved*). Well, then you're in the clear.

CLAIRE. Just because I don't have a lover doesn't mean I'm not a lesbian.

BEA (*quickly*). Still in my book you don't qualify to go on this piece of paper.

CLAIRE (*quietly*). Can't you see that I have to.

BEA. 'A man's got to do what a man's got to do.' Hardly seems the logical or appropriate cliché for your argument. Claire, I won't let you throw your career away like this.

Long pause.

CLAIRE (*tentatively*). You don't have to.

BEA. What option have you left me?

Pause.

CLAIRE. The same one I had.

BEA. I don't understand.

CLAIRE (*deep breath*). Forgive me. I think you do.

BEA. I'm all ears.

CLAIRE (*bravely*). Come on. Everyone knows you live with Miss Hemingford.

BEA. Really!! For your information Florrie's fiancé was killed in the war.

CLAIRE. That was forty-five years ago.

BEA. She was devoted to him. Absolutely devoted to him.

CLAIRE. I'm sorry but . . .

BEA. As well you might be. Marching in here suggesting that I am the Queen Bea of this business. I suppose according to you, we should get the authorities to rename this school 'Radclyffe Hall'. Have you any idea of what you're saying?

CLAIRE. I think so.

BEA. Do you really expect me to take this on board?

CLAIRE (*clearly*). Yes. (*Slight pause.*) Yes, I do.

Long, long pause.

BEA (*quietly*). Florrie and I do live together but not for as long as you would think. Before that, I had a very long-standing friend (*She corrects herself.*) relationship, but she died in a car crash in 1956.

CLAIRE. There really is no need.

BEA. Apparently there is. (*She shrugs.*) Long time ago now, probably the year you were born. I threw myself into my work and I am aware that I sail round the place with an air of bright bluffingly calm, occasionally desperate authority, but it is an act I can hide in and indeed at that time I relied on it for the sake of my sanity. I cannot afford to let myself get caught in the undertow. Do you understand?

CLAIRE. That. Yes. But, Bea . . .

BEA. After the accident she was in hospital for three weeks before she died. During that time my presence went unacknowledged. I wasn't allowed to see her. (*With irony.*) – only close family. And I was left with a sense of grief that couldn't be shared and an overwhelming feeling of utter – (*But she stops herself and then, firmly.*) And today, twenty-seven years later I am certainly not about to jeopardise my pension.

CLAIRE. But, I don't see . . .

BEA (*coldly*). So if you persist in this course of action you leave me very little alternative other than to ask for your resignation.

CLAIRE. You could sack me.

BEA. No, Claire, don't ask me to do that. Please think about it over the weekend.

CLAIRE. Will you?

Exit CLAIRE.

Immediate blackout.

PART TWO

Scene One

CLAIRE *has collected* POPPY *from school. On their way home they have stopped to feed the ducks in the park.*

CLAIRE. Poppy, you're very quiet. Has something happened? (*Pause.*) Did you get told off today? (POPPY *shakes her head.*) Well, that's good. It wasn't swimming today, was it? We didn't forget your swimming things? (POPPY *shakes her head.*) You've not said much about the weekend. Tell me a bit more about the fair.

POPPY. It was okay.

CLAIRE. Poppy, what's the matter?

POPPY. I think I'm depressed.

CLAIRE. Oh dear. Why do . . .

POPPY (*blurts out angrily*). Dad said I was going to live at his house forever and that you were a filthy pike.

CLAIRE (*gently*). What did you say?

POPPY. I said, 'She hates fish and you can go stuff yourself.'

CLAIRE. Poppy!

POPPY. Well, you aren't dirty, I didn't tell him about you leaving your knickers in the sink.

CLAIRE. Did he say anything else?

POPPY. Yes, lots, I nearly forgot that I loved him.

CLAIRE. I know we've talked about this a lot before, and you know I don't like your father much.

POPPY. He can't stand you either.

CLAIRE. That's sort of fair, isn't it?

POPPY (*agreeing*). S'pose so.

CLAIRE. And I left him when you were young and nobody ever asked you what you wanted.

POPPY. Huh, I was only a baby.

CLAIRE. Do you understand why all this happened?

POPPY (*flatly*). No, I don't.

CLAIRE (*smiles*). I mean what's happening?

POPPY. Dad is going to court because he wants me to live with him.

CLAIRE. Yes . . .

POPPY. But I've told everyone that I want to stay with you.

CLAIRE. And that's what I want – more than anything – but other people are going to decide for us.

POPPY. Why? It's none of their blimming business.

CLAIRE. Because your Dad won't give in and neither will I.

POPPY. I don't know why they're bothering because I'm staying put. Nobody can make me go.

CLAIRE. What I'm trying to say is that we don't have the power to decide.

POPPY. It's all such a mess.

CLAIRE. Yes. (*Smiles.*) You know, sometimes you sound just like your Nan.

POPPY. Why don't you and Nan have a fight with Dad? Nan would win 'cos she told me she keeps a Jif lemon in her handbag for muggers.

CLAIRE. Sometimes I don't know whose side she's on.

POPPY. Mine. I'd run away, you know. (*Emptying the last few crumbs from the bread bag. Then to the ducks:*) Okay, swim off. It's all gone.

CLAIRE. Perhaps we'll have a longer chat after supper. Do you want to go home?

POPPY. Yeah, the ducks are bored of us now.

Exit CLAIRE and POPPY, hand in hand.

Scene Two

Staff room. Lunchtime. MARION and ANNETTE are seated, packed lunches in Tupperware containers on their laps. CYRIL stares into space, a CND pamphlet in his hand. ROGER eats a banana. LINDA is mechanically bouncing a tennis ball against the wall.

ANNETTE. Frankly, I'm surprised she bothered to turn up at all.

MARION. The nerve. It was an oversight on Miss Grimble's part not to have suspended her in the first place.

ANNETTE. Linda, could you stop that please, the continuous thud, thud, thud is giving me a head.

LINDA stops.

MARION. She was obviously behind them.

LINDA throws the ball once again against the wall.

ROGER (*with a mouthful of banana*). Surely that only applies to queer males.

ANNETTE. I'm sorry to have to say this, Roger, but your mouth should carry a government health warning.

Enter CLAIRE. Silence.

CYRIL. I must congratulate you on your new life, I never realised you had that sort of bent. Mind, it's very precarious trying to make a living out of the stage.

ROGER. No, Cyril, she's not a thespian, you dozy cart-horse.

CYRIL. Oh, that's funny . . . there was this girl at college . . .

CLAIRE. Thanks, Cyril, but I don't bother with jock straps, not in the warm weather, you know.

CYRIL (*shrugs*). D'you know something, nobody ever bothered much about sex until 1960.

ANNETTE. People have been bothering about reproduction since long before you or I were born.

ROGER. We don't need any reminding. It's us that educates the product.

CYRIL (*incensed by the atmosphere*). Shall I tell you something? I might as well because I retire at the end of the summer term, and the nub of it is that I've hated every day of it.

ROGER. Steady on, Cyril.

CYRIL. Oh yes, and I know what they call me – Polly Mr Barrett, Polly Parrot and the only privilege I ever enjoyed was reading their names out of the detention book in assembly. I've seen generations of kids when all LSD meant to them was pounds, shillings and pence through the acid summer, when all that conjured up for them was litmus paper. Eras have come and gone. And what happens? They internalised the cliché of our times and spend their lives running scared. And whose fault is it then that they vote Tory? Ours.

ROGER. Not all of them are Conservatives.

CYRIL. Not for the want of ramming an ever-narrowing definition of choice down their necks so that it can be interpreted for 'status quo' and today, today, I took this (*Indicating the pamphlet.*) to discuss nuclear physics with the A level group and they looked at me as though I'd just announced the Pope had the clap. All but two of them thought the nuclear deterrent absolutely necessary and those two are in Mrs Anderson's tutorial group. Teaching is supposed to be about enabling development to make choices, not being trained by a parrot to recite received information. I don't care what you are, Claire, you're a bloody good teacher, which is more than anyone will ever say of me – surgical support and all.

CYRIL *gets up – crosses to the door.*

ROGER. Where are you going?

CYRIL. Pub.

ROGER. I'll stand you a pint.

ROGER *and* CYRIL *exit.*

MARION. Seems the whole place is erupting. I for one can't loll about here all day. (*She gets up.*)

ANNETTE. Neither can I. (*Crossing to the door with* MARION.)

MARION *and* ANNETTE *exit, leaving the door ajar.*

LINDA. Was it worth it?

CLAIRE. I almost got a standing ovation from Cyril.

LINDA. So what? I didn't exactly see him making a bee line for Grimble's office.

CLAIRE. Or Roger Cunningham leaping up and down about NUT regulations.

LINDA. Actually, I don't know why they're here.

CLAIRE (*shrugs*). Nor do I. Except to give Annette and Marion something to cling on to.

LINDA. Them, they're so . . . words fail me . . .

CLAIRE. They do take the theory of false consciousness a bit far.

LINDA. That's a polite way of putting it.

CLAIRE. Marion is jealous – she thinks she should have been made acting deputy – and Annette is afraid.

LINDA. Yes, much too dangerous an atmosphere for the likes of us. Why did you do it?

CLAIRE. I was beginning to feel very guilty about being a Judas.

LINDA. I wouldn't have imagined you worrying about any character in the Bible.

CLAIRE. If I'd had the courage of those girls, at their age, everything would have been different.

LINDA. You think? This won't make any radical change except to the lives of those involved, they'll have to leave, eventually get one job, if they're lucky, after another, until they learn to conform. Go and explain to the Queen Bea that it was a mistake, an experiment, in pupil–teacher empathy.

CLAIRE. No. I've said what I've said.

LINDA. Now you're quoting Pontius Pilate, only at least he didn't crucify himself.

CLAIRE. All I did was tell the truth.

LINDA. Claire, please don't drag me into this. I couldn't cope.

CLAIRE. I'm not about to drag anyone anywhere.

LINDA. It would be much worse for me.

CLAIRE. How do you make that out?

LINDA. Use your head, I see them in the showers for Christsake, besides it would kill my mother.

CLAIRE. And I've got to fight for custody of my daughter.

LINDA. Christ, Claire, I didn't realise.

Enter ROGER. *He hovers. Exit* LINDA.

ROGER. Err, hi, you still here?

CLAIRE. No, this is an apparition. I thought you were supposed to be down the pub.

ROGER. I changed my mind. Claire, I know you won't believe me, but I'm sorry, I mean, I've always liked your spirit, always have, but I overheard about your daughter.

CLAIRE. You're the limit.

ROGER (*long pause*). Look, Linda, well, she's one thing, you're different.

CLAIRE. You're not . . .

ROGER. No, I've told you. Her secret's safe with me, you forget I'm one of the Rolling Stones generation. I've done things that would make your hair curl.

CLAIRE. Save it for your memoirs.

ROGER. Linda, well, it's obvious about her but you, I mean, you've been married, got a little girl, we all fancy a change from time to time. Monogamous sex can get boring.

CLAIRE. I'm sure you'll understand that I don't have any energy to put into your problems.

ROGER. Okay, I know you're bitter but I do like you. You must know I've always been attracted to you.

CLAIRE (*genuinely aghast*). I had no idea. I thought our feeling for each other was one of mutual dislike.

ROGER. Ah, this sad little boy's inability to express himself.

CLAIRE. Please spare me.

ROGER. Claire . . .

CLAIRE. Perhaps we could change the subject?

ROGER. Listen, if I was to say on oath in court that I was having a relationship with you, there would be no problem.

CLAIRE. You'd do that for me?

ROGER. Yes, I would. We'll have to go out to the pictures or somewhere and then the evidence would tally.

CLAIRE. I've misjudged you. (*She turns.*)

ROGER. And then perhaps, depending on evidence, genuinely consummate it.

CLAIRE (*almost speechless with rage*). You bastard. (*She exits, slamming the door.*)

Scene Three

CLAIRE's living-room. POPPY, in dressing-gown, sits on CLAIRE's lap.

POPPY. Can we get on with the story now?

CLAIRE. Where are we? (Opening the book.)

POPPY. We haven't even got to the bit about what they chose for themselves.

CLAIRE. Are you ready? (She reads.) Psyche went home to plead for a husband. Demeter and Persephone were astounded by such a strange desire, yet they knew it must be satisfied. In secrecy, for such a thing had never before happened, Psyche was married to Eros – to Love himself, to Cupid, Aphrodite's son. Psyche lived alone with her husband, in a splendid palace, set high on a nameless mountain. Silent, invisible servants brought her whatever she wished. At night, and only at night, Love came to visit: Psyche's husband, but she didn't know who he was or what he looked like. Love had warned her never to look at him, but to love him in ignorance.

POPPY (sleepily). What is ignorance?

CLAIRE. It means not knowing.

POPPY. Go on.

CLAIRE. Athena never returned to her mother's house. Instead she went straight to Zeus, the god of gods, and proposed a bargain much to his vain and clever liking: to be reborn of him. She asked him to become her mother. And so Athena became twice-born, the second time of a man. She emerged fully grown from Zeus's head, wearing the armour she so desired. This daughter of Demeter seemed to have no memory of her earthly female origins. (Pause.). Are you asleep?

POPPY (almost asleep). No, no. Go on.

CLAIRE. Artemis, the youngest of Demeter's daughters, returned to her mother's house. First she had Demeter consecrate her to the moon, so that no matter how far she'd have to wander, she would never forget, never betray. (*She looks at* POPPY.) Poppy? (POPPY *is asleep.*)

CLAIRE *carries* POPPY *out in her arms.* LAWRENCE *enters followed by* JEAN.

JEAN. She's upstairs with her daughter.

LAWRENCE. Good, excuse me.

JEAN *stands in front of the door.*

JEAN. She'll be down in a minute.

LAWRENCE. Let me past.

JEAN. Lawrence, you shouldn't be here at all.

LAWRENCE. Just keep out of this.

JEAN. Sit down if you must but you're not getting past me – not unless you want to appear twice in court on Friday.

LAWRENCE (*reluctantly sits down*). Your affidavit had better be good because we're going to make mincemeat out of the fact that you chose to live with a sordid pervert.

JEAN (*moves away from the door*). I am quite capable of holding my own, Mr Anderson.

LAWRENCE. I'm sure you are.

JEAN. Look, Lawrence, Claire hasn't done anything wrong.

LAWRENCE. Oh no? Only turned my own daughter against me.

JEAN. That's not fair, she's always seemed very unbiased. Much more than I'd have been.

LAWRENCE. You just keep out of this or I'll drag you in.

JEAN. Don't be ridiculous.

LAWRENCE. You won't be so smug if you get publicly labelled a 'practising lesbian ed. psychologist'.

JEAN. I am practising as neither. I am a fully fledged educational psychologist and a sordid, perverted heterosexual.

LAWRENCE. You'll have difficulty proving it.

JEAN. I have a well-oiled boyfriend.

LAWRENCE. That wimp from some 'Men Against Sexism' group. The only thing you two practise together is probably Yoga positions.

JEAN. In your position perjury is not going to . . .

Enter CLAIRE.

CLAIRE. Lawrence? What are you doing here?

LAWRENCE. A word with you. In private.

CLAIRE. It's all right, thanks, Jean.

Exit JEAN.

I think you've caused enough trouble.

LAWRENCE. Me? I've caused enough trouble?

CLAIRE. Yes, I didn't know you'd turned into a parrot.

LAWRENCE. It's not me who's taught Poppy to be foul-mouthed.

CLAIRE. I beg your pardon?

LAWRENCE. My own daughter, my own flesh and blood, told me, her own father, to get stuffed.

CLAIRE. She was upset.

LAWRENCE. So, when she's upset, she goes round telling everyone to get stuffed?

CLAIRE. I suppose you like her to bottle it all up, smile sweetly and pretend nothing's wrong, like your idea of the ideal model for adult behaviour.

LAWRENCE. She's too old for her years. The kid's had no life, no childhood. A mother who has no time for her.

CLAIRE. That's not true, Lawrence, and you know it.

LAWRENCE (*calmly*). I'm only thinking of Poppy, believe me.

CLAIRE (*quietly but firmly*). Why don't you ask her what she wants?

LAWRENCE. Waste of time, you've well and truly poisoned her mind.

CLAIRE. That's not fair.

LAWRENCE. Too right it's not.

CLAIRE. I know we haven't turned out the best of friends.

LAWRENCE (*sourly*). Ha bloody ha.

CLAIRE. But I never thought it would turn out like this.

LAWRENCE (*wistfully*). It was you who thought happily ever after was a cheap empty dream.

CLAIRE (*quietly*). And I was right.

LAWRENCE. It didn't have to be like that. I didn't go off with anyone else.

CLAIRE (*softly*). No.

LAWRENCE (*with total sincerity*). And I still miss you. You know, we had some good times together, didn't we? It wasn't all bad. You used to make me laugh. Sometimes, I still think you were the only real person I ever knew.

CLAIRE. Then why? Why put me through all this then?

LAWRENCE. Because I miss Poppy too. She's my daughter as well.

CLAIRE. But she's lived with me all this time, you agreed access when we got divorced.

LAWRENCE. I can give her so much more now and I want . . .

CLAIRE. You mean now you've got married again.

LAWRENCE. Yes, that's partly it.

CLAIRE. What can you give her, Lawrence, done purely out of motives of what you can take from me?

LAWRENCE. It will mean she'll have an ordinary home like other kids and not have to cope with snide remarks.

CLAIRE. She can fend for herself.

LAWRENCE (*reasonably*). Only because she doesn't know anything else. I love her.

CLAIRE (*firmly*). So do I.

LAWRENCE. I really don't want to put you through this, believe me.

CLAIRE. Then don't.

LAWRENCE. It's nothing to what you've put me through.

CLAIRE Don't be so stupid.

LAWRENCE (*bitterly*). Always quick on the put-downs, weren't you? Well, we'll see just how well they stand up in front of an audience.

CLAIRE (*awkwardly*). Please, Lawrence, you know I'm not . . .

LAWRENCE (*with conviction*). You know I'm going to win.

CLAIRE. You know Poppy means everything to me. You can keep anything, take anything, but not this, let me keep Poppy.

LAWRENCE. It's up to the courts to decide now.

CLAIRE (*with quiet dignity*). You can change your mind. Anything else, you can have anything else.

LAWRENCE. Can I have you back?

CLAIRE. Oh, Lawrence. That's impossible.

LAWRENCE. Well, then. Can't you see I have to go through with it?

Exit.

CLAIRE. Lawrence?

The front door slams. Pause. Enter JEAN.

JEAN. You all right?

CLAIRE. Yes, I think so.

JEAN. What did he want?

CLAIRE. I don't really know.

JEAN. What happened?

CLAIRE. I don't really want to talk about it. How was your weekend?

JEAN. All right, what did you do?

CLAIRE. Oh, I saw Val.

JEAN. How is she?

CLAIRE. She'll be home by the weekend.

JEAN. That's good. What will she do?

CLAIRE. I'm not sure, I don't think she is either. I couldn't concentrate properly because it looks like I earned the sack.

JEAN. What?

CLAIRE. It's still a no-win situation. Miss Grimble refuses to sack me. I refuse to resign.

JEAN. What?! What for?

CLAIRE. A small matter of non-pacification over Diane Collier.

JEAN. Are you a complete babbling wally?

CLAIRE *looks at her.*

And for what – for one moment's satisfaction – riding high on the crest of a wave of martyred idealism.

CLAIRE (*coldly*). I can do without the objective heterosexual polemic. Thank you.

JEAN. Claire, in the name of whoever, you're supposed to stand before agents of the state.

CLAIRE. Agents of the devil.

JEAN. That they might be but they won't take too kindly to you telling them to go to hell – you've got to say what a responsible job you've got – how you've got everything going for you and you chuck it all up for a moment's unstable heroism.

CLAIRE. That might be how it appears to you. Anyway the court shouldn't find out unless Lawrence has hired tell-tale Marion Landsdowne as a private detective.

JEAN. For God's sake, Claire, compromise your principles.

CLAIRE. It's not a principle we're talking about. It's me. And what do you think I've done. I've compromised myself so much I've lied my way out of existence.

JEAN. Then why wreck it over some headstrong schoolgirl who probably wouldn't bother to turn round to thank you?

CLAIRE (furious). Wreck it? Wreck what? Something I've got very little hope of and absolutely no control over when the system dictates the outcome before the ushers clapped eyes on you. When welfare officers write down the names of books with the word 'woman' in the title and incriminate you. To be humiliated and ridiculed by a group of men and to gradually believe that the only thing that would change them is a bullet through the head. What sort of world is it where I have to plead for my own daughter?

JEAN. Claire.

CLAIRE (angry). And I will not calm down. I stand to lose Poppy, and in the face of current opinion the only weapon I have is compromise and you think that's okay. And what the hell do you know, what difference does it make to you? None. None at all.

JEAN *does not respond.* CLAIRE *is too angry to apologise. Silence. The doorbell rings.* JEAN *exits.*

JEAN (off). Hello, Joyce.

JOYCE (off). Hello, Jean.

CLAIRE (doesn't attempt to get up). Oh no, please God no.

JEAN (off). Val's okay, I hear.

JOYCE (*off*). Yes, fine, she'll be home in a couple of days. Much more positive, so they tell me.

JEAN (*off*). That's good.

Enter JOYCE *with* JEAN. JEAN *exits, shutting the door behind her.*

JOYCE. Whenever I come round she goes out of the room.

CLAIRE (*snaps*). We share a house, not our relatives.

JOYCE. I saw Lawrence in his car as I was walking up the hill from the bus stop. I don't suppose he's reached a reconciliation?

CLAIRE. No, he bloody well hasn't and I don't want to hear a pack of rubbish about the sun shining out of his armpit either.

JOYCE. Well I never really got on that well with him, no not really. Certainly not after the divorce. He never even sends me a Christmas card now you know . . .

CLAIRE (*aggressively*). What do you want?

JOYCE (*very taken aback*). Claire . . .

CLAIRE. Oh stop dithering around and sit down now you're here.

JOYCE (*sits*). I haven't been able to sleep this week.

CLAIRE (*sarcastically*). Poor you.

JOYCE. I don't think I've had more than twelve hours' sleep in the last fortnight. So I've been to see a solicitor.

CLAIRE. Can't you understand, I've got enough on my plate? I don't care about your neighbours, there's no law against do-it-yourself mania.

JOYCE (*firmly*). Look, Claire, I'm very sorry we had words. I can't stop thinking about it. I saw a solicitor about you.

CLAIRE. What for? To charge me with slander? (*A look from* JOYCE *is enough to make* CLAIRE *say:*) But Mum, I already have a solicitor.

JOYCE. I know that, don't I? This one specialised in custody, you should have got one who knew all about it in the first place.

CLAIRE (*through clenched teeth*). I have got one who deals with custody.

JOYCE. Yes, normal custody. Not one who deals with . . . you know . . . special circumstances.

CLAIRE (*firmly*). It's too late now Mum.

JOYCE (*sighs*). I just wish . . .

CLAIRE (*cutting her off*). It's no good bloody wishing, is it? Please get on with it.

JOYCE. The solicitor I saw was a specialist in . . .

CLAIRE. In special custody cases. Yes, you said that.

JOYCE. And on top of that, she was one of your lot as well.

CLAIRE (*deliberately provocative*). What, a teacher?

JOYCE. You know what I mean. (*Then quickly.*) Anyway she was very nice.

CLAIRE. She told you just like that.

JOYCE. No, I asked her outright, didn't I? Seemed a waste of time talking to one who wasn't and apart from that she had very good qualifications.

CLAIRE. She had to tell you that as well.

JOYCE. I could see that for myself, couldn't I? For one thing the sign on the door had so many letters on it there was hardly any room for the name.

CLAIRE (*flippantly*). Maybe we went to the same university.

JOYCE. Oh, I shouldn't wonder at all. I've always maintained that's where all those ideas come from. Those individual tutorials and seminal thingeys seem to lead to nothing but indulgent self-importance.

CLAIRE. So did you ask her?

JOYCE. Of course not. It's up to her own mother to find out where she went wrong.

CLAIRE. Which university she went to.

JOYCE (*becoming angry*). You what? You take the biscuit, you do, you're enough to try the patience of a saint. Do you know that? I haven't trailed half way across the country to find a whatname solicitor to ask which university she went to – just what sort of moron do you take me for?

CLAIRE. Can you get on with it because I can't understand a word you're saying.

JOYCE (*angry*). Just who do you think you are, girl? Eh? Just who? You've always been just a bit too quick with the backchat. You might find me ignorant, but if I hadn't made those sacrifices to get you the education that I never had, at least I wouldn't be made to feel small now, by you and your clever talk. (CLAIRE *looks away but simultaneously mouths every word of the next sentence.*) That tongue of yours is so sharp that one day you'll cut yourself in half with it. (*Having caught a glimpse of* CLAIRE *out of the corner of her eye.*) Oh yes, and you think I'm shallow and boring and mentally rearranged.

CLAIRE (*winces*). I never said that.

JOYCE. Yes, but you've thought it. I've not had half of what you've had and it didn't fall out of the sky. I worked for it, only, only to have you march in so many years later on, and announce with glee that you were living as man and wife with a woman and I'm trying to change, trying to explain to family and friends. For me and my lifetime, I've had to adapt much more than you ever have.

CLAIRE (*quietly*). It was hardly gleeful.

JOYCE. Whatever, whatever, it's much easier living in ignorance but it's not so awful, harder, painful even but not awful trying to understand. What is so awful is, for all I've tried, I get told to shut up and get lost.

CLAIRE (*softly*). I didn't.

JOYCE. You might as well have done. But when all's said and

done, I'm still your mother and nothing is going to be able to change that for either of us.

CLAIRE (*smiles*). No.

JOYCE. And sleepless nights won't change anything, so I said to myself, Joyce, I said, worrying won't make it go away, get off your behind and do something, so I went to the top set of chambers they call them to find a solicitor.

CLAIRE. So far so good. I'm with you.

JOYCE. And I said, if it was your daughter and your granddaughter, what would you advise them to do?

Pause.

CLAIRE (*gently*). Yes.

JOYCE. She told me to tell you both to skip the country.

CLAIRE (*flatly*). I hope you didn't pay for that advice.

JOYCE. As it happens I didn't have to, no. But I was more than willing to, I might add, and for your information that's just what you're going to do.

CLAIRE. Don't be so . . . so . . . we'll just hitch out to the airport, and say what with having to appear in court and all would they just fly us out of the way. And where did you think we should go to?

JOYCE. Just hold your horses and while you're about it, that tongue of yours as well.

CLAIRE (*ignoring this*). Where? And where have you thought we'd go?

JOYCE. America.

CLAIRE. America??!!

JOYCE. I know it can't be done just like that. God knows you don't get nothing in this life that easily. (*Deep breath.*) So I had a long chat with Sybil and she will arrange everything that end and I've spoken to Mrs Cuthberts downstairs, you know, the one with the son who manages the travel agents and he can get the plane tickets and visa and I went to the bank to see about travellers' cheques.

CLAIRE (*exasperated*). But Mum.

JOYCE. And I've been to the building society today and I want you to have it. (*She takes out an envelope and puts it in* CLAIRE's *lap.*) That's all I wanted to say.

JOYCE *gets up to go.* CLAIRE *gently takes hold of* JOYCE's *wrist so her mother remains where she is. Long pause.*

CLAIRE (*almost inaudibly*). But Mum.

JOYCE (*stickily*). We have our differences – we'll probably have them until the day I die, but I do know this much, if we didn't have them, Lawrence wouldn't be able to use them to get back at you.

CLAIRE (*hands back the envelope.* JOYCE *will not take it.* CLAIRE *puts it on the floor between them*). I can't. (*Slight pause.*) You'd do this for me? (*Pause.*) There are laws, that would give them the power to bring us back.

JOYCE. They'll have to find you first, and all the time they're looking will cost Lawrence money and mark my words, he'll give up. If not, in a couple of years Poppy's age will make sure he has no say in the matter.

CLAIRE. And just what do I tell Poppy? That's no way to bring her up, living as a fugitive.

JOYCE. Fugitive nothing and it won't be the rest of your life, will it? It's only to see you over. You always over-dramatise things. How are you going to explain to Poppy anyway, Lawrence has everything to back him up. You've got to play a game by somebody else's rules just to keep her with you, which you both want but are unlikely to get.

CLAIRE (*flatly*). I think I've got to go through with it.

JOYCE. Why? Seems to me that nobody cares what a good mother you are. All they care about is the other thing. And wearing a dress from Marks and Spencer on the day is hardly likely to fool anyone either. And what about that welfare officer? No sooner was my foot in the door, when this voice booms 'And what do you feel about your daughter's homosexuality?' And I said, 'Could be worse, she could be dead'. Well, it was a joke, wasn't it, only every word got written down.

CLAIRE. Look, once in court I can take that report apart and show it up for what it is.

JOYCE (*agreeing*). I'm sure, I'm sure, and who will they believe? A lot rests on these people. No, look, it's taken me long enough to come round and I'm your mother so you're hardly going to persuade some Hoorray Henry judge with a broom handle up his backside, to your way of thinking, not in an afternoon anyway.

CLAIRE. No, I won't give in. If there's one thing I've learnt from you it's stand my ground and fight.

JOYCE. And if there's one thing I didn't teach it was to sink. This time you're up to your neck in quicksand and wrenching your own head won't help. You need a hand – somebody else's. Before you say anything, Sybil said that.

CLAIRE. Typical Sybil line that is. It's not what I want.

JOYCE. I don't want it either but it seemed to me that only by letting go of the two of you could any sort of solution be found.

CLAIRE. Thank you, Mum, but I can't.

Scene Four

BEA's *living-room.* BEA *shows* DIANE *and* TERRI *in.*

BEA. This really isn't on, you know. If you wanted to see me you should have come to my office.

TERRI. We wanted to talk to you urgently.

BEA. How did you know where I lived?

DIANE. The phone book.

BEA. I see. Well, now you're here, sit down.

DIANE *and* TERRI *sit nervously on the edge of the settee.*

But I'm not in the mood to listen to threats and ultimatums so if that's what you're about you can walk right out again.

TERRI. No, we realised that we'd done a lot of damage.

BEA. I'm listening. I would offer you a cup of tea only the water is temporarily cut off.

DIANE. We overheard something about Mrs Anderson.

FLORRIE (*shouts off*). Bea? Would you be a darling and bring me an adjustable spanner?

BEA (*gets up quickly*). One minute. (*To* DIANE *and* TERRI:) My lodger is changing a washer.

FLORRIE (*shouts off*). Thanks, darling.

BEA. Excuse me. (*Once out of the door we hear* BEA *charging up the stairs.*)

DIANE. Fancy calling your landlady darling.

TERRI. Must work in the theatre. They all do that.

DIANE. Yeah. (*She gets up and starts looking around the room.*)

TERRI. Sit down. If she finds you poking your nose into anything she'll throw us out.

DIANE. We'll know when she's coming back. She couldn't have made more noise going up the stairs if she'd tried.

TERRI (*gets up and surveys the bookcase*). Boring, boring, boring.

DIANE (*finds a small framed photograph behind a plant*). Hey, look at this, an old photo of Bea with her arm round a woman.

TERRI (*looking at the photo*). They all did that then. Gawd, look at those shoes.

DIANE. She's still got them by the sound of it. (*She opens the desk drawer and tentatively rummages around its contents.*)

TERRI (*alarmed*). Don't do that.

DIANE. She poked her nose into our lives.

TERRI. We shoved our lives under her nose, you mean.

DIANE (*pulls out a card*). Look, an anniversary card.

TERRI. Blimey. Maybe she was married then.

Both of them look at it.

DIANE (*reads*). What can I say after twelve years except –

TERRI. Don't read it out loud, it's embarrassing.

They both read it.

TERRI } (*exclaim in unison*). All my love, Florrie.
DIANE }

They look at each other.

TERRI } Miss Grimble's one.
DIANE }

Their discovery causes such elation that they jump and dance around the room, hugging each other, proclaiming 'Miss Grimble's one' until the sound of BEA clumping, in a rather more dignified manner, down the stairs. DIANE throws the card back in the drawer and shuts it. They sit on the settee as before. Enter BEA.

BEA. I'm sorry about that. Now where were we? (DIANE *and* TERRI *just sit and stare at her slightly open-mouthed.*) Mrs Anderson. Now what d'you know of Mrs Anderson's business?

DIANE. Mrs Anderson. Yes. Ummmm. We didn't realise about her custody case.

BEA. And how did you find out about it?

TERRI. We accidentally – (*She stops herself*) – we were eavesdropping, Miss Grimble.

DIANE (*having recovered herself*). In fact, we're thinking of setting up as a detective agency.

TERRI (*to* MISS GRIMBLE). We had to tell you about it. (*To* DIANE:) Be quiet, Diane.

BEA. Actually, Linda, Miss Fellows, put me in the picture this afternoon.

DIANE. We've come to make a bargain.

TERRI. She means to be flexible and apologise.

BEA. But what can I do?

DIANE. Go to court and testify for Mrs Anderson.

BEA. I don't know about that.

FLORRIE (*shouts off*). Water's back. Shall I put the kettle on?

DIANE. Two sugars for me, please, Florrie. Ta.

TERRI (*nudges* DIANE). Shush.

DIANE *grins*.

Scene Five

Outside the courtroom. Before CLAIRE *is about to enter the room. Enter* BEA.

BEA. Claire? Claire?

CLAIRE. Miss Grimble. What are you doing here?

BEA. I had no idea. Why didn't you tell me?

CLAIRE. How did you find out?

BEA. It's too long a story to unravel just now.

CLAIRE. I hope you've not come here to be defamatory about my character.

BEA. Quite the opposite. In fact, if I'd known about this I'd have made a change in direction earlier in the day.

CLAIRE. Meaning what?

BEA. I'm here to offer what support I can.

CLAIRE. Thank you. (*Pause.*) And what of Diane *et al*?

BEA. I'm still negotiating with them. Oh, absolutely no question of expulsion. We are simply haggling over the new section of the history syllabus. But I'm very much hoping for a settlement on the word 'spinsters'. But first things first. I've explained to your barrister that should it be necessary I will testify to the fact that you are my deputy and an excellent teacher.

CLAIRE. Thank you.

BEA. Whatever else, I do understand about loss especially when it can go unrecognised or without a glimmer of sympathy from those around you.

CLAIRE. I've got a lot on my side, a good home and career and, if I say so myself, I'm a very good mother.

BEA. You're not going to be judged on the quality of your parenting but on the basis of your sexuality.

Fade. Lights up on LAWRENCE *and his barrister. A* FEMALE CLERK *hovers in the background.*

BARRISTER. When we win, will you take your little girl straightaway?

LAWRENCE. No, tomorrow morning will suit me better. Do you actually think it's a foregone conclusion?

BARRISTER. Everything's in your favour. (*To the* CLERK:) Be a love and get an extra copy of the welfare officer's report.

Exit CLERK.

LAWRENCE. Even so, she is her mother, I suppose.

BARRISTER (*drily*). Now is not the time to doubt her parentage. (*Then.*) Mr Anderson, you must be prepared to explain everything to the court, if necessary in the detail in which you first relayed it to me, and then we will have dismantled every right she thought was hers.

LAWRENCE. I was extremely angry when I first sought your advice.

BARRISTER. But you still want your daughter.

LAWRENCE. Yes.

BARRISTER. Therefore you will have to be prepared to 'throw the book' at your ex-wife. (*Pause.*) Well?

LAWRENCE (*firmly*). Yes.

BARRISTER. Good. Then our case is watertight.

CLERK OF THE COURT (*voice off*). Custody Case Number Thirty-Seven – Anderson versus Anderson.

Fade. Lights on VAL.

VAL. I think now, that I knew I was getting ill, losing control. I remember when the boys were just babies and we lived in hard-to-let flats with the railway track running behind our block and lifting one of them up to see a train go past – it all seems so insignificant now. He was fascinated and as I held him I started to cry and repeat over and over 'This is a little person'. I felt happy and overwhelmingly sad at the same time, I don't know why and from then on it was like getting drunk. No, nothing dramatic, like swinging naked from chandeliers, not that I suppose I wouldn't have been tempted had any swung my way – like when you start to get drunk, you relax, tell yourself you can sober up in a minute, only you can't and when confronted with sober people you know you're losing ground, so you appear more drunk, not that you could appear sober if you wanted to anyway. It's very difficult to remember being unhappy – the actual feeling, like when you're freezing cold in the middle of winter – you can remember lying on the beach boiling hot but you can't imagine enough to feel it. And when you're lying in the sun you can only remember being cold but not what it felt like. (*Pause.*) I haven't got an old self. I haven't got a new self to be cast on and off like a winter and summer coat. What I am is me.

JUDGE (*voice off*). Custody, care and control are awarded to the natural father, Lawrence Anderson.

Lights up on CLAIRE and JOYCE.

JOYCE. Nobody would believe that anyone above those appointed to sit in judgement could ask such filthy questions. Those people are obsessed, they must be sick in the head. I might have difficulty saying the word lesbian but nobody makes me ashamed for loving my own daughter.

LAWRENCE *crosses in front of them.*

LAWRENCE (*to* CLAIRE). First thing tomorrow morning and have everything ready.

Scene Six

VAL, *ready to go home. Enter* NURSE.

NURSE. I'm just about to go off duty but your sister rang up with this message. (*She hands her a piece of paper.*) From New York. I hope it's not bad news.

VAL (*reads the note then looks up*). No, not in the circumstances.

NURSE. Val, I just wanted to say . . .

Enter the OLDER DOCTOR.

DOCTOR. Looking forward to going home, Mrs Jones?

VAL. I'm looking forward to leaving here.

DOCTOR. Now, you know where we are, should you ever need us. Must take it easy when you get home, not rush things, but I'm sure Dr March has explained that to you.

VAL. Yes, Doctor.

DOCTOR. Good. (*He looks at his watch.*) What time did your husband say he'd collect you?

VAL. My mother's taking me home.

DOCTOR. Right, I see. Well, I'd better go before I'm tempted to make a quip about women not being renowned for punctuality.

The sound of furious knocking on a door can be heard.

LAWRENCE (*off*). Come on. Open the bloody door. It's no use stalling for time.

DOCTOR. What on earth is that noise?

Neither VAL nor the NURSE have heard anything and both look blankly at him.

NURSE. What noise?

DOCTOR. Sounds like someone is pulling the whole place apart. Come with me. (*He turns to exit.*) All the very best then, Mrs Jones. (*Exit. The NURSE reluctantly follows.*)

VAL (*looking at the note again*). Poppy and Claire have arrived safely and Sybil sends her love.

Lights up on LAWRENCE trying to kick CLAIRE's front door down.

LAWRENCE (*shouts*). For the last time, open this door, Claire.

Then fade. Lights up on VAL. Enter JOYCE.

JOYCE (*holds out her hand to VAL*). Ready?

VAL (*taking her mother's hand*). Yes.

BYRTHRITE

Foreword

Brynhie is set in the seventeenth century, the time when control
over women's reproductive processes began to change hands from
women to men. The changeover began with the introduction of
new technology by male doctors, the use of forceps in childbirth.
The process continued, and gathered momentum, over the
following three centuries through the progressive introduction of
technological interventions derived from a science and medicine
organised to exclude women from significant positions within it.
The organisation and development of medicine, particularly
obstetrics and gynaecology, and science, particularly human
genetics, is fundamental to the situation we find ourselves in today.
Reproductive technology has been defined as:

"Covering anything to do with the manipulation of the
gametes (eggs or sperm) or the foetus, for whatever purpose
from conception other than by sexual union, to treatment of
disease in utero, to the ultimate manufacture of a human being
to exact specification . . . Thus the earliest procedure is
artificial insemination; next . . . artificial fertilisation . . . or maybe
artificial implantation . . . in the future total extracorporeal
gestation . . . and finally what is popularly meant by
(reproductive) engineering, the production – or better, the
biological manufacture of a human being to desired
specification."

This definition, taken from the Journal of the American Medical
Association was published in 1972 when the only technique that
could be used to alter conception and result in a live birth was
artificial insemination. Artificial fertilisation and artificial
implantation resulting in a live birth did not take place until 1978
when Louise Brown was born in England, the first so-called test
tube baby.

In 1986 we have three of these five processes. Total
extracorporeal gestation, the so-called artificial womb, followed by
the biological manufacture of human beings to desired
specification, of course, remain to be achieved. The development of
these processes depend upon each other. The definition gives us the
cumulative technological steps that need to be taken in order to
gain total control over human reproduction. It also exposed the

Foreword

Byrthrite is set in the seventeenth century, the time when control over women's reproductive processes began to change hands from women to men. The changeover began with the introduction of new technology by male doctors, the use of forceps in childbirth. The process continued, and gathered momentum, over the following three centuries through the progressive introduction of technological interventions derived from a science and medicine organised to exclude women from significant positions within it. The organisation and development of medicine, particularly obstetrics and gynaecology, and science, particularly human genetics, is fundamental to the situation we find ourselves in today.

Reproductive technology has been defined as:

> 'Covering anything to do with the manipulation of the gametes (eggs or sperm) or the foetus, for whatever purpose from conception other than by sexual union, to treatment of disease *in utero*, to the ultimate manufacture of a human being to exact specification . . . Thus the earliest procedure . . . is artificial insemination; next . . . artificial fertilisation . . . next artificial implantation . . . in the future total extracorporeal gestation . . . and finally what is popularly meant by (reproductive) engineering, the production – or better, the biological manufacture of a human being to desired specification.'

This definition, taken from the Journal of the American Medical Association was published in 1972 when the only technique that could be used to alter conception and result in a live birth was artificial insemination. Artificial fertilisation and artificial implantation resulting in a live birth did not take place until 1978 when Louise Brown was born in England, the first so–called test tube baby.

In 1986 we have three of these five processes. Total extracorporeal gestation, the so–called artificial womb, followed by the biological manufacture of human beings to desired specification, of course, remain to be achieved. The development of these processes depend upon each other. The definition gives us the cumulative technological steps that need to be taken in order to gain total control over human reproduction. It also exposed the long term planning and major resource allocation needed to achieve these ends.

The new reproductive technologies are one aspect of biotechnological developments that will affect every aspect of life from the growth of food to warfare. The qualities inherent in biotechnology are those of efficiency, speed and control. In human reproduction research women, our bodies ourselves, are the experimental material.

Amid the eugenic presentation of the new reproduction technologies by the mass media, 'perfect babies for perfect couples', lies the Governmental, and ethical discussion generally. This proceeds without reference to women. The influential British Government Report of the Committee of Inquiry into Human Fertilisation and Embryology (the Warnock Report) uses a scientific, knowledge-based way of discussing reproduction. They showed no understanding that they were discussing woman's life processes. In this, and the other reports around the world based on it, women are reduced to body parts: wombs, ovaries, and fallopian tubes or subsumed within 'the couple' or 'the family', which of course is always heterosexual. Women have no existence except as biology or in relation to men.

The use of medicine and science controlled by men to challenge the independence and subjectivity of women continues as does the challenge to it by women. The prize is total control over women's reproductive processes and the reproduction of future generations. Women may at last become the vessel, the carrier, if used at all, for the male creation. In *Byrthrite* we return to the origins of this struggle.

> 'We are living in an age where technology is outstripping science fiction in its possibilities and in its language of myth and symbol and where, in the world of reproductive research, the whole idea of fathering is undergoing a profound shift of meaning. It is still a culture whose most persistent myth is that of ultimate male procreativity in the shape of God who both created the world and fathered his son through remote implantation using the medium of woman. Scientists do not have to be mad to be informed by the prevailing mythology. The technology, given the system of ideas that underlies it, is

self generating, and generating new technologies at an extraordinary rate'.

(Claire McDonald, Letter, *Women's Review*, No. 4, 1985).

Jalna Hanmer
University of Bradford, 1987

Byrthrite was first presented at the Royal Court Theatre Upstairs on 21 November 1986, with the following cast:

ROSE, *17*	Eleanor David
GRACE, *70*	
BRIDGET, *19*	Maggie McCarthy
HELEN, *33*	
ANN, *30*	
PRICKER'S MOTHER, *55*	Holly Wilson
URSULA, *13*	
MARY, *18*	Meera Syal
JANE, *20*	
LADY H, *30*	Janette Legge
URSULA'S MOTHER	
A MAN, *various ages*	David Bamber

The action takes place in the seventeenth century in the county of Essex, during the Civil War.

Part One

Scene One: The lying-in	Scene Five: The pond
Scene Two: Outside	Scene Six: Outside
Scene Three: The meeting room	Scene Seven: The servants' attic
Scene Four: Grace's home	Scene Eight: The meeting room

Part Two (two years later)

Scene One: Outside	Scene Six: Grace's home
Scene Two: The church	Scene Seven: The inn
Scene Three: A rowing boat	Scene Eight: Grace's home
Scene Four: The pond	Scene Nine: The pond
Scene Five: The gaol	Scene Ten: Grace's garden

Directed by Carole Hayman
Designed by Jenny Tiramani
Music by Jo–Anne Fraser

PART ONE

Scene One

The lying-in.

Night. ROSE *and* HELEN *outside a house.* ROSE *has almost completed carving a wooden toy and* HELEN *is finishing a baby's garment. Presently* GRACE, *a midwife, comes out to them.*

GRACE. It be a girl.

Women's voices can be heard singing from inside the house.

GRACE, ROSE *and* HELEN *join in the song.*

ALL:

The Birthing Song
Unto you a child is born
Unto you a daughter given
From this time forth go and to all women tell;
That the daughter's inheritance shall pass
Through you all, to be kept forever
Women's rite, women's right for choice in birth.

HELEN. How is Ann?

GRACE. In best of spirits. Mary is with her.

ROSE. And is her mind made up to a name?

GRACE. Aye, Marion. Ah there you be, Rose, now be sure and let all the women know of our plans afore this night's celebrations addle their memories.

ROSE. I'll need you to lend weight to arguments.

GRACE. By and by.

ROSE goes inside.

HELEN. Grace, you'll not take umbrage if I avoid the revellin'?

GRACE. Even the most rigid men allow our sex attendance at lying-in.

HELEN. Is not that.

GRACE. Aye. I know too well who I shall find outside: Rose and thyself with not a word passed between you, no doubt.

HELEN. For our reasons could not be more contrary.

GRACE. Cam, I will walk with you.

HELEN (shakes her head). Let me be alone.

GRACE. I shall see you at the meeting?

HELEN. Aye. So thou shalt.

Scene Two

The meeting room.

A bare room. MARY stands in the middle. HELEN at the side, watching her. ROSE, at the other end, her back to both of them, staring out of the window.

MARY. I'll not stand here waiting for moon to turn to cheese.

HELEN. Is you to begin, Mary. Rose and I follow on.

MARY. Mind, if she doth 'Grace' us with an appearance I'll not start over.

HELEN. Will do harm to none of us to have our memories freshened.

MARY (sighs, takes a deep breath and starts). 'Verily, we enquire of the cunning woman, wilt thou pass on the knowledge of the longevity of life, and she does thus reply' (Trying to remember the next line.) 'and she does thus reply,' yes? (But she can't.) Oh, a pox on this. (So she ad libs.) 'And she does thus reply.' (Very fast.) 'I vouchsafe to thee daughter, tis not so much the abominable odious persistent attention of such lewde and filthye offenders as mankynde. Tis not . . .'

HELEN. Recoil thy tongue before it runs us to the rope. Do you want us hung?

MARY (*to* HELEN). Nay, those are not the lines either – still sounds good, specially as it rhymes.

HELEN. Is not for saying out loud and neither is what you just spake.

MARY. What I supposed to have said floated clean out of my skull and them others floated in.

HELEN. Well, they aren't for floating out of your mouth.

MARY. Who pray will be bowing over to correct us? At this pace not even Holy Ghost. (*Sullenly.*) Oh, what matter is it to anyone, any matter.

HELEN (*wearily*). Don't beset us with that all over.

MARY. You liked my words well enough didn't ye, Rose? (*Pause.*) Rose?

ROSE (*still with her back to them*). I can't keep watch and sort out quarrels.

MARY (*mumbles*). Plain folly.

ROSE (*turns round*). Let her say what she wants, Helen, we've not got time to be worrying over a few words.

HELEN. Let's start up one more time, Mary? I was out of course to reprimand you.

MARY. The mood has mislaid me.

HELEN (*snaps*). Seems like you had a big dump on you afore you cam.

MARY (*mutters*). Waste of precious female breath.

ROSE. Mary! How can you turn your mind round so?

MARY (*wearily*). In the first instance, singing, dancing, players, enjoyment of any kind is going against the law. (*Becoming angry.*) Second, women are never heard of doing it. And third, (*Shouts.*) one of our dramatis personae is missing!

HELEN. Keep your mouth level. Do you want for the pricker to have his irons clapped on us?

MARY Us! Us! Us! It's always us! Not a woman in the county not lying quaking tonight a-worrying at being swam and who's doing anything 'bout it – us! Always the same.

HELEN. We should be thanking luck we don't live such a distance from each other. No place else in this country could you find a handful of women with no children.

MARY (*holding up three fingers in disbelief*). This many? This many of us? I'll not swallow nature having so few singularities.

ROSE. And Grace. That's one more.

MARY (*exasperated*). And where is Grace? Where be she then?

HELEN (*with concern*). 'Tis unlike her not to cam at all. And there's no woman due.

MARY. Huh, the day that will be. (*Then:*) Oh Helen, forgive me, I was not thinking.

ROSE. Probably her cock got loose again. (*They laugh, ROSE turns back to the window.*) He's almost upon us. You and your fooling.

HELEN (*panicking*). Quick, quickly. Make haste. The psalms.

They all kneel.

MARY (*mutters*). If I try and sing a psalm in this humour it will all but burst my throat apart.

HELEN. Make any effort to look devotional at least.

MARY. I'm going to say my piece.

ROSE. Do not risk it for sake of a moment's irritation.

MARY. I don't need lessons in moralising from you, Rose Clarke, I'll do as I please. Verily, I say unto you that man not only wants power over woman but over life. His attraction for lust, power and violence is fatally entwined.

HELEN. Hush, I can hear his footfalls.

MARY. You must be a bat then. Rain has not stopped since harvest. He'll be paddling on mud.

HELEN (*sings boldly*). The Lord's my shepherd I'll not want. He maketh me to lie down in pastures green, he leadeth me the quiet waters.

She stops abruptly as the door opens revealing JANE, a woman disguised as a soldier.

MARY (*continuing where HELEN leaves off*). Wherein to drown.

ROSE (*surprised to see a soldier*). Oh, and who might you be?

JANE. And who might you be expecting?

MARY. Not you.

HELEN. This is a devotional meeting, sir. For women alone.

JANE. Ha. You'll be thanking Lord Jesus for that then.

ROSE. We have no account to make to you.

JANE remains where she is and ROSE continues to study her during the following dialogue.

HELEN (*quickly, wanting to pacify*). We are but bald women, sir, asking for God to look down on us in his mercy.

JANE (*heartily*). You look neither useless nor hairless to me.

HELEN. As ye must know, sir, t'is a quirk of our speech that the word for barren and useless be but the same.

ROSE (*sharply*). What business have you here?

JANE. I am a soldier.

MARY (*sarcastically*). Even that much the weaker sex are able to guess at.

HELEN (*kindly*). What can be your enquiry? This is Master Grimbold country . . .

JANE. I have some information which I am in two minds as to if I should impart it to you.

HELEN. Please leave us be.

JANE. Is a question of my sincerity then? Cam now you can trust me.

MARY. Aye, 'tis those assurances have led us to the gallows.

Silence.

ROSE. I am mad for I will say it. Is my guess you be either a vision or a woman.

JANE. Curses! 'Tis the first time I have been tumbled. Now, you have spoilt my revelations.

MARY (*in disbelief*). A woman?

JANE. In truth. Doing a man's job for a man's wage.

HELEN. A woman?

JANE. Aye.

Pause.

ROSE (*coldly*). And what of this information or was it merely a revelation regarding your wardrobe?

JANE. Hovel some distance from here with a tree hanging over, containing an old woman with a fierce mouth.

ROSE. Grace? Would be Grace. (*Concerned.*) What of her?

JANE. Seems she had a visitor cam to frighten her. Mind, she had banished him well afore I got close.

ROSE. And she?

JANE. She was well enough to spit in my direction leading me to conclude she wasn't too weakened by it.

ROSE (*shakes her head*). Can't be Grace. She'd not spit at a brave woman.

JANE. With other things to think on. She took me on face of my apparel.

MARY. Oh for shame of it.

JANE. Aye. I'm bound that be but half the tale.

HELEN. To my relief she's cam to no harm. For I must take leave now.

MARY. Where does your husband think you are?

HELEN (*didn't want* MARY *to mention her husband in front of* JANE. *She says casually*). He'd not notice, he's keeping an all-night vigil against the divel. But of my own accord I must take leave. (*To* JANE:) But my hope is that our paths will cross again, Mistress err . . .

JANE. Jane.

HELEN. I'm Helen.

ROSE. Rose.

MARY. Mary.

HELEN. I'll bid you goodnight. (*She goes.*)

JANE. Goodnight.

MARY. All night vigil against the divil. Ha! He'll not be so engrossed that her presence won't be missed when his belly rumbles.

JANE (*checking she has their names right*). Rose. Mary. Do sound like a herb.

ROSE. 'Tis Grace you should ask about that. Cam on.
They go.

Scene Three

GRACE's home.

It is not a hovel, although it is sparse and has a hole in the roof. A pet frog is kept in a box in a corner of the room. GRACE *is plucking a dead chicken. There are numerous jars and bottles containing every sort of herb around.*

GRACE (*mumbles angrily*). You wreck our lives leaving us no recourse but to curse, for which we are condemned. We go to the scaffold cursing for the crime of cursing, and would take only a chicken with life wrung from it to be silent from cursing at the injustice of it all.

Enter JANE, MARY *and* ROSE.

ROSE. Is us Grace.

GRACE (*lunging at JANE with the chicken carcass*). Do this look like a place stuffed with Royals. Be off with you.

ROSE (*standing between JANE and GRACE*). Don't take on, Grace – this, afore your eyes, be a woman. (*Slight pause but GRACE doesn't react.*) By name of Jane.

GRACE. What's she doing prynked out like a prick-eared cull?

MARY. For the war – is it not the most wondrous sight?

ROSE (*proudly*). A female soldier, wager you'd not thought you'd live to see the day.

GRACE. Par – you young women. There's no hope.

ROSE (*teasingly*). What relief to find your spirit unruffled by your visitation.

GRACE. I have righted mess he made. Though, warrant, this neutered cock has seen its day. 'Tis only small misfortune and we can make good by it. Pass that pot, Mary.

MARY (*in doing so she sees the frog*). Oh, no Grace, you don't still keep that frog.

GRACE. Good enough for most folks around here. Good enough for me.

JANE. In London they only keep cats and dogs.

GRACE. Cats and dogs cost dear to feed. Many's the time children go without while animals grow fat and full.

MARY. Asides, where would they get frogs from in London?

JANE. They have a fine river you know.

ROSE (*firmly*). We ent assembled here to bend our ears over who's got a frog or not.

JANE. I hear tell in France they eat frogs.

GRACE. Ha. Then I wish he would have took it into his skull to do away with the frog then. 'Twould have been a fair treat to see him climbing and jumping round the walls trying to grab and strangle it.

ROSE. Frogs! Frogs! Frogs! Is not frogs we're concerned for.

GRACE. Would have broke my heart to lose old croker.

ROSE (*impatiently*). What was *his* purpose?

GRACE (*quietly*). He has got his courage up. Seems I am not so far off next choice to swim. (*Silence.*) Well, is not so remarkable, merely the same road as several of my years have trod before me.

MARY. Hasn't he made enough money from these parts?

ROSE (*gently*). So how cam he left you?

GRACE. Not bargained for the dish of tongues I served him. Made off in a rush of great frustration.

JANE. Wager he'll be back.

MARY (*flatly*). What a comfort you turned out to be.

ROSE. She be right well enough though.

MARY (*panicking*). So what are we to do?

JANE (*brashly, one hand on her sword*). I'll stand behind the door and slice his brain-pan off his shoulders.

ROSE (*with admiration*). Did I not tell you she was a good woman. Is she not a good woman Grace?

GRACE. Rose!

MARY. As stars hang in the sky then so should we.

GRACE. And another pricker wilt up in the place of his martyred master.

ROSE. Aye. He'll not be 'man enough' to return hisself so soon. Most probably pay a man tricked out like the divel.

JANE (*cheerfully*). My cuttle don't care which prick's head it cuts off.

GRACE. Their tools, mistress, are best kept from them. Tis not our way.

ROSE. And what pray is our way? (*Sarcastically*.) Cast a spell?

GRACE. Rose, how many times will you need telling not to lark in such a sour humour.

ROSE. So how are we to prepare ourselves for when the divel cams knocking?

GRACE. This business of carnal copulation with Satan is all new.

MARY (*shakes her head*). The curse of printing. Ideas spread faster than the plague.

GRACE. Printing is not the curse but them who decide what's on the lines.

JANE. I have heard tell of a pamphlet which shows more truth of the writers' blighted minds than of women's nature.

MARY. And what do you know of their working pattern?

JANE. A man pricked out as the divel cam to alone old woman and does say, 'I am the divel and I am cam to sleep with thee'. Aye, it sound like a noddy idea but 'tis enough to frighten many out of their wits. And if but a fly cam within arm's length will be proof enough of imps, but is when he stabs her flesh over and over with a blunt nail to find marks of the divel, do most give in.

GRACE. Aye, the pricker's not so called for nothing.

ROSE. Is little use us sat recounting our plight, we must prepare for his entrance. (ROSE *opens the door a little to keep watch*.)

MARY. Save your breath to tell us how.

GRACE. Laughing.

ROSE. Laughing?

GRACE. Aye. 'Tis my new plan. To laugh.

MARY (*flatly*). I don't feel like laughing.

GRACE. Takes courage beyond man to carry out duties amidst raucous ridicule.

JANE. Take a courageous man carry out his duties with a rum cuttle ran through him. (*She puts her hand to her sword*.)

GRACE. That war's done you no good, girl. Now, this is the plan. You three climb up the tree outside and observe scene through unmended hole in the roof.

MARY. Oh Grace, Thatcher still not cam?

GRACE. Thatcher don't care 'bout poor folk on parish welfare.

ROSE. For mercy's sake, I can hear horse hoofs.

GRACE. Signal be, if he so much as poke his finger in my direction – laugh.

ROSE. Right. (*She bundles MARY and JANE out of the door.*)

MARY. But . . . Grace. (*ROSE pushes her.*) But Rose.

ROSE. Get up that tree. (*They all climb into the tree.*)

MARY. But Rose. Point is, we have nothing to laugh at.

ROSE (*whispers*). Shush. (*She points off.*) There he is.

JANE (*whispers*). Worry not on that matter. I know something their adled brains think we do that will make you giggle till your bladders give way.

ROSE. What?

JANE. 'Tis not so funny in second telling. So wait for signal but be warned not to heed your aching sides but cling firmly to these branches.

Disguised as the devil, the Pricker's Apprentice has tethered his horse and walks the rest of the distance. Although this is his first mission, he has been well primed and is confident that his mere presence will scare GRACE half to death. Consequently he is unnerved by her response.

APPRENTICE (*enters, announcing grandly*). I am the divel and I am cam to sleep with thee.

GRACE. If the divel has desires for the flesh he must be made of blood and bone.

APPRENTICE (*not the reaction he'd expected; still he must try harder*). I see you have several familiars.

GRACE (*pulling the chicken out of the pot*). You be telling me you be the divel and yer never spied a capon before. Now there's a thing.

APPRENTICE (*confused now, so more aggressively*). I am cam for a place in your soul.

GRACE. Stop making a cod's head of yourself, man. Behave and take thyself off.

APPRENTICE (*taking a step nearer*). Don't prank with me, I am the divel.

GRACE. So maybe you think you are. Delusions of this nature, especially of men believing themselves to be a character from the Bible are not uncommon. Would it be a relief to talk about this affliction?

APPRENTICE (*is now hard pressed for things the devil might say*). You are in my pay.

GRACE. Well, truth to say, I've received none of it to date. I am a healing woman, a good one but a poor one.

APPRENTICE. Oh shut thy twittering. (*He advances another step closer.*)

GRACE. And *pray* – oh, I see that word don't shock you none. What have I done that you should pester me so?

APPRENTICE. You are evil.

GRACE. The divel is calling a mere mortal evil?

APPRENTICE. I'll teach you to mock my powers.

He tries to grab her but she nimbly avoids him.

JANE (*to MARY and ROSE*). They are of firm belief that women collect male organs and keep them in birds' nests where they move about by themselves and eat corn and oats.

The three of them screech with laughter.

APPRENTICE. What is this divelry? (*He hesitates. The laughter continues.*)

GRACE. Run along with you, mister, and tell who ever's paying you there's no business for him here.

The Pricker's Apprentice turns tail and swiftly exits. When he is out of sight, MARY, ROSE and JANE descend from the tree and return to GRACE who is tending to the stew.

ROSE. A wondrous plan, Grace.

MARY. Aye, my face is wet from laughing.

GRACE. You have some peculiar ideas, young Jane but I'll like you yet, and you took a risk revealing yourself to the meeting.

JANE. I have a text Grace. 'Where two or three women are gathered together 'tis a risk worth taking'.

ROSE. Tell us of the war.

JANE. The war? The war, Rose, is a fuckin' bore. Tonight I'm more interested in the conflict around your necks and the purpose of your meeting.

ROSE. The idea belongs to Grace.

MARY. We're trying to put some words together so we can perform them.

JANE. I've not heard of women doing that.

ROSE. We'd not heard of women passing as men till today.

JANE. And when?

MARY. At next lying-in.

JANE. For what purpose?

GRACE. Is the only time women are allowed to be together.

ROSE. So we can feel less afraid of these evil times against our sex.

JANE. How can it be women of our time are stronger than ever before and yet persecuted worse at same time?

GRACE. When those who are accumbred kick back, the oppressor kicks harder.

JANE. But they pick on frail, defenceless old women. Oh begging your pardon, Grace, but usually by their very age they can offer least resistance.

GRACE. First there is your reason, is easy. Second, some have power, such as they see it in health and advice over women's bodies, particularly in childbearing. And they want power over that.

MARY. Only there's not enough of a complex nature about their own bodies to keep their minds occupied.

JANE. But the doctors are not the prickers.

GRACE. New inventions and persecution step together, in time.

ROSE. At least they're not hypocrites and do call themselves doctors.

JANE (*confused*). I know not what the word means.

ROSE. To cut up. To doctor – to tamper with in an unnatural way.

JANE. So then – put a stop to me if you've heard it – This doctor goes to a cunning woman with a frog on his head and the cunning woman asks, 'How long have you had that?' and the frog says, 'Long since, it started as an abcess on my arse'.

They all laugh including JANE.

GRACE. I see, if nothing else, you have some store of jokes in your head, mistress.

JANE. Aye, well, I know this much. 'Twill be a long time afore the likes of us have money for a doctor to lay his hand on doorpost never mind else.

MARY. And who do you think they'll practise on?

JANE. I'm not so easily convinced, I've heard tell . . .

GRACE. You seem to have heard tell a lot for a woman of your years.

JANE. The war, Grace, it gets you around. Is best education a girl can have.

GRACE. Par – Glory and killing would seem to my mind to lead to dead end.

JANE. In France.

ROSE. France? How d'you know about France?

JANE. Loyalist always going there.

GRACE (*slightly mocking*). Oh aye and they confide in you?

JANE. I am nobody's halfwit. I have change of clothes and curls under this headpiece. I choose safest disguise depending on company I keep.

GRACE. Probably you're keeping war going single-handed.

ROSE (*prompting JANE.*) So in France . . .

JANE. In their history they did burn four hundred women in town square, in one hour, all over country and many low countries besides. Whole villages left with one woman. Just one alive. Was not the doctors' doing, was the church.

Silence.

GRACE. Certainly sad to say 'twas better when we was all Catholics. At least Virgin Mary was sacred. There's not a good word to be said for Eve. Though where men reason they cam from if not Eve, I don't know.

ROSE. They name the name, if it don't fit they name it again.

GRACE. It won't stop. Not here nor now. Will not stop till they can give birth and then have choice to do away with us altogether.

JANE (*laughs*). Oh aye Grace. And when will that be? Before or after they walk on the moon?

GRACE, MARY, ROSE, JANE *sing:*

And a Man Named Armstrong Walked Upon the Moon
So you think that's an ironic joke?
At NASA's celestial poke.
They thrust up a man into space,

But you won't even think
That they're on the brink
Of finishing off half our race.

For women have the bodies that breed
And the men just provide her the seed
So love guides the stars in our eyes,
    With feet on the earth,
    Men can't control birth,
And a man on the moon is all lies.

For men have ejaculated onto the moon
By rocket, and phallic intent
Has given new meaning to that old famous rune
That for men's domination the great moon was meant.

There's a warning here, sisters, let's take heed of this,
That man on the moon came to earth:
And fucking and love may start with a kiss
And you may control your kids' birth
But not for long now, they're taking our place.
Fashioning Star Wars in labs. Winning the race
To eradicate us and give birth by men
Fashioning new wombs inside of them.
So don't laugh at the technological joke
Of scientists' long-reaching poke
They're doing the same thing now with their reproductive
    technology
And Neil Armstrong gives the Man in the Moon no apology.

Scene Four

Outside.

The same night. Behind an inn. A WOMAN, hands tied behind her back, feet bound, is slumped in a cart. Her daughter, URSULA, watches from a distance. When she perceives no one else is around she runs to her MOTHER, lightly jumps onto the cart and starts to untie her hands. URSULA was born deaf. She makes no sound when she communicates but uses sign language and mouths the words simultaneously.

MOTHER. Oh child, go. Go back lest they find you here.

URSULA, *having untied her* MOTHER's *hands, proceeds to loosen the ropes around her feet.*

(*Knocking* URSULA's *hands away.*) No, no, it's of no use. (*She holds out her hands, which are numb.*) My hands are all but dead. Where rope has bitten into them.

URSULA *starts to rub her* MOTHER's *hands until she can flex her fingers, then she goes to untie her feet. Taking* URSULA's *hands away, her* MOTHER *speaks softly, signing at the same time.*

Is no good. Go now and save yourself.

URSULA (*signs*). Cam, cam back with me.

MOTHER (*continuing to sign as she speaks*). I cannot. My leg is broken. Is too painful.

URSULA *brings out a leather bottle from her skirts. Her* MOTHER *angrily snatches it away from her and throws it to the ground.*

What did I counsel you? You know nothing of herbs or healing. Remember nothing.

URSULA *holds her* MOTHER's *head in her shoulder.*

(*To herself*). Better to let the water take me and give them proof of my innocence. They cannot then cam looking for you. Born deaf to them is sign of divel's work.

She gently lifts URSULA's *head, so that she can sign and says:*

Go to the big house and I will pray the lady take pity on you and give you work. Quickly afore my gaoler return from his aledrinking.

URSULA *lingers.*

Please go now.

She kisses URSULA *and then gently pushes her away.* URSULA *looks at her* MOTHER, *turns, jumps down from the cart and runs.*

(*To herself*). Please God keep her safe. Spare her.

Scene Five

The pond.

GRACE, ROSE, HELEN *and* MARY *stand on the edge of a large crowd. All that can be seen is the cross-bar of the gallows with the top of the rope hanging from it. At the moment the box is kicked away they turn and face outwards, eyes down, unable to look at each other, isolated by a sense of powerlessness and grief.* GRACE, HELEN *and* MARY *go off in different directions. The only sound is that of the rope straining against the wood.* ROSE *is alone. She sits as far away from the scene as possible and picks up two stones, idly knocking them together. Enter a fellow worker, a* MAN.

MAN. That be a fine way to spend an afternoon off now, Rose. Cam. Let's make the best of the sunshine and take us a stroll together. (*Silence.*) Maybe I'm not earning up to your expectation and it be the farmer hisself you're hoping for, eh?

ROSE, *fists flying, goes for him.*

He steps out of the way, laughing.

Oh, I'll have to be telling the pricker I've found one that can fly without a broomstick. Heh, heh.

He wanders off still chuckling. She throws the stones ineffectually after him and then sits down again. URSULA *enters, unseen by* ROSE, *stands some distance away, trying to summon the courage to approach* ROSE.

ROSE (*becoming aware that she is being watched, turns*). Who are you? (URSULA *doesn't move.*) Don't worry, I won't fly at you. What do you want with me? (*Pause.*) Well, if you don't speak up how am I to know?

ROSE *turns back and resumes staring ahead.* URSULA *takes a couple of steps towards* ROSE *but sees* JANE *approaching and takes fright and goes off.* JANE *sits next to* ROSE.

JANE (*gloomily*). Seems we didn't give his apprentice fright enough. (*Then:*) What are you doing sat there, Rose?

ROSE (*flatly*). Waiting for the stars to cam out.

JANE. Won't right yourself by sulking. Is not *your* tongue that has been stopped in your throat today.

ROSE. Easy words for you. Who was it spoke out last time? Grace.

JANE. Aye. (*Pause.*) I'd like to see her again afore I go.

ROSE. Go? When?

JANE. With the sun. And hoping it will prompt me to rise afore I'm missed.

ROSE. But I will see you again.

JANE. That be another thing I am hoping for.

ROSE. Can I get word to you?

JANE. Via another soldier perhaps. Though messages are apt to be long forgotten afore they arrive to those receiving them.

ROSE. I will write to you.

JANE (*incredulously*). You can write?

ROSE. Aye, and read.

JANE. You can read and write?

ROSE. Aye. Can you not hear under that helmet?

JANE. But how?

ROSE. Oft I go over to Grace and we stay awake all night. Her teaching me. Mind, is hard to set to work the next day without falling asleep over my pail.

JANE. Grace can read and write too?

ROSE. Course. I didn't learn from air. When her father saw he wasn't to have no sons, he taught her instead. She knows all manner of things that she taught herself besides.

JANE. Like what?

ROSE. Names and properties of herbs and plants and different ways to help heal the body.

JANE. So tell me about them.

ROSE. All that be of more interest to Grace than me. But I know the names of the stars.

JANE. So what are they?

ROSE. I can't show you now, can I? (*Pointing to the sky.*)

JANE (*carefully casual*). Maybe if we couldst meet at night you'd tell me.

ROSE. About best one is named Ursa Major.

JANE. Never heard of it.

ROSE. It means the Great Bear.

JANE. You ever seen a real bear?

ROSE. I cannot say I have.

JANE. I have, some miles back, chained up in an inn garden.

ROSE. A bear?

JANE. Aye.

ROSE. A proper bear? A live bear?

JANE. Aye. (*Teasingly.*) Maybe you'd like to borrow my helmet to aid your hearing.

ROSE (*jumping to her feet*). Meet me here as sun goes down. I've got a new plan. (*She starts to go.*)

JANE (*disappointed*). You mean we're not going to look at stars together after all.

Scene Six

Outside.
   Night. ROSE and JANE lead or rather are lead down the street towards the PRICKER's house by a dancing BEAR.

ROSE. My hope is that Grace is late. I didn't find courage enough to tell her about this.

JANE. She'll be pleased with us right enough. Surely.

ROSE. We don't even know if our friend Ursa is male or female.

JANE. Well, I ent getting down on my hands and knees in the dark to have a look. Should it make a difference?

ROSE. It might to Grace. She don't hold with violence for our sex.

JANE. What do she hold with for bears?

ROSE. I don't rightly know.

JANE (*unconcerned*). We're sure to find out by and by.

ROSE (*worried*). I don't doubt.

JANE. Look, I don't hold with violence myself (ROSE *looks at her in disbelief.*) against our sex and that is for why Ursa must try and kill him and nature take its course and the blame. Now quit worrying Rose. Look at it – not stopped dancing all the way – most probably be too wore out to piss.

ROSE. S'pose then it don't kill him?

JANE. At very least it will give him shock enough to soil his breeches.

ROSE. My hope is, 'tis not accustomed to being shut behind door and 'twill run amok.

JANE (*pointing*). That is pricker's residence, is it not?

ROSE. S'pose . . .

JANE. Now ent time for s'posing, now's the time for doing.

JANE *opens the door, puts her shoulder against the* BEAR's *back and shoves it inside.* ROSE *and* JANE *then crouch beneath the window. The* BEAR *lumbers towards the* PRICKER *and sits on the end of the bed. The* PRICKER *remains asleep. After a moment* ROSE *puts her head on the window sill.*

JANE (*whispers*). What is it? Has the shock laid him out dead?

ROSE. I'm surprised the shock ain't laid the bear out dead. It just slumped on the bed. Not even awoke the pricker.

JANE gets up and shuts the door with an almighty slam, then runs back and crouches under the window.

PRICKER (*wakes, startled*). What the? Who's there? Who is it?

ROSE (*deep booming voice.*) I am the biggest imp of all and I am cam to be familiar to you.

The PRICKER jumps out of bed, screaming. JANE pulls ROSE down.

PRICKER. Leave me be. Leave me be. (*He tears around the room in a mad panic, screaming, the BEAR loping after him.*)

JANE (*puts her head up, to ROSE*). Oh no, the lumping great noddy has put its arm round him. (*In a deep voice:*) The divel has sent me for you are his most trusted worker.

JANE ducks down. ROSE puts her head up. The screams reach an unbearable pitch as the BEAR tries to dance with the PRICKER.

ROSE. Oh no. It's trying to dance with him.

JANE sinks down as the PRICKER frees himself from the BEAR's grasp, jumps through the window and runs, without looking behind, until he is out of sight.

JANE (*gleefully*). Well, that's that.

ROSE (*giggles*). Leastways he won't be queueing up to stay in that room again in a hurry.

JANE. And we don't have to worry about sex of the bear for it did only dance and I'm sure even Grace holds with dancing.

ROSE. I have no mind about that now. Fact I wish it had done away with him.

Enter GRACE.

GRACE. Look at you pair of leverets, giving yourself hemorodes under the pricker's nose.

ROSE. Grace. Oh, Grace, you just missed picture of a lifetime.

GRACE. Get yourselves off that wet grass afore you grow any protrusions that he'll use as evidence of imp suckling. Is that I cannot bear.

JANE. Now, I'm glad you brung bears into the conversation.

ROSE. Pricker has fled.

GRACE (*confused*). Bears? Pricker fled?

JANE (*halfway through the window*). Cam, look for yourself. (JANE *and* ROSE *help* GRACE *through the window.*) Well, has made good use of bed. Is asleep.

ROSE. Best day's work it's ever done, in moons I'll warrant. More the shame that it never gobbled him up.

GRACE *laughs.*

JANE. We thought you'd be vexed at plan, not laughing.

GRACE. Brown bears are vegetarians.

ROSE. Are what?

GRACE. Only eat greens. Turn nose up at flesh.

JANE (*defensively*). Well, it danced with him.

GRACE. It would have been trained by players to do that.

JANE. Well, it don't look like it's about to take a bow. It won't budge. And I'm loathe to prod it in case it turns on us.

ROSE (*pointing*). And it can't sleep there a night or we're done for.

GRACE. Let's find some edible foliage suitable to its diet in pricker's garden. And we'll lure it out.

JANE. Leave me to rummage through this pit. There may be papers of interest to you, Grace.

ROSE *and* GRACE *leave the room.* JANE *makes a search of the room and finds a sum of money hidden under some papers. She hesitates. Looks up, but* ROSE *and* GRACE *aren't watching so she puts the money inside her jerkin.* ROSE *and* GRACE *come back inside the room armed with lettuce leaves.*

ROSE. You find anything?

JANE (*holds up some papers*). These, but I can't choose which to take, on account of I can't read.

GRACE. Let me see.

ROSE. Take them, Grace. We dare not wait here longer.

GRACE *takes the papers and waves the leaves under the* BEAR's *nose. It wakes up and nibbles at them.*

JANE. See, all it wanted was a nap.

GRACE *entices the* BEAR *out of the room.*

ROSE. Must be feeling sorry for itself that its dancing partner was so unsuitable.

When they are all outside.

GRACE. Would be best course to return this noble creature while its owners still slumber.

JANE. I am headed in that same direction and will be thankful in morning to have curtailed my travelling distance.

ROSE. But . . .

JANE. And none of your protests for it would be foolhardy man who attacked a soldier with a bear for a guard.

ROSE. Will we see you again?

JANE. When is next meeting?

GRACE. Not till full moon.

JANE. So, 'tis true covens meet by full moon.

ROSE. How else can you see foot in front of ditch?

JANE. If I'm still drawing breath and sword I'll hope to attend.

Exit JANE *pursued by a sleepy* BEAR.

GRACE. That is either a very hammerheaded woman or a very brave one.

ROSE. 'Tis a bit of both to my reckoning but that don't alter my opinion of her one jot.

GRACE (*laughs*). Aye.

GRACE *and* ROSE *continue on their way in silence.*

GRACE (*cheerfully*). You've not got a lot to say for one just performed historic service to womankind.

ROSE (*flatly*). I am pleased enough.

Silence.

GRACE (*sits down on a tree stump*). Cam on girl, spit it up.

ROSE (*sitting down next to* GRACE). Surely there are more problems facing us than brown bears left in the world.

GRACE (*smiles*). When did you learn to place such melancholy humour in your turn of phrase? Surely we can afford to smile at our triumphs?

ROSE. I want you to make a potion for me.

GRACE (*concerned*). Oh Rose, I knew not. Who did get away with that?

ROSE. Nay, not that. Though is connected but not in a straight-line way.

GRACE. What is? The hour is late and I have no eye to see into your brain.

ROSE. Is difficult.

GRACE. Aye.

ROSE. I do not want to grow into a woman.

GRACE *laughs.*

(*Angrily.*) Is not something to ache your jaw over. (*Then calmly.*) I am not womanly enough for farmer's liking but soon as I becam ripe enough for all to see he'll pluck me too. I eat so little, Grace, I would rather wilt than grow.

GRACE. That course can only do you harm. Short of poisoning yourself there is no way halt you becoming a woman.

ROSE. Sometime he cam so close I feel his breath on back of my neck and have to cast up behind a tree.

GRACE. That be customary put off. The farmer is the problem not your body.

ROSE. Easy words. For I hate him. I hate the work. And I hate my body also.

GRACE. You been on earth long enough to know choices are few. Least milking cows keep you free from pox.

ROSE. Milking farmer won't keep me free of other pox.

Silence.

GRACE. I am old woman now. I can't live forever.

ROSE. Don't say that Grace. As if I am not maudlin enough.

GRACE. Is a truth you'd best prepare for. I'd be honoured to teach you about the herbs and matters for body's well-being such as I know.

ROSE (*bursts out*). Oh no Grace! I don't want to know none of that. I am best not knowing. I have plenty more preference for making a play than a child. Be the worst thing that could happen to me, and I would rather be on parish, or in stocks than tend women in labour – yeuk, how could you suggest such a thing?

GRACE. These things seem not vital when you're young and have rude health.

ROSE. That has nothing to do with it. I tell you, Grace. I hate mere thought of touching bodies never mind else. Don't ever speak of it again to me.

GRACE (*sadly*). Rose.

ROSE. I won't blight this day with any more talk of it. Cam now, let's make off to Ann and Mary.

GRACE. Have we not put ourselves in enough danger this night?

ROSE. We have a lucky star to protect us.

GRACE. Oh aye?

ROSE. Make cheerful, for these dumps have left me. If I can make a plan to rid us of pricker, can only be a matter of time afore I do away with farmer.

They go.

Enter DOCTOR.

DOCTOR (*sings*).

God and the Technodoc

What is life but for creating
   Other life to carry on,
Churches and religion taught us
   We are made to marry one
Who like God can create babies
   Embryos of human form,
Where is life and science going
   Who decides the foetal norm?

Medicine is a new religion
   Opium to the childless pair
Who can judge when what's on offer
   Gives to them an equal share
Of the right to bring forth babies
   Perfect creatures shaped by man,
What will happen to the others
   Miscarried in the master plan.

Eradicate all forms of illness,
   Handicap and brain disease?
No one will be born disabled
   The technodoc is out to please.
Join the doctors and the medics,
   Scientists of the human life
Babies are essential for them
   To sustain the perfect wife.

Science has at its disposal
   Power to reproduce the race.

All the kindly interventions
   Are the subtle saving face
Of the other side of medicine.
   Interference is the plan.
Making life by experimentation
   Women's bodies controlled by man.

The DOCTOR *goes.*

Scene Seven

The servants' attic in LADY H's *house.*
   MARY *and* ANN *are sewing, mending a variety of garments from an assortment scattered around them.*

MARY (*stopping to rub her eyes*). Is no good, Ann, I will have to sleep else when morning comes my eyes will resemble two pissholes in the snow.

ANN. Sshush, don't make so much noise.

MARY. I am sewing as quietly as I can. (*She grins.*)

ANN. You'll be grinning when Lady Wipe-my-arse catches you awake at this hour.

MARY. She has never caught me awake or in any other position at this hour. (*Then:*) Aye. This day hast been bitter enough. Let's shut our eyes on it.

ANN. If we was to keep vigil for every woman killed, we'd not get sleep for many years hence.

MARY. Aye. (*She yawns.*)

ANN. Our time will come for their accusations and you cannot shut your eyes on that.

MARY. I have said I will mind child whilst you can go to the meetings.

ANN. All you do there is argue over who does it right way or wrong way – I'd rather keep my precious free time to myself.

MARY. Is not all like that. Asides is important to sort out differences.

ANN. Seem a mighty luxury to my mind. Risking everything to meet, causing you to be half-asleep at your work. We are not granted privilege of living quarters big enough to stand up in, never mind liberty to run around the village half the night. If you are caught will only confirm their suspicions that you are up to no good.

MARY. We cannot do nothing.

ANN. On that we are agreed, so we must leave.

MARY. Would be treacherous, we have no money.

ANN. As if I know not that. For if we did we'd not be sat here tickling each other's ears about it. I know it be a gamble we must take.

MARY. Gamble? Sheer peril. And what of the child?

ANN. You let me worry over the child. I am her mother.

MARY. Don't start that up.

ANN. You are the one most free to go and yet is you who are most scared. Can you not understand our safety here hangs by a thread.

MARY. We'd not find a position like we have here.

ANN. So it's not Grace nor Rose nor the rest keeping you here but the high time you have in your master's house.

MARY. With a footman and a stable boy who are partial to each other, and they are happy to keep up pretence of a bogus alliance with us to keep themselves from prying eyes. We would not find another position so favourable.

ANN. Bachelors aren't hung for their sex.

MARY. Ones of their leanings are neither embraced by their fellows. Cook says she heard talk of a cunning woman who arranges sham marriages between folks like us. So we can carry on our lives as we wish without tongues wagging.

ANN. What might you be suggesting now? That we all bed down together?

MARY. Merely that, is safer here than you s'pose.

ANN. I have no faith that when the rope grips our throats we shall hear but even a squeak of rebuke from either footman or stable boy.

A knock at the door makes them start. They both stand. MARY picks up a piece of wood.

(*Behind the door*). Who is it?

ROSE. Rose and Grace.

ANN (*opening the door, ushering them into the room*). What trouble has brought you here at this hour?

GRACE. No trouble. Set your mind at rest.

ROSE (*shouts*). We have rid . . .

MARY. Quietly now for we cannot afford whole household to know our affairs.

ROSE (*grandly*). We have rid this place this very night of the pricker.

ANN. How? (*Delighted.*) Rose, how?

ROSE. We frighted him with a bear. (*Pause for effect.*) A dancing bear.

MARY. I can guess whose cunning was behind that.

GRACE. Oh no. All young Rose's doing.

ROSE. And Jane.

MARY. Aye, from the moment I set eyes on her I knew she had spirit.

ANN (*smiles at MARY*). Jane? And who might she be?

MARY. That young mistress dressed as a soldier.

ROSE (*to MARY*). Aye and the moment you laid eyes on her you thought she was a man.

ANN. So, is he dead?

ROSE. No.

GRACE (*sharply*). Rose!

ROSE (*she looks at* GRACE). Aye and perhaps that is best. But is my guess he will not show his face round here lest the vision of his massive grizzly imp haunt him.

GRACE. Will mean a new start.

MARY. Do you hear that, Ann?

ANN. Aye. (*With delight.*) We are free. We are free.

Enter LADY AITCH (LADY H). *She barges into the centre of the room and so has her back towards* ROSE. *They are all rather shocked and a bit frightened by her presence.*

LADY H. There is more of you than I remembered.

MARY. If it please, my lady, these are two women from the village who are err . . . cam to err . . .

ROSE (*quickly*). Give the child lucky charm for its christening.

LADY H. Strange rituals.

GRACE. No, Lady H, 'twas a present. Not a charm. Rose, we do not want Lady H to believe we are ignorant, superstitious people.

ROSE (*mutters*). What we want don't come into it.

ROSE *and* GRACE *make to leave.*

LADY H. No, please, don't leave. I have had some sorry news. Seems my husband's guts got spilled in battle.

ROSE (*from behind* LADY H's *back holds up two fingers and mouths*). Two down.

MARY. We are sad for your distress, my lady.

LADY H. He was away much anyway, but there are certain responsibilities I cannot undertake unaided.

ANN. That is sorry news, my lady.

LADY H. Rumour hath reached my ears that meetings happen in the village for women without menfolk and, further, you attend them.

ANN. Only at night, my lady, and we do not sleep in your work.

LADY H. That I am not disputing, though God knows I should be. I am enquiring as to when, so that I might join you.

ROSE. You would not care for them, lady, we are a very rough crowd.

MARY. Begging your pardon, but I don't see how they could help you, with all respect.

LADY H. But I am given to understand that each gains solace for your life's lost happiness and further find husbands for one another and other lonely widows.

ANN. You would not like it.

LADY H. How am I to judge until . . .

GRACE. We know of no men suiting to your station and your ladyship would not care to be married off to any old cobbler would she?

LADY H. Certainly not.

Pause.

Alas, I am so confused, and in your debt for righting me, I have quite forgot my status. I'll bid you all goodnight.

(*She turns. Then as an afterthought:*)

Oh Ann, cam and see me first thing in the morning. I will need you to wetnurse the youngest heir. I am much too hard pressed for time myself.

She goes.

ANN (*ironically*). Now, where were we? Oh, yes, as we were saying. We are free.

Scene Eight

The meeting room.
GRACE, ROSE, HELEN *and* MARY.

ROSE (*to* HELEN). Least you can do is open your mouth and give us a half-good word of praise.

HELEN. You shad never have done such a thing, Rose. He'll only be more vengeful than afore.

ROSE. You have faith he'd have stopped afore we was all rotted at bottom of the pond?

HELEN. You've placed the rest of our lives in jeopardy.

ROSE. They was in jeopardy anyway.

GRACE. Leave her be, Helen. The pricker has not been seen since. Was a very brave thing Rose done.

ROSE. And Jane.

MARY (*teasing* ROSE). Oh aye and Jane.

HELEN. Fine for Jane, being as she's not from here. No nail nor noose will reach her – a mere lark to her mind.

ROSE (*losing her temper*). Don't you go putting her under. You a fine one to say such things yourself. No one cam looking for you, being married as you are. I am cam to accept that I would never get a pat on the head or back from you, but you never open your mouth except to drench other's suggestions.

MARY. I agree on that.

GRACE. Let's us get on with the play.

MARY. I'm sick of the bleedin' play. It has taken so long. Will look out of fashion now we have rid ourselves of the evil.

GRACE. We have rid ourselves of all evil, eh?

MARY. Oh, I'm not going to ache my brain reasoning with you, Grace. I'll do my bit so long as Helen promises to keep silent.

GRACE. We have enough wishing that on us in every waking hour, to be guarded enough not to ask it of each other.

HELEN (*pathetically*). I cannot help being married. Is difficult to shake off accumbrements of parson.

ROSE. Nobody asked you to marry him.

HELEN. He did.

MARY. You should have said no. You are not a lady of wealth enough to have it arranged for you.

HELEN. I have always wanted children but it was not to be. Even Grace cannot tell me why and it can't be his fault for men of the cloth are not prone to pox.

ROSE. Ha ha.

HELEN (*brightly*). Cam, I am still committed to our endeavours and will hold my tongue still from anything but praise.

GRACE. Right, now, Mary. I hear you have some wonderous new words to add.

MARY (*hesitates but then stands*). 'Verily we enquire!'

Enter JANE.

JANE (*jocular as ever*). Me again, you bundle of old maids, the soldier returned to your arms.

ROSE. You came!

JANE. Flying pitchforks couldn't keep me away. I cannot tarry long.

GRACE. You are in time to see our play.

JANE (*alarmed*). Has the pricker returned then?

ROSE. No. Sent for his belongings and has settled elsewhere.

GRACE. He was but part of our troubles the rest have not vanished.

JANE. Truth to say, that's, in part, reason why I'm stood here. Is about his belongings. I have grown accustomed to poking through purses of dead men and that night when you and Grace was coaxing the bear I found some money in Pricker's house.

She throws it down.

Do not be sore with me for I have righted myself. Is not mine.

GRACE. Nor ours.

JANE. Is now. And I have delayed too long already.

MARY. Surely half the money is yours.

JANE. I want nowt of it. That is my payment to myself for concealing it from such friends. I am away and don't say goodbye for it would not do for a soldier to be seen with misty eyes, for I will see you again soon.

She goes.

GRACE *is about to say something but she has gone. The others sit staring at the money.*

MARY. Really, by rights, it belongs to Rose.

ROSE (*shakes her head*). It is soiled. I did not earn it by torturing women.

HELEN. True place then would be the pondbed.

GRACE. Where it would not even be of benefit to duck's diet. Surely 'tis the property of the relatives of the women whose lives paid for it?

MARY. The factor that they had no relatives sped him in his work.

ROSE. Then maybe is ours to share? How much is there, Grace?

GRACE. You can count good as I. See for yourself.

ROSE (*carefully counts it*). Five and twenty shillings.

HELEN. So what does that work out at each?

ROSE. I just managed to count it – do you want miracles from me?

GRACE. Six shillings.

MARY (*whistles*). Six shillings?

GRACE. And threepence, but wait on, aren't we going to use it for something for all of us.

HELEN (*jokingly*). Like what – buy an inn?

GRACE. What do each of you want then?

MARY. Ann would like to go to London and my excuse has all but disappeared with this windfall.

HELEN. That be no place for a child.

MARY. I have told her but it seems women are kicking up great protest there and would be fine thing to be part of. So you, Helen? What would you have?

HELEN. A child.

ROSE (*not nastily*). That might cost you dear but you don't need to part with no money.

HELEN. With money I can afford a doctor from the town.

ROSE. Oh no, tell me my lugs have turned to liars.

HELEN. To me is worth trying.

ROSE. Par. You would willingly give them power over us by offering yourself up for their butchery.

GRACE (*sternly*). Is all right for you Rose. You do not entertain thought of having children, but it be a severe mistake to dismiss them what do.

MARY (*gently*). There are plenty of motherless children in the world.

HELEN. But I wish for one of my own. Only what most women take as given. Oh aye, and a great burden to many but 'tis something I want for myself. Am I to be denied that?

GRACE (*carefully*). And s'pose there is no cure for you, Helen?

HELEN. Then I will buy a babe.

MARY
ROSE } (*outraged*). Buy one!

HELEN. Plenty of women have so many they don't know what to do with them.

MARY. Buy one off Lady H, then. She's always farming them out.

HELEN. Money wouldn't induce her, she don't need it.

GRACE. Aye.

Silence.

MARY. And what then are your dreams, Rose?

ROSE. I will buy some men's clothes and then I'm off to find Jane and fight alongside in the war.

HELEN. But you'll have to charge about with a pike.

ROSE. Is no heavier than a scythe and a lot less wieldy to use.

Pause.

Grace?

GRACE. I am too saddened to reason further.

HELEN. Seems the only thing left is to share it.

ROSE (*goes to pick it up, then*). We've not heard from Grace yet.

MARY. Oh aye. What's it to be for you, Grace?

GRACE. I all but feel out of turn now. For I wanted us to remain together and form a band of travelling players to go from county to county entertaining women . . . Making them laugh, dispelling myths and superstitions and fears so that life and health and well-being were no longer mysteries but understood by one and all.

Silence.

Rose?

ROSE. My mind is set but after the war . . .

GRACE. Always taken as given you are living.

ROSE. I want to be equal, Grace. Treated the same.

GRACE. But not in war – in peace. We are becoming stronger, now is not the time to throw it away.

ROSE. I am throwing nothing away 'cept my servitude.

HELEN. We should pledge now to meet two years from hence and find what has becam of our dreams.

Silence.

GRACE. I cannot say goodbye in this room. Let us walk as far as the house together afore we go our separate ways.

MARY (*off*). I can't wait to tell Ann.

HELEN (*off*). I'm not telling Parson.

HELEN *and* MARY *go off.* ROSE *and* GRACE *linger.*

ROSE. You are sorely disappointed in me, Grace?

GRACE. I know well enough once you have idea stuck in your head, take the divil to shift it.

ROSE. I will cam back and when I do I'll have written a play all myself, Grace, for you. I won't forget you.

GRACE *turns away.*

Are you all right?

GRACE. Aye, just tired.

ROSE *takes* GRACE's *arm and they go. Presently* LADY H *enters looking rather the worse for the weather.*

LADY H. Yoo hoo. Cam on now. Show thyselves. I know this is where you meet.

Enter the PRICKER.

PRICKER. I have you now.

LADY H. Ah ha, now are you looking for a woman?

PRICKER. Which woman?

LADY H. Was your intent to pose that as question or accusation?

PRICKER. Oh, begging your pardon. I didn't realise it was you, Lady H.

LADY H. Oh, 'tis but you, Master er . . . How remiss of me, I cannot recall your name. I thought you'd left this part of the country long since.

PRICKER (*doffs his hat*). Newly appointed Woman-Finder General and you do well to take my advice, Lady H, and not lurk around this place at night or I might mistake you for a hag.

LADY H. I am apt to overlook your insult as my appearance is somewhat impaired by the elements and I don't suppose with your newly acquired grand title you'll be having much to do with a muddy rut like this village now.

PRICKER. On the contrary. Soon I am to be stationed by here for good. Alas, there is evil in the air.

LADY H. I need no reminding, for why do you think I look like I've been wrestling with a hawthorn bush? As you are so concerned with the air you'd not mind giving me your cape for it's a fair walk back to my house.

She takes the cape before he can protest and goes, leaving him standing alone in the room.

PART TWO

Scene One

Outside.

Two years later. ROSE, *now a soldier, is on watch duty. She stands alone, occasionally adding a branch or log from the pile of dry wood beside her to the small fire in front of her.* JANE *enters, bounds over to* ROSE *and slaps an arm around her.* ROSE *looks up surprised and pleased and then looks around her nervously.*

JANE. Never worry. They are always slapping arms round each other. Why aren't you down yonder (*Nodding down the hill.*) fighting with the foliage to ferret out the spy?

ROSE. Why aren't you?

JANE. I am to deliver a message and waiting on a fresh horse.

ROSE. Oh.

Pause.

JANE. To my reckoning this war will soon be finished with.

ROSE. You've been saying that with the same regularity as moon waxing and I know 'tis only to keep me cheerful.

JANE. Nay, I do feel it in my bones.

ROSE. We can only pray you don't feel a bullet in your bones as proof of your miscalculation.

JANE. There is much talk of it.

ROSE. And where will they seek their enjoyment and bragging then?

JANE. Is but their bluff and relief on feeling of having cheated death. For if you have lived through the bloodiest battle, the possibility of tripping over a stone and getting a broke neck do seem remote.

ROSE. Par, that explanation be too generous by half.

JANE. So then, and I've been thinking on this, maybe is compensation for their inabilities. Alarmed that they cannot give life they do find glory in death. Surely that serves as explanation enough as to why they oft set themselves dangerous tasks for no other purpose than to prove themselves – 'tis envy of birth. There now would not Grace be proud of my reasoning! Maybe could even go in your play.

ROSE. I had a dream of Grace. Seems I was calling out her name – much to all else's amusement.

JANE. If you callest out the name of every woman you know, you'll be gaining a reputation of a real ladies' man.

ROSE. You be almost as bad – you view everything in jest.

JANE. Oh Rosie, you would have me leave with face down to my knees?

ROSE. No, for if you leave I am afraid, and by staying here I am afraid. I do spend all my time in fear.

JANE. Tell me then what is without fear. You can lock your life away behind four walls and still be murdered in your bed.

ROSE. That is of little consolation.

JANE. I do miss you.

ROSE. And supposing we never see each other again?

JANE. Now ain't the time for supposing.

ROSE. Oh and why not?

JANE. Supposing you'd choked to death in your cot, supposing life got crushed out of you by a cow toppling on top of you?

ROSE (smiles). The likelihood of that has lost me no sleep.

JANE. Supposing farmer bedded you and you died in childbed? Suppose you'd been swam and hung? Suppose I'd not met you, then we'd not be supposing.

ROSE. Suppose some sword run through your breast.

JANE. Then.

ROSE. Then won't be the time for supposing.

JANE. Where is the bravery of the bear baiter?

ROSE. It got lost in some ditch, or behind some wall. I don't know anymore and if you lay dead or dying I would have no knowledge of that either.

JANE. If I am alive I will find you and if I die I shall remember to do so thinking of you. So you will know and you must do the same for me.

Pause.

Though I don't think you should put that in the play. Would make my character sound damaged in the brain-pan.

ROSE. You silly mome. Is not your character I want to keep alive. Is you. And me.

JANE. I know. Rosie, I know.

JANE *hugs* ROSE. *Enter male* SOLDIER. ROSE *and* JANE's *body language and posture change in front of him. They 'act' and talk like men.*

SOLDIER. I thought you was to keep watch, not cling to each other like a couple of wet nurse-maids.

JANE (*turning to face him*). What business be it of yours?

SOLDIER. Plenty if we are attacked because of your tomfoolery. I am cam through to report, friend, that your horse be ready.

JANE (*nodding towards the fire*). Log burst. (*Nods towards* ROSE.) Embers caught him full in face.

SOLDIER (*sarcastically*). Nasty.

ROSE (*turns*). I be fine now.

(*To* JANE:) Thank you for your comfort.

JANE (*patronisingly, to* SOLDIER). Don't fret yourself little man, I'll not dally further, so if I'm late will be my jig roasting, not yours.

ROSE. Ride with care, sir.

JANE. I will that too, sir.

She turns and goes.

Silence.

SOLDIER (*making conversation*). Folly pure folly, is it not, leaving you and I alone. I thought orders was for others to return at dusk.

ROSE. Their orders was to return with spy dead or alive with preference to the latter state.

SOLDIER. Aye, well, by my reckoning commonsense should sometimes give leeway to orders.

Pause.

Or do you not agree?

ROSE. Aye.

SOLDIER (*moves closer*). I was apt to thinking you a bit queer but now I see I am mistaken, are you not the one fancying himself for having cuckolded the parson?

ROSE. I think not.

SOLDIER. Aye – is you – crowing in your sleep thrice 'Grace, Grace'.

ROSE. That be twice. Thrice is this number. (*She holds up three fingers.*)

SOLDIER. She be your sweetheart then? Is she? She is that, I can tell. What's she like then?

ROSE. You think this war will soon be over?

SOLDIER. You missing it that much then?

Pause.

Aye, by my reckoning we have the better of them, but war will not end for me whilst notion of Royalty still kicking. Is the thought of those wastrel bastards getting their true deserts keeps me going.

ROSE. Then you are n'ere beset by fear?

SOLDIER. Me? Nay?

Pause.

Why then, are you?

ROSE. Aye.

SOLDIER. Well, sometimes my gut do behave of its own accord like it was nothing to do with my head. But I think that be the same for most.

ROSE. I don't know.

Silence.

SOLDIER (*almost mumbled*). First time I did kill a man I did cast up. I had no notion of how bloody the mess would be.

ROSE. Did you never see death before?

SOLDIER. Aye, my sister died when I was but not five years old. But it was more like seeing a body asleep.

ROSE. And did you never see a woman swam?

SOLDIER. Oh aye, but that was more sport, she was a lewd-tongued old woman used to frighten me as a boy.

ROSE. You still look like a boy to me.

SOLDIER. By looks on you, you be even younger than I.

He moves closer.

God knows I've seen more hair on a woman.

ROSE *moves out of the light of the fire.*

Whilst we are about speaking the truth, I've never known a woman. I do pretend I have but I've not.

ROSE. Did you not know your mother?

SOLDIER (*scoffs*). Aye. Not by that meaning. (*He nudges* ROSE.) You know.

(*Then piteously:*) I suppose I might die not knowing.

Pause.

What's it like then?

Pause.

What's the game? I've all but laid my soul bare to you.

ROSE *gestures to him to be quiet. And points to a* LOYALIST SOLDIER, *standing, some way off, back to them and out of breath.*

(*Handing his pistol to* ROSE). Have that cocked. (*Creeping up from behind he seizes the* LOYALIST.) Cam along with you, sir, where we can see you better. (*Dragging his victim in a stranglehold towards the fire.*) Now out with it, what is your business?

ROSE. He can't speak for your arm crushing his apple.

SOLDIER (*shoves his opponent, who is face up, to the ground*). And looks like a jerkin stuffed full of documents. Let's see what secrets we have in here.

He bends, puts his hand inside the jerkin and pulls it out again quickly.

It be a wench. (*Then with glee to* ROSE:) We have ourselves a wench here.

(*To the* WOMAN:) Aye and now I see your face, you be pretty in spite of your costume.

He kisses her roughly. She turns her head and spits in his face.

What sort of whore runs with Loyalist bastards eh? No need to answer on that for we're about to find out.

ROSE. No.

SOLDIER. Fair's fair, me first. (*Sitting on the* WOMAN. *He takes his sword off and throws it aside.*)

ROSE, *remembering* GRACE's *advice, lets out an unnerving howl of laughter.*

Don't take on, you'll get your turn. (*Then on seeing* ROSE *advance, pistol in hand.*) And it's not that gun you'll be needing, son. (*The* WOMAN *takes this moment to struggle from underneath him but he restrains her.*) Not so fast.

She scratches his face.

You little vixen.

They struggle on the ground in front of the fire. ROSE *realises that should she shoot, she might hit the wrong one. Putting the pistol down she goes to the fire and tearing a red hot branch, waits till the* SOLDIER *is on top of the* WOMAN *and puts it down his back. He screams and lets go. A shot is fired. And it is the woman,* BRIDGET, *who stands shaking, but her pistol pointed at* ROSE. *They stand in silence, the body of the* SOLDIER *between them.*

BRIDGET. So it was to be your turn next?

Pause.

ROSE. You will not make your way alive from here without my help.

BRIDGET. You must take me for a halfwit. I will not leave you here whilst you still have tongue in your head.

ROSE (*looks at the body*). I will ride with you.

BRIDGET. Aye. In front – this pointing to your back, and if I am brought down, I shan't be alone.

Scene Two

The church.

HELEN's *husband a* PARSON, *is sitting in the pulpit making notes.* HELEN *enters, pausing to give the inside of the font a wipe. She walks down the aisle towards the pulpit.*

HELEN. May I be granted words with you husband?

PARSON. Presently, dear. Not now for I am too busy.

HELEN. And what is this task?

She starts to step up in the pulpit.

PARSON. Women are not allowed in the pulpit. Take thy foot off from that step.

HELEN *obeys*.

I am recording events in my diary.

HELEN. You don't need to do that perched up there.

PARSON. It serves to keep me ever mindful of my responsibility to my congregation.

HELEN. But you can't have anything to record other than 'today I wrote in my diary' for you've done nothing else.

PARSON (*impatiently*). I won't be a moment, I am just writing history.

HELEN (*wandering over to the lectern*). And where is the reason behind that?

PARSON. In many years hence, men will want to read it and find out about the accounts and happenings of our time.

HELEN. You only know what goes on inside a church. Could I not help you with it?

PARSON. A woman cannot write, for even if she has a mind to understand the lines on paper, her emotions get in the way of truth.

Pointing to his diary.

This is plain statement of fact so it will not be questioned as to its accuracy in the future.

HELEN. What does it detail?

PARSON. You need not be troubled with it.

HELEN. I'm sure t'would improve under my guidance.

PARSON. Don't be foolish, women don't make history.

HELEN. Best read me your version before my curiosity causes me to test if the bird can fly.

Meaning the lectern, which is a wooden eagle.

PARSON (*sighs*). Very well. If it will mean some peace for me and be of some amusement to you.

HELEN (*mutters*). It will be of little else I'm sure.

PARSON (*reads as though delivering a sermon*). 'The war has rid us of many evils not least of the evil embodied in some of the female sex who were weighed in the balance and found wanting. Suitably dealt with through rigorous court procedures and brought to justice either swum or hung.'

HELEN (*curtly*). You've repeated the word evil twice.

PARSON (*casually*). 'Tis part of women's nature since life began with Eve.

HELEN. I have heard that so many times the words form wax and block my ears.

PARSON. God's word writ since time began. Is not for mortals to meddle with.

HELEN (*wild with rage, sweeps the bible from the lectern to the floor, smashes her fists on the lectern and jumping and down shouting*). Why can't you change? Why can't you change?

An elderly WOMAN PARISHIONER enters from the main door at the back, scurries to a back pew and kneels, hands tightly pressed together, eyes firmly shut. On seeing her, the PARSON scrambles from the pulpit, crosses to HELEN.

PARSON (*in hushed whisper*). Do not take on in such a hysterical humour, calm yourself. Do you want for us to be footing another bill from the quack?

HELEN (*calmly*). Pray continue.

Simultaneously the PARISHIONER starts to mumble a jumbled up, only half-remembered version of the Lord's Prayer.

Our father witch chart in heaven

Hello to thy brain
Give us this day our daily bread
Forgive us our panes
As we forgive those will be done
Thy kindom be done
As now or never
Lead us up to temptation
Deliver us from weevil
Thine be the glory every lasting son
For ever and ever, Amen.

The words cannot be heard clearly, i.e. it should not compete with the following dialogue, but should continue until HELEN speaks directly to her.

PARSON. This is but a humble clergyman's account.

HELEN (*nods*). Aye. (*She waits, tapping her foot.*)

PARSON (*scrambling with his notes; reads in hushed tones*). Some of these women were unfortunate. (*Looks up.*) See, I too can find sympathy. (*Continues reading.*) In fact many were merely harmless, repulsive, foul-smelling hags who cursed everyone who cam near and were quite mad in the head.

HELEN (*aggressively*). Can you not know what a dangerous thing you write.

PARSON. You are rapidly putting me in bad humour. Now I have quite lost the flow, please content yourself to leave me be.

HELEN (*coldly*). Presently, dear, for I wanted to speak with you.

PARSON. Well, speak then and leave me in peace.

HELEN (*calmly*). Have no fear. Firstly, are you a Quaker?

PARSON. In our Lord's name what blasphemy are you asking of me? You know my religion. Steady as the rock of St Peter.

HELEN. Even he was known to quake in a cock's presence.

PARSON. Do not play games with the scriptures.

HELEN. Well, I am a Quaker.

PARSON. You cannot be, you are wed to me.

HELEN (*serenely*). Oh dear. Now a Quaker must be married to another Quaker.

PARSON. Have you been victim to bites from mad dog?

HELEN. I must make sure. You say you are not a Quaker?

PARSON. You know I'm not.

HELEN. Then I cannot stay married to you.

PARSON. Have you lost all sense?

HELEN. No. The dilemma is solved. I wilt leave you to your solitude now husband. Thank you for sparing me the time.

She turns on her heel and strides down the aisle.

PARSON. But you can't.

HELEN (*on reaching the praying PARISHIONER, stops briefly and taps her on the head*). That pes would be put to better use saving your knees whilst scrubbing floors. Take it with you.

She continues walking.

PARSON (*trying to catch up with his wife whilst retaining his dignity*). Helen? (*On reaching the PARISHIONER he lays his hand on her head so she sinks back to her knees.*) Bless you, child.

(*Continues to follow HELEN.*) But you are my wife.

Pausing only to spit in the font, HELEN goes, shutting the door behind her. Once outside she laughs.

Scene Three

A rowing boat on the river.
    ROSE and BRIDGET *are seated opposite each other in a small rowing boat.* ROSE *sits back trailing her burnt hand in the water.* BRIDGET *rows but cannot take her eyes off* ROSE *which proves a preferable pastime to rowing.*

ROSE (*sitting up*). Shall I take my turn now?

BRIDGET. Your hand is too sore. Besides I am far from tired.

ROSE. What ails you then?

BRIDGET (*blurts out*). I thought I must be only one of my kind under the sky, and now I have found you – is that joy which distracts me.

ROSE (*laughs*). Will be short-lived if it prevents you from pulling on the oars – for we shall perish.

BRIDGET. I am too happy. I care not.

ROSE. Well I do. Here. Stand up and change places.

They both stand. The boat rocks. ROSE holds onto BRIDGET to steady herself. BRIDGET kisses ROSE. Both slightly surprised and shocked and sit down again without having changed places.

BRIDGET. Rose, cam home with me.

ROSE. Home?

BRIDGET (*starting to row with renewed vigour*). You'd not want for anything again.

ROSE. You must have wanted for something – to leave its comfort.

BRIDGET. Was for something I didn't want, namely a rich toad with his brain in his stones and one thought between them.

ROSE. And if he still waits for you? Your mother will put me to work in her garden no doubt.

BRIDGET. She'll be only too overwhelmed with joy to see me alive and that you have no money will play no part when I tell you saved my life. Rose, you will have riches and servants such as you never imagined.

ROSE. And do you imagine that this war with its blood and death and gore has meant nothing to me? For it is about no one being a servant to another. No more rich and idle by virtue of their birth but every person equal.

BRIDGET. Every man. For they might each have equality but they still take upon themselves, rich or poor, a wife who is but a slave and not paid into the bargain.

ROSE. But now it is you who talk of servants. I am a servant. Do you think I'd take it upon myself to treat my kind likewise?

Pause.

BRIDGET. Then I shall share with you all I have.

ROSE. Then cam back with me?

BRIDGET. Back where?

ROSE. To my village.

BRIDGET (*shakes her head*). I'd be out of place.

ROSE. I'd not be out of place with your kind?

BRIDGET. Money can buy a person any place.

ROSE (*ironically*). Oh Aye. Money.

BRIDGET. Please think on it Rose.

ROSE (*shakes her head*). My longing to see my friends again be too strong.

BRIDGET. They will be asleep now.

ROSE. But the morning will unite us.

Pause.

BRIDGET. Then spend this night with me.

Scene Four

A misty day by the pond.
     Enter ROSE, *on foot. She can just about see* HELEN *standing on a tree stump and* MARY, ANN *and an unknown* WOMAN *standing motionless beside* HELEN.

ROSE (*approaching slowly*). So none have mislaid our pledge.

HELEN (*shouts*). Cam closer, sir, show yourself.

ROSE *moves closer and finds the only person there is* HELEN.

ROSE (*to herself*). Two years and I'd quite forgot tricks marsh mist could play.

HELEN. You be a stranger here?

ROSE. No more stranger than you, Helen.

HELEN. Who are you? (*She takes two steps towards* ROSE.) Rose? Young Rose?

She hugs her.

ROSE (*laughs and frees herself*). Steady, lest the village tongues have us tied in holy state afore we can be acquainted again.

HELEN (*stands back*). My, what a handsome fellow you make. I hope two years at war has not turned you to the habits of other young men.

ROSE (*quietly*). I am home.

HELEN. Rose. Oh Rose, I am pleased to see this day. What have you done to your hand?

ROSE (*putting her hand behind her back*). Nothing. And how have you fared these two years since?

HELEN. You have been constant in my thoughts, Rose, not least because you were right. My dealings with doctors served only to punish and humiliate me. I do swear they loathe us worse than the rest of their kind. But, for me now that is finished.

(*Carefully.*) And what news of Jane?

ROSE. I know not where she is. So make cheerful with your tales, for there must be some event you can recall which will warm my heart.

HELEN. Rose . . .

ROSE. Helen, tell me only of cheerful things. Tell me of London and the jick-a-joy women kicked up there.

HELEN. Oh aye, and why would you be interested in peace protests when you was making money in the war?

ROSE. Oh rouse yourself.

HELEN. Was all but wonderful, Rose, how we wished you'd seen it.

Slight pause.

Mary (*She falters but continues.*) becam so carried away with her protesting against violence that she broke the Duke of Richmond's staff over his own head.

ROSE (*laughs*). That do sound like her.

HELEN. That is not but half of it. The chant went up over and over 'We will not be wives and tie up our lives to villainous slavery'.

ROSE. So another war broke out at the moment I'll wager.

HELEN. The retort was varied but in the usual manner. From contemptible vileness to what they deemed as reasoned arguments like 'Go home and wash your plates'. But you have never heard women's voice so strong. One immediately rejoined 'You give us something to put on our plates and then we'll wash 'em'. While another cried 'We ent washing no more plates for you'. And another much to Ann and Mary's delight screamed 'When I have your head on a plate then I'll wash it off'. I had to keep reminding the other two that our purpose there was to ask for peace. And we met there women and, Rose, they had so many ideas like yourself you'd have talked till your clacker fell apart. Cam home with me so we can eat and talk at leisure. Is too cold standing on this spot.

ROSE. But first you must reveal to me, what are these clothes you have on?

HELEN. I have become a Quaker.

ROSE (*alarmed*). You mean thou has the shaking pox? I thought you looked in peculiar shape tossing your arms on this stump.

HELEN (*laughs*). It is but the new religion.

ROSE (*more alarmed*). That is good news? The misery religion has wrought us. Helen, what folly is this?

HELEN. Afore you lambast me hear me out, for in this new religion I am a preacher.

ROSE. You?

HELEN. Any person who feels so moved can be.

ROSE. No doubt St Paul's corpse be a-quaking too.

HELEN. I'll have you know I can draw quite a crowd with details of my visions, which I can reveal to you, are well structured so as to be precise on pointing out the nature of women's accumbrements.

ROSE. But what of your husband? I perceive your walls would crumble under strain of two preachers practising their sermons within.

HELEN (*gleefully*). The way of this new religion be if your spouse be not of the same persuasion, you can leave for another who shares your beliefs.

ROSE. Is far less of an evil solution than ridding yourself of a wife by getting her hung.

Pause. HELEN *does not respond.*

So you have some bad news? You have taken yourself a Shaker husband?

HELEN (*smiles*). My visions are such that I cannot seem to find a suitable one. You wait, we shall stir up this country in this time of unrest, till woman shall laugh till she cries at very notion of being pinned down to man.

ROSE. I will fetch the others and we shall have a meeting like never afore.

HELEN. No. (*Gently.*) Rose, you can't.

ROSE (*ruefully*). Oh, waste no worry over me. Dressed as a man has given me wonderful freedom to go charging about where I want.

HELEN. Let's sit down.

ROSE. For why? We're not in church. (*Pause. So she sits on the tree stump.*) Right, I am sat down. Oh, Mary and Ann are still in London?

HELEN (*sits down next to her and holds her hand*). Rose, Ann and Mary are dead.

ROSE. Dead? They are dead?

HELEN. Yes. Hung.

ROSE (*in disbelief*). Hung? For what?

HELEN. For what else?

ROSE. We did rid this place of the pricker, did we not? I can't believe it. Did we not rid this place . . . ?

HELEN (*gently*). About the same time as we went our separate ways he returned with fame, fortune and self-appointed title and powers and set about his task more zealously than ever.

ROSE. But you said you all went to London.

HELEN. Aye but others returned for child, whilst I stayed on to waste money on their doctors.

ROSE (*letting go of* HELEN's *hand, stands and turns accusingly, raising her voice*). They are dead? And you are content to sit here holding my hand and say they are dead and you did nothing?

HELEN (*stands, angrily, almost shouting*). And what would you know of what's been done? There has been one hundred hung since you've been gone and to my reckoning double that number swam and drowned unrecorded. And you demand of me what has been done when women live in fear of drawing next breath for it bringing the noose closer to their windpipe. When women take to practising holding their breath in hope they might sink and be then dragged from the water alive.

(*Quieter.*) And you ask me what has been done in this place where we dare not even look at one another or, God forbid, converse for that be deemed conspiracy enough. And you will tell me the old story that love is as strong as death? For in these times, to my mind, life all but holds a weak flame to fear.

ROSE (*sits ashamed*). I did not know.

HELEN (*calmly but still angry*). And well might you brag of men's clothes. For it does not pay to be a daughter today. The child, aye, with not two years of life behind her was swam along with her mother for the crime – the crime of being descendant of Eve – which be but a mispelling of Evil to their minds. (*Sadly.*) Rose, they have all but bled our village dry of our sex.

ROSE. I dare but ask the question burning in my head.

HELEN. We know what they can do. We have paid for that knowledge at such cost that those remaining can no longer afford to be left divided.

ROSE. And Grace? Helen, what of Grace?

HELEN (*gently*). Rose, I know not whether she is yet living or has died from her sufferings.

ROSE. She is in gaol?

HELEN. Would be to no avail, Rose. 'Tis too well kept and her brain is worse scrambled than a broke egg.

ROSE. She is in town gaol?

HELEN (*sighs*). Aye. Where hangings are public sport. As the crowd never knows the victim, not a shadow passes through their eyes.

HELEN *goes off*.

ROSE (*sings*).

Rosie's Song

When I was fighting alongside the men
For the freedom they had taken by right,
I wondered if I'd visit my village again
And return to another dear fight.
The price I have paid to walk as a man
Has lost me the trust of my kind

And it had been part of a much bigger plan
But now I am back here I find –

I fought in their wars, and not with my sister,
My pay is in shillings and being called mister,
While women have hanged and drowned all the time,
And being a woman's a death-bringing crime.
I gave up my woman in wearing a disguise,
Partly by bribery, partly by lies,
And what they have got is a soldier to fight
And one woman less to defend her birthright.

The freedom to pass as a man is a curse –
No woman would choose that for her life –
And marriage to men is no better or worse
For bearing the name of a wife.
The only way through is to stand out and strong,
And not wear disguise in *their* fight,
But to be with the women here where I belong
And to call on our strength and our might.

I fought in their wars, and not with my sister,
My pay is in shillings and being called mister
While women have hanged and drowned all the time
And being a woman's a death-bringing crime.
I gave up my woman in wearing a disguise
Partly by bribery, partly by lies,
And what they have got is a soldier to fight
And one less woman to defend her birthright.

For they take the skills and the powers that we share
With women who trust in our healing.
For they cut and thrust, and no one will spare
So no woman dare speak what she's feeling.
But I shall take power and we'll start a war
Against doctors and soldiers and men
Who challenge our right and seize at the core
Of our birthright, our freedom. Fight again!

Scene Five

The gaol.

A very unpleasant gaol with an equally unpleasant-looking GAOLER. ROSE *approaches him, placing a flask of beer on the table. Although she is still dressed as a man she is no longer dressed as a soldier.*

GAOLER. And what's a young gentleman like yourself be wanting with me (*Sarcastically.*) sir?

ROSE. I'm a visitor to these parts and enquiring as to when the next hanging might be?

GAOLER. Luck's out, sir. Was this very morning two pretty young things drew a great crowd. You'll be cursing yourself if you missed it.

ROSE. So you'll be keeping an empty gaol, then sir?

GAOLER. Not in their interest or mine, if gaol was empty I'd not have work. Like days of cock fighting. No good if you finished off your last cock. Rest assured, no shortages of women round here, dare say we'll have more in by the end of the week.

ROSE. Is an old woman I'm after.

GAOLER (*firmly*). Now listen here, young sir. There's still plenty of young maids out there what would be happy to service a young man like yourself. I don't know what you gents think I'm running here.

ROSE (*abruptly*). I do not want that (*Spitting out the word.*), sir.

GAOLER. You don't look the sort, granted, but you can never tell, I am afraid to say. Some of them Puritans are the worse.

ROSE. You don't understand.

GAOLER (*mockingly*). Aye. I dare say.

ROSE. I do not want her for any purpose other than talking.

GAOLER (*seriously*). Forgive me, sir, I now understand. She put a curse on your family and you want one last chance to remove it, lest further tragedy strike.

ROSE. Aye, aye, that's right.

GAOLER. Well, out of luck again. That old hag wouldn't know if she was saying the Lord's Prayer or cursing a cow. Her brain's curdled worse than the milk she's bewitched.

ROSE. Has she been here long?

GAOLER. Some months now. Aye, they're hoping for a bit more life outta her. Now that's an arse-about-face idea if ever I heard one. Still these days crowd gets mighty despondent if them what's hanged be a corpse afore hangman even gets started.

ROSE. Take me to her.

GAOLER. Now hold still, young sir.

ROSE. Give me a cup of that and keep rest. (*She takes a cup of beer.*)

GAOLER. Through there and mind you leave her in the same state you found her in.

ROSE *finds* GRACE *chained at the feet and whispers for fear of being overheard by the* GAOLER.

ROSE. Grace? (*Gently trying to rouse her.*) Grace? Grace? Is me.

GRACE (*mumbles*). Oh another imp, a rat this time. Our father who art in heaven hallowed be thy name the divel. I have more imps than stars in the sky and they all seem to sleep here in my bed with me, so fly and take them with you.

ROSE. Grace?

GRACE. Young man, I am done, done with thee all.

ROSE *gently tilts the cup to* GRACE's *mouth.*

GRACE (*spits in back in* ROSE's *face*). Every woman has her breaking point and you have seen mine thrice over. Leave me be.

ROSE *doesn't know what to do or say. Impulsively she undoes her outer garment and takes* GRACE's *hand, placing it between her vest and outer garment, on her breast.*

ROSE. Grace, it's me.

GRACE (*looks into* ROSE's *face trying to recall who it belongs to. At last she says faintly*). Rose?

ROSE. None other.

GRACE. I knew you'd cam. (*Her hand falls and she slips into half-consciousness.*)

GAOLER (*shouts*). Shift your parliament, sir. You don't know what you'll catch in there.

ROSE (*returns to* GAOLER). I trust the ale is to your liking.

GAOLER. Not so much as to grant any further favours.

ROSE. And how would they know? If she died?

GAOLER. I've got a tongue in my head, ain't I?

ROSE. And they'd have to see the body?

GAOLER. You think stink's not bad enough when they're alive. I get the corpses shifted quick enough. Just get a doctor or a priest to sign paper.

ROSE. I would like to take her.

GAOLER. You're a strange one, you are, but I have no time for this riddle.

ROSE. And for you to tell them she died.

GAOLER. You would eh? Just like that I'd let a young gent whose tastes are out of course make off with a dying hag.

ROSE. How much? (*She drops a coin on the table.*)

GAOLER. It's more than my job's worth.

ROSE (*drops another coin in front of him*). And what's your job worth?

GAOLER (*flatly*). More than that.

ROSE *puts another coin down.*

Who'd sign the paper?

ROSE. I would.

GAOLER (*unsure*). Oh, aye.

ROSE. I'm a doctor. (*She puts another coin down.*)

GAOLER. A doctor you say now? And what would a doctor be wanting of a half-witted crone, with one foot in hell and the other on piss-soaked straw?

ROSE. Bodies are valuable to our science.

GAOLER. Aye, I have heard something of the like.

ROSE. So you'll do it?

GAOLER. Not for four shillings I won't.

ROSE. Five shillings. No more.

GAOLER. If you're caught I know nothing of this.

ROSE. Very well. Take her cramp rings off.

GAOLER (*throwing* ROSE *the keys*). Take 'em off yourself.

ROSE *returns to* GRACE *and undoes the chains.*

ROSE. You're as good as home, Grace.

A hand darts out from under the straw and grabs ROSE's *ankle.* ROSE *visibly jumps but keeps herself from crying out. The hand belongs to another prisoner who had completely hidden herself in the straw on* ROSE's *arrival. Now* ROSE *can see the hand belongs to a young woman –* URSULA.

URSULA *holds* ROSE's *arm and* GRACE's *hand.*

Who are you?

Pause.

For why am I asking when I know you are a young woman waiting to be hung.

She pulls herself free from URSULA's *grasp and returns to the* GAOLER.

GAOLER. Give over them keys and sign here.

ROSE. How much d'ye want for the girl?

GAOLER. Cam te yer sense then, sir, seen the prettier one? Now she's worth a lot more, that one, she is. You won't get no nagging out of her neither. Divel took her ears and tongue.

ROSE (*shouts*). What do you want for her?

GAOLER. You must be a young man of some wealth, your voice not yet broke neither, there's a thing.

ROSE (*calmer*). Two.

GAOLER. Don't mock me.

ROSE. Take it or leave it.

GAOLER. Too risky them both dying together as it were. Too suspicious.

ROSE (*snaps*). The plague didn't look suspicious, did it?

GAOLER. Your lot making money outta it did though. Three.

ROSE. Three. (*She gives him the money.*)

GAOLER. Ooh, make a hard bargain you do, sir. Best keep to your part and sign papers here for me.

ROSE (*does so*). If all the wrongs men had done to them were counted up and laid on doorsteps of where they came, not a man left in the land who not be quaking.

GAOLER. Ah, now that do go a long way to explain your oddity, sir. You be one of them new religious lot.

Scene Six

GRACE's house.
    ROSE *is trying, with little success, to get* GRACE *to eat some broth.*
URSULA *sits in the corner. There is a knock on the door.*
    ROSE *opens to a young* DOCTOR.

DOCTOR. You sent word for me?

ROSE. Aye and money too.

DOCTOR. I'll do my best for you, sir, on that you may depend. Well, let's go take a look, shall we?

ROSE. She is afore your eyes. (*Nodding towards* GRACE.)

DOCTOR. My mistake, young gentleman. I am used to tending livestock first and then asked to see to the wife. What 'tis the rhyme you farm people have – 'If the cow kicks off, mighty cross, if the wife kicks off, no big loss.'

ROSE. I am no farmer, sir. So it be a notion you'd do well to disabuse yourself of.

DOCTOR. So it is your wife first and foremost.

ROSE. No, not her. But her mother. (*Chronologically this would be doubtful so she corrects herself.*) Her mother's mother.

DOCTOR. You have paid me good money, sir, but in truth she is really too old to bother with.

ROSE. Not to me.

DOCTOR. She is weak and frail.

ROSE. That is plain enough. I don't have to part with payment for looking through my own eyes. She does talk nonsense, such words as she speaks come forth all jumbled.

DOCTOR. She has a fever. (*He opens his bag and produces a knife and* URSULA *starts screaming.*)

ROSE. Can you put the knife away, sir.

DOCTOR. If she is to be cured I am to bleed her and let the badness drain out.

ROSE (*gestures to* URSULA *to be quiet*). Please leave off that noise. I will see no harm comes to her.

DOCTOR. 'Tis your wife who needs attention, sir.

ROSE (*referring to* GRACE). Have you none of nature's remedies for this sickness, sir?

DOCTOR. I took you for an intelligent man, sir, and far advanced from the rubbish spouted by old crones. If I am to save your wife's mother's mother I am to cut her. (*He advances on* GRACE.)

GRACE (*barely whispers*). No.

ROSE. That is your answer.

DOCTOR. But you claim she knows not what she says.

ROSE. Her life's blood is not bad, it doesn't warrant flowing away. Leave her be.

DOCTOR. I have come all this way and as yet administered to no one. Shall I take a look at your wife?

URSULA *starts to scream again.*

ROSE. No. No, cam away. You only seem to aggravate her condition.

DOCTOR. Now you and I know, sir, women are bad led down with nerves. There are several cures for that.

ROSE. She has suffered, sir. Is natural to have nerves.

DOCTOR. But can you not see? Is but your unyielding obstinacy that hampers our work. Forward thinkers term us saviours of mankind. Our science is the new hope. Only thing your cure depends on is your trust in it.

ROSE. Take more than that to convince me that the knife is cure for anything, never mind everything.

DOCTOR. It is within my power to right the ills plaguing both these females and your belief in me will cause you to be grateful for the service I am about to perform. (*He shrugs.*) Most likely their faith in the old hocus-pocus herb medicine that has landed them in this state of ill-health.

ROSE. Aye. Most probably was, though not in the way you're meaning. Thank you for your trouble, door is behind you.

DOCTOR (*scoffs*). Natural remedies. (*He takes out a knife.*) This won't hurt.

ROSE (*drawing out her sword*). Is there something amiss about your lugs or would you like me to perform on you your own style of cure and in the mark of St Peter?

DOCTOR. 'Tis not my usual reception. Many are overcome with gratitude to see me.

ROSE. I'll not be overcome with gratitude until you step other side of the door.

DOCTOR. I would just like to say . . .

ROSE advances, sword in hand. The DOCTOR's knife looking quite pathetic by comparison, causing him to make for the door.

ROSE. Sling thy hook.

DOCTOR (*with as much dignity as possible*). Goodnight.

He goes.

ROSE. Cut the badness out? With their judgement, soon enough there'd be none left of us. (*To* URSULA:) Do you have any idea what would make her well?

URSULA turns away.

Oh, what have they done to us? What have they done? (*She turns away and cries.*)

Pause.

URSULA turns, shocked and confused by ROSE's tears as she thinks she is a man. Gently she approaches her. ROSE looks up.

URSULA (*confirming*). I am free.

URSULA takes ROSE's now festering hand, and holds it open. ROSE pulls back. URSULA waits. ROSE holds it out again. URSULA cleans her hand, places Calendula leaves on the sore and bandages it.

ROSE. Thank you.

URSULA takes the water over to GRACE and starts to bathe her hands and face, then rolls up the sleeves of GRACE's garments. Realising that ROSE (a man) is watching, she turns ROSE round so she faces the door and has her back turned to GRACE. *Enter* LADY H. URSULA, *unaware of her entrance, continues with her task.*

LADY H. Oh, I was given to understand an old woman lived here.

ROSE. She is not fit to receive visitors.

LADY H. Is it not customary for a gentleman to bow when a lady enters his abode?

ROSE. Is it not customary for a lady to knock when she enters a gentleman's abode?

LADY H. Who are you?

ROSE. Never you mind. Please state your business here.

LADY H. You are a bold fellow. Be this your wife, timid from your tyranny?

ROSE. No, this be my sister.

LADY H. My, this is a rum household. (*To* URSULA:) How would you like to cam and work for me, girl? 'Tis utterly tiresome, most of my staff have kicked off or been knocked off. There's not a bod willing to take care of my babes for love nor money.

Silence.

You'd do well to answer me.

URSULA *does not turn round.*

ROSE (*mockingly*). Forgive me. I was but musing on our language. Where the words 'for love' mean 'for nothing'.

LADY H. I cannot tell which is most addled, your mind or your mouth. No matter, I am not here to solve the riddle for you. And 'twas not you to whom I was addressing myself in first place.

ROSE. If your household is so depleted you'd have been better preventing the deaths of those who so inconveniently got knocked off.

LADY H. Simple folk full of superstition and nonsense. And for certain, not my place to interfere in their squabbles or rituals.

ROSE. Then is not your place to put your nose in this dwelling.

LADY H. It was the old woman's help I sought.

ROSE. Where were you when she needed help? She's too ill even to speak.

LADY H. A great pity, for these times are harsh set against my sex.

ROSE. If you feel them harsh, lady, may the divel take the rest of us.

LADY H. I have cam to accept that men have no understanding of bonds of accumberment between rich and poor amongst our sex.

ROSE. I will lend you half an ear.

LADY H (*gently*). My sister died in childbirth last week and babe was torn limb from limb in the name of their science with these barbarous instruments. (*She throws down two evil-looking hooks.*) There, that is their substitute for the midwife's hands of flesh.

ROSE. And you have borrowed them?

LADY H (*back to her old self*). Aye. If only to dispose of them. He will not use them further. After he committed foul deed I whopped him one over the skull with a poker, such was my temperament. 'Twas a blow from which he didn't recover.

ROSE. You killed him?

LADY H. Doesn't the good book say an eye for an eye, and a tooth for a tooth? Should be made to think afore he wields his authority in such a murderous manner.

ROSE (*despite herself is beginning to admire* LADY H). But you could be hung?

LADY H. These doctors can't find their way round a woman's body never mind a village on the marshes. Will be no shock to anyone that he disappeared.

ROSE. I hope it is not that you have cam to set the blame at this door.

LADY H. My sole purpose was to talk to the old woman and get these evil ways stopped before there is neither mother or babe left in the land.

ROSE. If Grace becomes well I shall be sure to tell her.

LADY H. Aye and to ask her advice about setting up schools for midwives. For rumour has it that one man has instrument which is true aid for difficult births such as were cause of anxiety to best-experienced midwives. But such is the nature of these bastards' code of conduct that he will only pass secret of it on to his son for no one has offered a high enough price. Ha, he has not bargained for what I will offer him, should I track his whereabouts down.

ROSE. I wish thee luck.

LADY H. Now I am off to hear that Quaker lady speak for I am half-way committed already. But if I might be permitted to make one last observation – it would be to note your sister's rudeness for she has not so much as acknowledged my presence.

ROSE. She is unaware of your presence for she cannot hear.

LADY H. Oh then I must make my case to her face. (*She taps* URSULA *on the shoulder.* URSULA *jumps with surprise.*)

ROSE. No.

LADY H (*to* ROSE). You must allow your sister to do as she pleases. We have noted too much the desires of your sex and it has not served your health. (*To* URSULA:) How would you like to work for me child?

URSULA (*not understanding, looks at* ROSE *and signs*). What she say?

ROSE. Bear her no mind. (*Using dismissive arm-waving gestures.*) Nothing. Nothing.

LADY H (*to* ROSE). Let her choose for herself. (*Saying and miming to* URSULA:) You want to work for me? Sewing, cooking, cleaning, looking after my children? For money.

URSULA *nods enthusiastically then looks at* GRACE *and then back at* LADY H.

(LADY H *nods.*) Aye. You may continue to nurse the sick woman also.

ROSE. She does not want to work for you.

LADY H. Seems you are mistaken.

GRACE (*whispers*). Rose. Rose.

ROSE (*goes to* GRACE.) Grace?

GRACE. I knew you'd cam.

LADY H (*sighs*). Be of no use, sir. Her mind still tricks her mouth.

Enter the DOCTOR. *The* DOCTOR *and* LADY H *sing*.

From a Dish to a Dish

DOCTOR (*sings*).
We're here to stay, no more witches and midwives
With potions and herbs and wasting of lives.
We're gaining control and refining our tools
Creating a science, replacing these fools.

LADY H (*sings*).
Three centuries ago they started with hooks,
But the medicine man will next control our looks –
For they have moved on from bleeding out our life
To creating the next generation of perfect wife.

DOCTOR (*sings*).
Fertilised in a Petri dish as a result of egg donation,
Transplanted by the doctor, father of the future, perfect nation,
Completed the laparoscopy, done with amniocentesis,
Will abort if results show a less than first-rate foetus.

Have mastered techniques of *in vitro* fertilisation,
Surrogacy, ectogenesis and superovulation,

Won't stop now, intrauterine surgery will enrich our lives,
And cloning will ensure that males outnumber wives.

For women's dispensability will not hamper surgery,
Experiments will never end the bank of frozen embryos
We divided at the 4-cell stage
For chromosome analysis and sex preselection.
We don't admit that no one knows
The results of trans-species fertilisation.

And hormonal manipulation is bombing women's ovaries
And it's unethical not to experiment on spare embryos.
We're in charge of the future, the future perfect nation,
We're in charge of women's bodies, and isn't she a sensation.

I look at her in the Petri dish
And I fuck her with scientists' wish
That I'll create a full-grown dish
Who'll satisfy my every wish
And I'll father the perfect nation.

LADY H (sings).
From witches and midwives, they raped us with hooks,
Created their science, wrote us out of their books,
And now they're in charge of more than our looks –
Our future's in the hands of their reproductive technology.
And there's more at stake now than the right to children and
   gynaecology.

Scene Seven

The inn.
   HELEN *stands on an upright barrel,* LADY H *next to her. Several*
women crowd round. The PUBLICAN, *relieved that the bar separates*
him, fidgets nervously.

HELEN. I speak not of Holy Ghost.

WOMAN 1. Thank God for that.

HELEN. Nor spooks or superstition, nor the fear of the immortal or invisible but of those who have taken it upon themselves to think they are the God-only-wise.

WOMAN 1. Who?

HELEN. The wreckers of earthly beauty and nature herself.

WOMAN 2 (*to* WOMAN 1). Oh, men.

WOMAN 1. Oh aye, if my husband had another brain it would be lonely.

HELEN. The battle of men against men is not the war of our time but the fight women have had for their lives. We have shaken their opinion of us as the weaker sex . . .

WOMAN 3. Weaker sex ho ho.

HELEN. And they have responded with ways more forceful than ever before. Now is not the time for slowing down, for our lives swing more lightly in the balance than ever before.

PUBLICAN. Now then 'mistress', I'm sure your husbands must be fretting as to where you are. And fretting all the more I dare say if they knew.

WOMAN 1. If you know what's best for you, you'll keep your jaws still.

HELEN (*continues*). Women will flee for the lives of their unborn children from the spittle-house rather than endure birthing at the mercy of the doctors' tools. The disease that follows will be worse than any plague yet known, except it remains unchartered for 'tis our sex alone again that will suffer and die from it.

LADY H. Listen to her, she speaks absolute truth.

WOMAN 2 (*to* WOMAN 3). If Lady Horse-face has got herself here, is not for the likes of us. Let's make off.

PUBLICAN. That's right dear, you do that, you're frightening off my customers.

They all turn and stare at him.

WOMAN 1. Sit down.

PUBLICAN. Aye. Maybe I need a rest.

WOMAN 3. Certainly your mouth does.

The PUBLICAN sits, disappearing from view.

LADY H. I have a pamphlet here written by two women and I'd like to read . . .

WOMAN 2. Do we want a reading from her?

WOMAN 3. Let her speak, for is not writ by her and how else can we learn of its contents?

WOMAN 1. Who was it writ by then?

LADY H. They couldn't use their own names for front page, but ones they chose were better than any family name in the land. 'Mary Tattlewell' and 'Joane Hit-him-home Spinster'.

PUBLICAN puts his face above the bar.

WOMAN 2. How does 'Ann Hit-him-over-the-brain-pan-with-a-tankard' sound?

The PUBLICAN promptly disappears from view.

WOMAN 3. Tell us what they have to say then.

LADY H. If women were ever allowed to be taught singing and dancing 'twas only to please men's licentious appetites. That women are taught nothing than to get a husband, and what life could a woman ever expect if marriage was the be all and end all of existence. At same time they cite how female character is preferable to the male.

WOMAN 2. What did you do when we was begging and them refused was cursing?

WOMAN 1 (*to* WOMAN 2). She didn't so much as lift a chicken leg off her table, that's what she did.

HELEN. The hanging and butchering of women is part of the same hatred. We must make certain that we be the last generation to bear witness to the wrongs done to us in name of science. That our daughter's daughter and her daughter too will know what we know.

WOMAN 3. She is right and 'tis not only labourers' daughters what need telling. I say Lady H should join us.

LADY H. We will be despised, ridiculed and deemed mad but I vouchsafe that I am prepared to forgo my privilege in the name of truth.

WOMAN 1. Aye let her be part of us for we can no longer do nothing but pray.

WOMAN 2. And not rest until we have won back our bodies for ourselves.

Scene Eight

GRACE's home.
Physically weak but mentally alert, GRACE is reading ROSE's play. ROSE paces the floor.

GRACE (*puts down the play having finished*). Rose, this is more than reward enough for teaching you to write.

ROSE. What did you like best? I saw you grinning like your mouth would crack.

GRACE. A fine story Rose. Aye and funny.

ROSE. Perhaps the best thing you have read by one of our sex?

GRACE. Rose, it is the only thing. But that makes it no less wonderful.

ROSE. Talk to me more about it, Grace.

GRACE. Presently. First, while it is just you and I, I want to tell you to take it on yourself to let Ursula know who you are. Well, you don't have to tell her you write plays but the least you can say is you're no man.

ROSE. I'll think on it. Now what did you think of your character?

GRACE. No you will not think on it, you'll do it. It's not fair to abuse her trust in this way.

ROSE. Trust, ha, took her time enough to reveal to me her understanding of healing.

GRACE (*coldly angry*). Rose, she saw her own mother hung for her pains. Do you think she'd want any part of that knowledge?

ROSE (*sulkily*). Then she went to work for Lady H.

GRACE (*abruptly*). Aye and have you not stopped to wonder on why? For why would a man buy her? She is working to repay the debt. And is for you to tell her money was hers by right. (*Then with warmth:*) And what of Jane – when she breezes in her confusion will know no bounds, and trick even I into believing my mind is blown away again.

ROSE (*quietly*). Grace, I know not if she is still living.

GRACE (*gently*). You would know if she were dead.

ROSE. I never felt Mary and Ann were anything but alive.

GRACE. You knew when death had all but closed in on me.

ROSE. I had but one dream, Grace. Only that.

GRACE. But, I knew you'd cam.

ROSE. Several events cam between you and the dream. I do not now want to dwell on Jane, for all manner of ills my running off may have caused her.

GRACE. Cam, that one could talk herself into the King's privy and out again. There are enough causes of death in war besides yourself. So you'd be as well not to beset yourself with guilt.

ROSE. Supposing?

Pause.

Oh let us talk about my play.

GRACE. Aye. Well, I have several recommendations that may improve it.

ROSE (*defensively*). What is wrong with it?

GRACE. Don't take on like a child. Is not in the writing, Rose.
Though story is apt, like its mistress, to wander. But the ideas.

ROSE. Like what?

GRACE. If you keep interrupting I cannot collect my thoughts.
Firstly I am very proud of my part. Is a very generous picture
you paint of me, but you give impression that I was able to cure
all manner of ills which is more like the story of son of God than
me.

ROSE. But . . .

GRACE. I wasn't able, nor am I still. True I have perfected the use
of some herbs and given some advice but I have no power over
life and death. Your portrait of cunning women is too glowing
for truth. So many have been killed in this purge who didn't
know a sprig of dill from a cauliflower. They were chosen
because they were women not because they were special. When
we have received foul attentions from lord and from farmhand
alike, 'tis because we are women. It's a danger to claim it is
because we are different in some way.

ROSE. Who did they start on first, old women, cunning women,
women alone, Mary and Ann. They were independent and did
not carry on as men wished them to.

GRACE. But it didn't stop there, did it?

ROSE. No.

GRACE. Our sex with its single power to give birth, pose a threat
to men's power over whole order of villages, towns, counties
and countries. That control depends on women cur-tailing to
men's ideals of how they should behave.

ROSE. So, if it is fact you want from me, happen there was
women enough to cause trouble against each other.

GRACE. Because not only are men set against the woman named
wicked, but also the women and children whose livelihood
depends on the approval of men.

ROSE. So the condemned woman is special. She has freed herself as much as is possible and will not keep her mouth still about it.

GRACE. What I am saying is that the tests and methods by which they decide who is evil are without two solutions. They are designed only to condemn. When they look for a witch they are looking for a woman and do not mistake thyself, any one of us will do.

ROSE (*impatiently*). Is a story, Grace, not a pamphlet nor a broadsheet. Is a story.

GRACE. Religion has given us enough martyrs and saints. Is for us to do away with them, not create our own.

ROSE. Is not s'posed to be a list of facts and dates. There must be other women interested in recording exact history. I cannot do all. Is a story I have written, out of my imagination, to entertain. Not a bible.

GRACE. That leads me to other thing I want to say.

ROSE. Oh no, will mean I will have to start whole thing over.

GRACE. There is too many scenes of hanging and swimming and is not for us to present as entertainment.

ROSE. But that is the truth! One breath you say 'not accurate' the next you want women to sprout wings and fly out of the ponds. And next, no doubt, you'll tell me that the pricker's character is not light enough. Well, I care not. He is writ as he is. And what difference if he suffered from corn-toes or was kind to his dog. It does not lift weight off his wrongs.

GRACE. I have no quarrel with pricker's character. Though there will always be those who refuse to believe the worse has been done to us. But, Rose, do not give him all the weight. What of the fight back?

ROSE. But we've not stopped it. (*Then:*) I put bit about the bear in.

GRACE (*impatiently*). We? We've not stopped it? Look at you. What are you still doing in men's clothes?

ROSE. And how else am I to hold down job as shipping clerk and how else are we to be afforded protection. My clothes are of no matter. You don't like my play. Nothing matters.

GRACE. You will have to learn to take criticism with a little more dignity. Do you think they'll not be shouting at you from all sides?

Enter JANE.

JANE. I'm back. (*Sees* GRACE.) Christ Jesus, Grace, you look far from the best of health.

GRACE (*dryly*). Still got the same sweet, sensitive nature I perceive.

ROSE *rushes to* JANE *and hugs her,* JANE *lifting* ROSE *off the ground and swinging her round. Enter* URSULA, *her expression of agitation turns to confusion on seeing* ROSE *and* JANE. ROSE *wriggles out of* JANE's *grasp. An embarrassed silence ensues.*

JANE. I don't mind you have a new love, Rosie, but didn't you ever speak of me to her?

ROSE. Ursula is not my love as you term it.

JANE. Notice she's not jumped to a denial.

GRACE. She cannot hear Jane – she is deaf.

JANE (*casually*). Oh Aye?

(*Signs to* URSULA *and says*.) Is not Rose a wonderful woman?

URSULA (*signs*). Woman? Woman?

GRACE. Where on earth did you learn to do that girl?

ROSE. The one time I thought your big mouth could go unheeded.

JANE. Just because I can't read and write, Grace, doesn't mean I can't converse in other ways.

(*To* ROSE.) You daft cony – is a wonder, your modesty's not brought bladder trouble on yourself.

URSULA (*signs to* JANE). If I'd known, she could have come to the meeting by the pond.

JANE (*to* ROSE). If she'd known, you could have come to the meeting.

ROSE. Oh we all been there before.

JANE (*to* ROSE). By the pond. (*Pause.*) Oh no, the man of hanging tree is alive and pricking.

ROSE (*agitated*). When? Who was swam? What was her name? Is she alive?

GRACE. Keep your clacker still, Rosie. Let Ursula tell us in her own way.

The others have made a model pricker by stuffing straw into a spare jerkin and a pair of breeches. They perform a 'dumb' show which URSULA *narrates in sign language. (It should be accompanied by a taped voice over.)*

URSULA (*with voice over*). We met the night before. Women from near and far and a very long and angry meeting it was; only one thing was agreed on by all – that we would meet in the morning and no woman that day would lose her life. So now we are stood at the pond. Our blood tingling and the pricker preening himself on drawing such a large crowd.

GRACE *stands the dummy pricker up and makes it take a bow.*

Everything still and I had half a thought of worry that we would take root in the ground. The feeling vanished when her body hit the water, we joined hands and by a force unspake floated through the crowd, each silent till she was set free.

The other three mime pulling the woman from the water.

ROSE (*to imaginary woman*). Take off there that wet cloth. Pass me those blankets. Who will take this woman home?

GRACE. I will, I be her sister.

JANE. And what will we do for him?

ROSE. Smash his brain-pan and have done.

GRACE. Nay, we agreed not to do that. He must take his own medicine.

JANE. Cam on. Help me put this sheet over him.

They put the sheet over the struggling man.

GRACE. No, he must be prepared in same detail. Left thumb tied to right toe and right thumb tied to left toe.

JANE. Should be right thumb tied to left stone.

ROSE. I, for one, wouldn't be disappointed, if he were two stones lighter even if it did mean he did float.

They mime throwing him into the pond.

GRACE. Seems he has floated.

GRACE *and* JANE *pull the dummy pricker up and drag him out of the action.*

ROSE. And he is yet living.

JANE. Then who amongst us is agreed that he should complete the course of punishment?

URSULA (*voice over*). We did not kill him. We are not the same as him. We left him, still tied, in the place where women's bodies are left to be claimed by their loved ones at night.

End of show.

ROSE (*shouts*). Aye bodies. Bodies of dead women. Deemed then innocent for an invented crime. Dead to be collected and buried! How many of us will have to die while our good natures get the better of us?

Silence.

GRACE (*quietly*). Then take that pistol and shoot him through the head. For is that not what they do to sick animals? And tell him from me, 'tis offer of death more humane than ever he has dealt in.

It is JANE who turns with the purpose of doing so. ROSE remains, stunned by GRACE's change in attitude.

URSULA *places her hand on* JANE's *arm to restrain her.*

ROSE. Oh take heart, Jane, he has yet to escape his fate. He'll not get far tied and bound. Cold and dripping.

GRACE. Aye, then, so be it, let nature deal with him in her own way.

Scene Nine

The pond.
  Night. The dummy has been replaced by the PRICKER, *tied in the manner described and shivering uncontrollably. A* WOMAN *approaches.*

MAN. Mother? Is that you?
  She comes closer.
  Oh, Mother, what has kept you so long?

MOTHER. The hardest hours of my life, far harder than the few before you were born.

MAN. Untie me, Mother. I shall perish of cold.

MOTHER. How many times have you done the same for me, son?
  She turns.

MAN. Don't leave me.

MOTHER (*turns back*). And still you show no remorse.

MAN. Hurry. Please hurry, Mother.

MOTHER. Have you no word of shame?

MAN. Have I not had all day to think on my plight and shame enough, aye, to know I cannot live here. I will follow my brother to New England and make there a new life for myself.

MOTHER. And what of me?

MAN. You're to say I died of consumption. You have access to parish register. Therein record my death.

MOTHER. And what of me?

MAN. You can't let me die. Mother, help me.

MOTHER. The cord which once bound us did not even enter your head whilst you hung many cords around my neck.

MAN. I vouchsafe I will ne'ere show my face here again.

Pause.

MOTHER. You will not return?

MAN. Ne'er, untie me please.

MOTHER (*stooping to untie him*). I would that you had never been born, but I cannot take life from you.

URSULA (*voice over only*). We all knew what she'd done and that she aided his passage to Salem, but we never heard of him again and we never spoke of it again. We spoke to her, she was one of us.

Scene Ten

GRACE's *garden.*
GRACE's *burial.* HELEN *and* ROSE. LADY H, *obscured from their view, is digging the grave.*

HELEN. I know it is but small comfort, but Grace does now merit a grave within the churchyard.

ROSE. The comfort is she died peacefully. Was her own wish to be buried in her garden. And we'd best rouse ourselves, for one thing church'll not be lending us gravediggers.

HELEN. Oh Lady H is seeing to it.

ROSE. Lady H?!

HELEN. I tell you she is turning over a new leaf.

ROSE. She'll be turning over a site more than that.

They find LADY H *who has almost completed the work.*

LADY H (*wiping her muddy face with an equally muddy hand*). Will this do?

HELEN. Thank you very much, Lady H.

LADY H. H only from this day forth. For I am hoping to have proved myself a lady no longer.

ROSE. And thank you all the same. We are waiting now on Jane, and Ursula but I know not where she is.

LADY H. She will be here presently for she wants to pay her own tribute to Grace. I will take my leave now, for I sense it is not my place to be here longer. (*Exits.*)

HELEN. Thank you.

A fussy little PARSON bumbles breathlessly towards them.

ROSE. Don't look now but God's little flea has cam to bug us. (*She walks towards him.*)

PARSON (*breathlessly*). You can't take burial services into your own hands. This place is unconsecrated ground. Do you want for her neighbours to . . .

ROSE (*firmly*). To say that she was a wise woman? An outlaw. Aye, I do.

PARSON. I forbid it, in the name of God the Father, God the Son . . .

ROSE. If God the Father and God the Son care to intervene on their own account that is up to them, but on your own you'll not be able to sway us.

PARSON. You will bring nothing but an eternity of hell's fire and damnation on your head.

ROSE. That will be all? Then I'm laughing. (*She laughs. He exits. She returns to HELEN.*) Still they will not leave us alone.

HELEN. Aye but Grace would've approved of manner in which you sent him off. She didn't want for today to be dreary.

ROSE (*sighs*). Aye she says 'Rose is to take form of celebration' but is not an easy feeling to capture, Grace. Oh, Grace.

HELEN (*gently*). Why not see if Jane is far off. I will tend to what has to be done.

> ROSE *walks until* HELEN *is out of view, and sits by a tree, head in her hands. Enter* JANE *carrying a metal box.*

JANE. Rosie?

ROSE (*looks up*). What kept you?

JANE. A dog collar with a person inside.

ROSE (*smiles*). I hope you made him no offer of aid.

JANE. Indeed I did, in form of my foot, but alas he didn't note it till he was on his face. That is enough talk of parsons. We are here to say farewell to Grace.

ROSE. Seems so final.

JANE. Supposing you'd never known her? Would you have known how to read? Or name the stars? Or tamed a bear? Or written a play? Or been as strong?

ROSE (*smiles*). So now is the time for supposing?

JANE. Is not her memory a part of our lives and are we not better for it?

ROSE. Aye.

> *They join* HELEN *and* URSULA *for the ceremony.* URSULA *kneels throughout, and plants various herbs in the fresh earth.*

HELEN/ROSE/JANE (*sing*).

The Burial Song

Death comes swiftly
Life on earth
Is ended, ending
All together we are sending
One another to ourselves
Not forgotten, undertaking
To remember, not forget
Life does end but celebrating
One we knew and won't forget.

ROSE (reads).

    With you I learnt the stars at night
    We named the Bear, who gave a fright
    At last I see that my disguise
    Hid me from men who tell their lies
    In bed and gaol and with their blades
    Their war, their fear, their rape and raids
    Our knowledge we have always shared
    With our own sex for whom we cared
    Men take from us the power to cure
    By brutal means, they make a war
    On what we held as our birthright
    They cut us up, but we will fight
    Not in their wars, dressed up as men,
    Not by the pond when they say when,
    But by the very deed they fear,
    Deny their power to leave us here:

    Pause.

HELEN. Grace, your life occurred with the passing of women's healing to men's doctoring. Now their inventions continue without intervention. How many charms have we played with to guess at the sex of the unborn child? Their science will conquer the problem and what will become of our sex, for there can be no place in the world where daughters are valued above sons as first-born child. We will miss you not only for your vision, Grace, but for your strength and it is in your memory we struggle to arrest the weapons from the masters' violent hands.

ROSE. Thank you Helen.

    Silence.

HELEN. Rose, now I'm wanting to ask if you've had new thought on the school for midwives.

ROSE. How many times are we to buy back our birthright?

JANE. She'll not be swayed from teaching girls to read and write.

HELEN. Aye, that will be task enough.

JANE. Lady H has agreed to help us, but Rose has to help her with her education first. Her family have all that money and they know nothing.

ROSE. You are welcome to join us, Helen.

HELEN. Thank you but I shall carry on with the Quakers.

JANE. Now, that do sound like a good title for your next play, Rose.

HELEN. And what of your play? I hear it is very good?

JANE. Aye and we should know, Ursula and I have learned our writing by copying it out – every word.

HELEN (*to* ROSE). So you will choose a man's name?

ROSE. No. My own.

HELEN. No doubt I'll see it anon then.

JANE (*remembering*). That's why I brought this box for copied version to be secured within and buried next to Grace.

ROSE. But it's not had a life yet.

HELEN. So if it doesn't cam to pass in your lifetime one day when you're long gone it'll be uncovered.

ROSE. But s'pose it never gets unearthed?

JANE (*turning to face* ROSE). You're not the only woman in the world, Rose.